AN OMEGA BOOK

This New Age series of Paragon House is dedicated to classic and contemporary works about higher human development and the nature of ultimate reality. Omega Books encompasses the fields of mysticism and spirituality, psychic research and paranormal phenomena, the evolution of consciousness, and the human potential for self-directed growth in body, mind and spirit.

Ask your bookseller for these other Omega Books:

LIFECYCLES

Reincarnation and the Web of Life

by

CHRISTOPHER M. BACHE, PH.D.

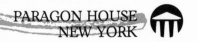

PARAGON HOUSE
NEW YORK

First edition 1991

Published in the United States by

Paragon House
90 Fifth Avenue
New York, N.Y. 10011

Book design by Felecia Monroe

Library of Congress Cataloging-in-Publishing Data
Bache, Christopher Martin.
    Lifecycles : reincarnation and the web of life / by
Christopher M. Bache. — 1st ed.
    p. cm. — (An Omega book)
    Includes bibliographical references and index.
    ISBN 1-55778-350-0 (HC) : $18.95
    1. Reincarnation. I. Title. II. Title: Life cycles.
III. Series: Omega book (New York, N.Y.)
BL515.B23   1990
133.9'01'3—dc20   90-37096
                                                        CIP

Manufactured in the United States of America
10 9 8 7 6 5 4 3 2 1

The paper used in this publication meets the minimum require-ments of American National Standard for Information Sci-ences—Permanence of Paper for Printed Library Materials, ANSI Z39.48-1984.

*This book is dedicated
to my students*

*and to the memory of
Martin A. Greenman, Ph. D.*

CONTENTS

	Acknowledgments	*xi*
	Foreword	*xiii*
CHAPTER 1	Introducing the Issues	*1*
CHAPTER 2	About the Evidence	*26*
CHAPTER 3	Karma and Rebirth	*62*
CHAPTER 4	The Oversoul	*105*
CHAPTER 5	The Rhythms of Life	*128*
CHAPTER 6	A Reincarnationist Christianity?	*149*
CHAPTER 7	Reincarnation and the Family	*175*
CHAPTER 8	The Web of Life	*185*
CHAPTER 9	The Field Effect	*201*
CHAPTER 10	Postscript	*215*
APPENDIX	Reincarnation in Early Christianity	*219*
	Bibliography	*225*
	Index	*231*

ACKNOWLEDGMENTS

No book is one person's project alone, and this is perhaps particularly true for someone's <u>first book</u>. I would like, therefore, to thank a few of the many people who have contributed directly and indirectly to *Lifecycles*.

At the top of the list are my students. The ideas presented here were first developed in conversation with them. If it were not for their questioning and their willingness to consider new ways of envisioning their lives, there simply would have been no book. Not far behind them is my wife. Carol buffered me from domestic responsibilities while I worked long hours at the computer and scanned each chapter with her fine editorial eye. More importantly, she has been my companion in all things. I also wish to thank my brother and his wife, Bill and Gayle Bache, for their enthusiastic support when the book was still in its infancy and most vulnerable to criticism. It was through their eyes that I first saw myself as a writer, and their eyes were kind.

The core of *Lifecycles* was written while I was on sabbatical leave from Youngstown State University, and I wish to thank several persons from the university community who supported my work along the way. David Cliness contributed not only some of the ideas found here but something uniquely valuable to me personally—the opportunity to explore my own deeper past. His many years of clinical experience were a valuable resource as I pondered the philosophical implications of the literature on past-life therapy. My chairperson, Thomas Shipka, read a portion of the manuscript and though he did not share my enthusiasm for reincarnation, he nevertheless gave me strong administrative and moral support. Veterans of university life know that controversial research does not always receive such even-handed treatment, for which I am indebted to him. Martin Greenman (1917–1989) was a colleague and dear friend with whom I spent many hours discussing reincarnation and related topics. Martin was well known at YSU as an outspoken proponent of rebirth, and while he did not live to see *Lifecycles* published, he was surely present at its inception. Finally, the University Research Council supported both my sabbatical travel and preparation of the manuscript for publication with grants.

I also wish to thank my editor at Paragon House, Andy DeSalvo, and John White, the general editor of the Omega series, for their many helpful suggestions for improving the manuscript. And lastly, I wish to thank my trusty computer, which never let me down or lost a precious byte from start to finish. If you have ever had a head crash in the middle of a major project, you will understand why this particular acknowledgment is included.

FOREWORD

<hr />

Christopher Bache and I have traveled different paths, but after
reading *Lifecycles* it is evident that they have led to the same
destination.

Chris's took him through the study of philosophy, religion, and
eventually to a reincarnational view of life, which is the subject of this
admirably lucid and cogently reasoned book. Mine led through the
thickets of social psychology into the clearing of transpersonal psychology and finally to the luminous fields of near-death experiences, the
study of which has, more than anything else, informed my own world
view.

My teachers have been the hundreds of near-death experiencers—
many of whom have become my good friends—I have been privileged
to interview during the past twelve years.

What they have taught me stems of course from their near-death
experiences; and what they teach will also be found in this book.

What accounts for this unmistakable convergence between the
lessons of reincarnation and the implications of near-death experiences?
To me, the answer lies in the fact that the transcendental *state of
consciousness* that a near-death crisis elicits is the *same* one that points to
the reality of reincarnation. Certainly, many of the near-death exper-

iencers I have interviewed have told me that following their NDEs they became, if not believers in reincarnation, then at least more convinced of its plausibility and eager to learn more about it. Through the event of nearly dying, then, near-death experiencers come to see directly what the reincarnationalist has always held: that the spiritual world is our true home, that what we call death is only a flip into this spiritual realm, and that in fact life is eternal.

And—the reincarnationist would add—*we come back.*

The evidence for this basic proposition of the reincarnational position is, as Chris Bache shows, impressive and impossible to dismiss. But this is *not* a book primarily about the evidence for reincarnation. Rather it is about how our human life might be better understood and more fully *lived* if we were to become more cognizant of the implications and tenability of a reincarnational world view.

Make no mistake about it: While the first part of this book provides a persuasive and engaging presentation of the author's formulation of contemporary reincarnational thought, his ultimate aim is to bring home the lessons for self-awareness and spiritual growth in daily life that are inherent in a reincarnational world view. And this, as you will see, he does with masterful clarity and compellingness.

In making his case, Chris Bache has wisely drawn upon and beautifully synthesized the findings from those areas of current research and exploration that are helping to fashion a new, more spiritual, view of ourselves: reincarnation research, past-life therapy, the experiential therapy of Stanislav Grof, research into out-of-body experiences, near-death studies, and so on. To my knowledge, this is the first time a writer has woven these particular experiential and empirical strands into the fabric of reincarnational design, and for this achievement alone many readers will find themselves in the author's debt.

Even this contribution, however, must not be construed as simply interesting reportage. What it reflects is something far more significant. Indeed, it must be understood as an expression of the contemporary reemergence of the view, long out of fashion, of a *meaningful cosmos.* All of us, of course, are familiar with Camus' *The Stranger*, that bellwether of the modern age, and all of us who absorbed that book have, consciously or otherwise, found ourselves dwellers in Camus' universe of "benign indifference" where life is stripped of any inherent meaning or purpose.

But now, finally, in the last decade of the twentieth century, this dark cloud of existentialist nihilism is beginning to dissipate as the findings and implications of today's consciousness researchers become known to ever-increasing audiences.

And Chris Bache with this, his first, book here establishes himself as an important transmitter of the postexistentialist perspective that is beginning to permeate our thinking as we approach the next millenium of the human future. For from his reading of the findings of consciousness research pertaining to reincarnation, Chris's conclusion is that "meaning pevades the *entire* universe," that reincarnational experiences lead one "to *know*, not just believe, that life is eternal and that the ultimate purpose of human existence is learning to love," and that "above all, we should know that we are safe, that nothing could possibly separate us permanently from the source of life, and that the rigors of life are ultimately for our own benefit."

This is precisely what my near-death experiencers have told me, too.

Now I invite you to walk along Chris Bache's path to see how he ineluctably found his own way to these conclusions. By doing so, you may well be led to take a similar journey of your own.

KENNETH RING
Storrs, Connecticut
May 1990

1

Introducing the Issues

Romy Crees was born in 1977 to Barry and Bonnie Crees of Des Moines, Iowa. She was a charming little girl, a typical whirlwind of curiosity and mischief. Her parents were both devout Catholics and so were completely unprepared for what happened when Romy began to talk. Mixed in with the usual childhood chatter were details about her previous life as Joe Williams. She had grown up, she insisted, in a red brick house in Charles City, a town about 140 miles from Des Moines. She said that she had married a woman named Sheila and that they had had three children together. Both Joe and Sheila had been killed in a motorcycle accident that Romy described in considerable detail. "I'm afraid of motorcycles," she said. Among the many incidents she recalled from Joe's life was a time Joe had started a fire in his home; Mother Williams had burned her hand throwing water on the flames. "Mother has a pain in her leg—here," she pointed to her right leg. "Mother Williams' name is Louise. I haven't seen her for a long time." She often asked to be taken back to Charles City because she wanted to reassure Mother Williams that "everything was OK."

Romy's parents were understandably upset and confused by these revelations and tried to discourage Romy from indulging in what appeared to them a bizarre fantasy. Yet her description of Joe's life and the accident that ended it were so detailed as to give them pause. Eventually they agreed to a visit from Hemendra Banerjee, a professional investigator of children who appear to have spontaneous memories of former lives.[1] In the winter of 1981, Banerjee and his wife came to Des Moines, accompanied by two journalists from the Swedish magazine *Allers*, where they met and interviewed Romy and her parents. Later they set out with the family for Charles City to determine whether any of Romy's "memories" could be verified.

Romy was quite excited on the drive and very much looking forward to finally being reunited with Mother Williams. As they drew near to their destination, the four-year-old climbed into the front seat and said "We have to buy flowers. Mother Williams loves blue flowers. And when we get there we can't go in through the front door. We have to go around the corner to the door in the middle." After consulting the telephone directory, they soon pulled up in front of a white bungalow on the outskirts of town. Romy jumped out of the car and dragged Banerjee up the walk. It was not the red brick house Romy had described, but on the walkway was a sign that read PLEASE USE THE BACK DOOR.

The elderly woman who answered the door on the side of the house walked with the assistance of metal crutches and wore a tightly wrapped bandage around her right leg. Yes, she was Mrs. Louise Williams and, yes, she had had a son named Joe, but she was leaving for a doctor's appointment and did not have time to receive this unusual party of visitors. Romy was crestfallen, and her eyes brimmed with tears. An hour later, however, Romy, her father, and the Swedish journalists returned and were welcomed inside.

Mrs. Williams was startled by Romy's gift of blue flowers and revealed that her son's last gift to her had also been a bouquet of blue flowers. As Romy's father told Mrs. Williams of Romy's "remembrances" of Joe's life, her astonishment grew. "Where did this girl get all this information?," she asked. "I don't know you or anyone else in Des Moines." She explained that she and Joe had lived in a red brick house, as Romy had said, but this house had been destroyed by a tornado that had damaged much of Charles City ten years ago. "Joe helped us build this house and insisted we keep the front door shut during the winter."

---

[1] See his book *Americans Who Have Been Reincarnated*. (References will be kept as short as possible throughout the notes. Complete bibliographical information on all works mentioned will be found in the bibliography.)

Romy and Mrs. Williams quickly took to each other. When Mrs. Williams stood up to get something in the next room, Romy rushed to follow her. They returned hand in hand, Romy trying to help the old lady walk. Mrs. Williams was carrying a framed photograph of Joe and his family taken the Christmas before he and Sheila died. "She recognized them," said Mrs. Williams with surprise. "She recognized them!"

Mrs. Williams was able to confirm many details of Romy's narrative about Joe, including his marriage to Sheila, their three children, the names of other relatives, and the fire in her home in which she had burned her hand. She was also able to verify Romy's precise description of the motorcycle accident in 1975, two years before Romy was born. Despite this confirmation, neither she nor Romy's parents were prepared to accept the possibility that their daughter was the reincarnation of Joe Williams. "I don't know how to explain it," observed Romy's mother, "but I *do* know my daughter isn't lying."[2]

Romy's remembrances are not as rare as her parents may have thought. As we shall see in the next chapter, hundreds of cases have been documented in which children have spoken in great detail and quite accurately of a life they feel they lived before their present life. Cumulatively, these children are forcing us to reexamine one of the oldest and most tenacious beliefs in human history, the belief that we live on Earth not once but many times.

But should we really trouble ourselves a great deal over these children's claims? The vast majority of us have no recall whatsoever of having lived a life before this one. Moreover, the evidence of our physical senses is that we disappear from Earth when our bodies fail us. Whether we simply cease to exist or go "someplace else," the conscious experience of the majority of humanity speaks against return. Why, therefore, should we not simply dismiss these children as strange anomalies we cannot yet explain and stick with what appears to be the simpler alternative?

Some may be moved to take these children seriously by considering the number of noteworthy individuals who after careful thought have chosen to believe in reincarnation. The list includes such diverse figures as Plato, Schopenhauer, John McTaggart, Benjamin Franklin, Leo Tolstoy, William James, Henry Wadsworth Longfellow, Ralph Waldo Emerson, Henry Thoreau, Walt Whitman, Saul Bellow, Richard Wagner, Gustav Mahler, Jean Sibelius, Paul Gauguin, David Lloyd George,

---

[2] Romy's case is summarized from *The Case for Reincarnation* by Joe Fisher, pp. 5–8.

George S. Patton, Charles Lindbergh, Henry Ford, and Carl Jung. But then again, the list of Western intellectuals and creative artists who have rejected the concept of reincarnation is longer still.

Others may be moved by the simple fact that reincarnation has been accepted by approximately half the human race for thousands of years. This too ought to give us pause, but soon we will remind ourselves that many old and venerated ideas have proved false, such as the notion that the sun revolves around the Earth or that the Earth itself is flat. Age and popularity are no guarantee of truth and are not strong enough by themselves to cause us to override our powerful everyday experience that we are who our bodies say we are and no more.

In the final analysis, the strongest reason for not dismissing the experience of children like Romy Crees is the children themselves, everyday children who are completely normal in all respects except for this one curiosity—they appear to remember what most of us for some reason have forgotten. If twentieth-century Westerners are ever to take reincarnation seriously, I believe it will be due primarily to the patient and critical study of these little ones. Before going further, therefore, let us look at a second case—one researched by Dr. Ian Stevenson of the University of Virginia.[3]

Prakash Varshnay was born in August 1951 to a family in Chhata, India. As a child he showed no unusual behavior other than perhaps a tendency to cry more often than most children his age. When he was about four and a half years old, however, he woke from his sleep in the middle of the night and ran out of the house. When his parents caught up with him, he insisted that his name was Nirmal and that he "belonged" in Kosi Kalan, a town about six miles away. He also said that his father's name was Bholanath. For four or five nights in a row, Prakash repeated the same performance, waking up at night and running into the street, and then less frequently but still occasionally for a month.

During the day he began to speak about "his" family in Kosi Kalan. He said he had a sister there named Tara, and he named several neighbors. He described his house there as built of brick, in contrast to his present house in Chatta, which had mud walls. He said that his father had four shops, including a grain shop, a cloth shop, and a store where shirts were sold. He also spoke of his father's iron safe in which he had a drawer with his own private key.

For reasons his family could not fathom, Prakash became quite

---

[3] For the complete case, see *Twenty Cases Suggestive of Reincarnation*, pp. 19–34.

obsessed with this other life he had suddenly begun to remember, repeatedly begging them to take him to Kosi Kalan. He made such a pest of himself that one day his uncle gave in and said he would take him, though only after trying to trick him by getting on a bus heading in the opposite direction. Prakash caught on to the deception, however, and his uncle yielded. In Koshi Kalan they did find a shop owned by someone named Bholanath Jain, but as the shop was closed, Prakash and his uncle returned to Chhata without meeting any members of the Jain family.[4]

After his return Prakash continued to maintain an unusually strong identification with Nirmal. He often insisted on being called Nirmal and would not answer to his own name. He told his mother that she was not his real mother and complained about their modest house. He begged repeatedly and with tears to be taken back to Kosi Kalan. One day he simply set out on his own, carrying a large nail which he said was the key to his drawer in his father's iron safe. He got a half a mile down the road before he was caught and brought back.

Prakash's parents were understandably upset by this sudden change in their son. They wanted their old Prakash back without these disruptive memories, which they had no interest at all in attempting to verify. Eventually their patience ran out and they took matters into their own hands. Following an old folk custom, they spun him on a potter's wheel hoping that the dizziness would cause him to forget his past, and, when that failed, they beat him. Whether or not these actions actually caused Prakash to forget his life as Nirmal, they did cause him to stop talking about it.

Meanwhile, there was in Kosi Kalan a family who had lost a child to smallpox sixteen months before Prakash was born. His name had been Nirmal. Nirmal's father was Bholanath Jain and his sister's name was Tara. Nirmal's father was a merchant who owned four shops— one cloth shop, two grocery stores, and one general-merchandise shop in which were sold, among other things, shirts.[5] The Jain family lived in a comfortable brick house, and the father did have a large iron

---

[4] Prakash had never been outside Chhata prior to his first visit to Kosi Kalan. Kosi Kalan (population 15,000) is the commercial center of the area and Chhata (population 9,000) is the administrative center. They lie on the main road connecting Delhi and Mathura.

[5] Bholanath Jain had owned these four shops while Nirmal was alive. At the time Prakash was telling his stories, however, two of the shops had been sold. This feature of being unaware of changes that have taken place after the death of the first personality occurs in several places in this case and is an important consideration when deciding whether this is an instance of actual reincarnation or perhaps extrasensory perception.

safe there. Each of his sons had a drawer in the safe with his own key.

The Jain family soon learned about the visit of the child claiming to be Nirmal and his uncle but made no attempt to investigate the matter for five years. In the early summer of 1961, Nirmal's father was in Chhata on business with his daughter, Memo, when he chanced to meet Prakash and his family. (The two families had no prior knowledge of each other before these events brought them together and no acquaintances in common.) Prakash immediately recognized "his" father and was overjoyed to see him.[6] He asked about Tara and his older brother, Jagdish. When the visit was over he followed his guests to the bus station, begging in tears to return home with them. Prakash's behavior must have made a deep impression on Bholanath Jain; several days later his wife, his daughter Tara, and his son Devendra returned to meet Prakash for themselves. Prakash broke into tears when he saw Nirmal's brother and sister, particularly Tara, and identified them both by name. He also recognized Nirmal's mother. Sitting on Tara's lap, he pointed to her and said "This is my mother."

The Varshnay family were not pleased with the events that seemed to be overtaking them, nor were they pleased to have Prakash's memories and longings reawakened, for reawakened they were in full force. Nevertheless, they were eventually persuaded to allow Prakash to visit Kosi Kalan one more time. That July, when Prakash was not quite ten years old, he was taken to Kosi Kalan for a second visit. He led the way without assistance from the bus station to the Jain home, a route of about a half a mile with many twists and turns, despite Tara's attempts to trick him by suggesting false routes. When he finally reached the Jain house, he hesitated and was confused. It turned out that the entrance to the home had been changed since Nirmal's death and the door moved considerably to one side. Inside Prakash correctly identified the room Nirmal had slept in and the room he had died in. (Nirmal had been moved to a different room just before his death.) He found the family safe and identified a small cart that had been one of Nirmal's toys.

Prakash also correctly identified a large number of people. In addition to recognizing "his brother," Jagdish, and two aunts, he recognized numerous neighbors and family acquaintances, identifying

---

[6] Prakash mistakenly identified Memo as his sister Vimla. Memo had been born after Nirmal's death. However, when Prakash met Memo in 1961 she was about the same age Vimla was when Nirmal died.

them by name or by description or both.[7] When asked if he could identify a particular man, for example, he correctly gave his name as Ramesh. When subsequently asked "Who is he?" he answered "His shop is a small shop in front of ours"—an accurate observation. He identified another person as "one of our neighbors of the shop" and gave the correct location of his shop. He spontaneously greeted a third man as though he were a familiar acquaintance. "Do you know who I am?" the man asked him, to which Prakash correctly replied "You are Chiranji. I am the son of Bholaram" [sic]. Chiranji then asked him how he knew him, and Prakash replied that he used to buy sugar, flour, and rice from his shop. Chiranji confirmed that these were Nirmal's customary purchases at his grocery shop, a shop which he no longer owned as he had sold it some time after Nirmal's death.

The Jain family eventually accepted Prakash as the reincarnation of Nirmal, a fact that increased the already considerable level of anxiety in the Varshnay family. They had resisted verification of Prakash's claimed memories every step of the way and in the end yielded only to silence his continual pleading. In the face of Prakash's obvious attachment to the Jain family, they began to fear that the Jains were going to try to take him away from them and adopt him permanently. They were also extremely suspicious of the researchers who investigated the case, believing them (falsely) to be covert agents of the Jain family. Prakash's grandmother even went so far as to encourage some of her neighbors to beat up the party of investigators.

In time, however, the tension between the two families faded. The Jain family had no plans to steal Prakash away from his family and were quite content with the visits that were eventually permitted. The Varshnay family's fears gradually subsided, as did the intensity of Prakash's emotional attachment to his past.[8] When researchers returned three years later for follow-up interviews, they were greeted much more cordially and with greater cooperation.

Another child with startling knowledge of someone else's life. Another set of confused and upset parents. We will return to the

---

[7] Two of the women Prakash identified were in purdah. Women practicing purdah are hidden from the public eye by seclusion and by veils worn over their face when they go out. They are seen only by their husbands, children, and close female relatives, and therefore their features are unknown to outsiders. Recognition of these women would be virtually impossible for someone outside the immediate family.

[8] It is typical in these cases for the children to spontaneously lose their memories of their previous life as they grow older. The memories simply fade as the children become more deeply entrenched in their current life situation. See Stevenson, *Children Who Remember Previous Lives*, pp. 106–107.

question of the evidence for rebirth in the next chapter. Here I would like to pursue a different line of questioning, using Romy's case as a reference point.

What would it *mean* to Romy if Joe Williams turned out in fact to be her former life? As she grew up and became old enough to reflect on her experiences, would it change how she thought about herself or how she lived her life? And if her parents had accepted the concept of reincarnation, would this have influenced how they raised their daughter? Would it have influenced how they thought about children in general?

Whether or not it would have, I think it should. In fact, I can think of few questions that have such far-reaching implications for how we understand ourselves or how we view life as whether reincarnation is true or not. Perhaps I see the contrasts sharply because I came to accept reincarnation only after living and thinking for many years within what I now call the "one-timer's perspective." Reincarnation was not part of the southern Catholic world I grew up in, nor was it taken seriously in the academic world where I pursued my professional training. Through eleven years of higher education, I do not remember hearing a single lecture on the subject. I knew that Hinduism and Buddhism taught the doctrine of rebirth, but I had only distant contact with these traditions at the time. All the thinkers I studied—both religious and secular—pondered the riddles of existence assuming that life was a one-time-only experience. For all their differences, they accepted this common starting point. Only after completing my graduate studies in philosophy of religion did I become convinced that rebirth was a fact of life. When I shifted to seeing life as a repeated experience, a very different world began to open to me. If reincarnation was one of the fundamental rules of life, we were playing a game very different from what I had thought we were playing.

The question of reincarnation is in essence a question of our life expectancy and through that it becomes an inquiry into the basic nature and purpose of human existence. One of the most basic questions we can ask ourselves is—How much time do I get? How much time do I get to be alive, to take in experience, to learn? How much time do I get to make mistakes and to correct my mistakes, to discover what it is I most want from life and to pursue it? Are we beings that live at best a hundred years, or are we beings that live, say, ten thousand years—through many hundred-year cycles? These are critical questions because how we answer them will profoundly influence what we understand ourselves to be and what we take life to be about. We cannot become more than we have time to become, nor can we expect more from life than it has time to give us. Everything hinges on how many years we have to work with.

If we live only one lifecycle on Earth, this constricts what we can expect to realize out of life. We are given just enough time to sort out our individual identity from our family's expectations, train ourselves in some trade, find a mate and raise the next generation, accomplish something professionally, and, if all goes well, relax for a few years with our grandchildren before we die. Along the way we may look up occasionally to marvel at the universe in which we live. We may cry in awe of the miracle of birth or the beauty of the Milky Way. We may even spend years contributing to our collective understanding of some aspect of its wonder. But always we know that no matter how hard we try, we do not have the time to truly explore the extraordinary cosmos we find ourselves in or to participate to any significant degree in its grandeur. On the other hand, if we live many lifecycles on Earth all this changes. Our roles in the cosmic drama expand in proportion to the time we are on stage. Reincarnation weds our individual evolution to the larger evolution of the universe, and we become more significant participants in everything that is taking place around us. This inevitably will cause us to raise our philosophical estimate of the purpose of human existence.

How we answer the question of reincarnation determines our answer to many other important questions. Take, for example, the problem of suffering. Each one of us knows that our world can be shattered by just one phone call, one doctor's visit, or one careless driver. How are we to respond to the seemingly inexplicable tragedies that so easily cut through our lives, severing relationships and shattering our dreams? The inequities surrounding us in life are so great and the injustices so terrible that they challenge any claim that we live in a universe which permits meaning, let alone a universe which supports our deepest yearnings. On the surface of things, life appears cruel and devoid of compassion. We appear to live at the mercy of whimsy and fortune, to have no control over our fate.

The litany of events that can crush our lives is rehearsed on our television screens every evening. Someone drives home still angry with her boss, runs a red light, and hits a car in which a couple is bringing their newborn child home from the hospital. The wife and baby are killed. Someone else's sanity finally snaps, and he goes on a killing rampage at a nearby shopping mall. As we listen to these stories day after day, how can we not come to feel that we are walking a tightrope over an abyss of random chance that constantly threatens to swallow up everything we love in life? If these tragic events are truly without meaning, then there is no order to our lives and no logic to our fate. Without order, life is random, and if random, tragic. We can survive without the reassurance of meaning, but we can never relax. We can never feel safe in any ultimate sense because we know life cannot be trusted. It pays no attention to our deepest needs, nor does it honor our heartfelt efforts. If even one human life is wasted, if even one human being is treated shabbily by life, then the universe is unjust and none of us can trust it.

How we respond to the questions raised by humanity's suffering will differ profoundly, depending upon whether we start with the assumption that we live on Earth only once or whether we view this one life as part of a chain of many lives. If we see life as a one-shot affair, we have essentially two options. First, we can accept the premise of randomness and make do as best we can. If we are only complicated physical beings brought into existence through spontaneous mutation, as so many believe today, then of course there is no genuine meaning to our lives or to the events in them other than what we can give them through a heroic act of will, as the existentialists recommended. If the physical universe is the only universe that exists and if we perish with our bodies, then we live in a world guided only by necessity and chance, operating without purpose or project. We simply must make the best of our luck and keep developing technology to reduce our risks.

The second option is the traditional Western religious one that sees us surviving the loss of our bodies and inheriting a compensatory afterlife that balances out life's injustices in eternity. Unfortunately, this approach leaves the reasons for the original injustices unexplained. They are taken as reflecting the will of God, yet ultimately we cannot understand God's reasons for allowing them. Despite centuries of debate, Western theology has never been able to explain satisfactorily how we can reconcile humanity's suffering with the belief that God is all-loving, all-powerful, and all-knowing. Thus the problem of suffering has become part of the mystery of God.[9]

Yet the anguish that has traditionally surrounded the problem of

---

[9] Attempts to make Satan carry the responsibility for the world's pain eventually fail because Satan draws his existence and life force from God and can act only with the implicit permission of God. Attempts to make humans responsible for it through Adam's primal sin will also fail for similar reasons. What kind of architect would God be if his carefully planned creation were to fail his first major test? No, ultimately the riddle of suffering must be laid entirely at God's feet.

suffering in Western theology and the resulting inscrutability of God have been forced upon us not by revelation but by the questionable assumption that we live on Earth only once. When we introduce the alternative hypothesis that we live many lifecycles here and that our experience in any one cycle can only be comprehended within the context of the others, the world suddenly becomes more complex but also more humane. When we begin to look at the rhythms of life through reincarnationist eyes, the chaos that surrounds us changes into a symphony of exquisite complexity and beauty. Themes started in one century are developed in another and closed in yet a third. The consequences of choices made in one life register in others. All is conserved; nothing is wasted.

For several centuries, scientists have been showing us the incredible splendor and magnificence of the physical universe we live in. From the macro level where galaxies are born and die to the micro level where particles show only "tendencies to exist," the universe demonstrates not only an uncanny precision but also an ingenuity and beauty that cannot fail to move us. Nature is a work of art at every level. Wherever we look in the physical universe we see a world pervaded by order and intelligence.[10] Yet when we turn to consider our own lives, this order seems to disappear, or at least this is how it has looked to us since the Age of Enlightenment. Everywhere around us is the lawful progression of cause and effect, yet at the existential level our lives appear to be riddled by chance. Cause and effect may govern our weather, our physiology, even our psyches, but they do not appear to govern our fate. Thus where it counts most to us, we are cut off from the order that saturates the world around us. If this is the way things are, then the beauty of a spectacular sunset is a cruel joke, for ultimately our lives do not participate in that beauty any more than they participate in the order that produced it.

Yet the proposal that the existential flow of human life shares nothing of the order and majesty that permeate the physical universe is not forced upon us by the evidence but by the assumption that our lives end when our physical bodies fall apart. When we shift to a reincarnationist perspective, we discover the causality we could not see before. The concept of reincarnation is almost always paired with a concept of cause and effect that orchestrates our many lives into a

---

[10] The intelligence inherent in nature is obvious, it seems to me, regardless of how we explain it—whether we attribute it to an intelligent Creator or to the ingenious mechanisms of evolution.

meaningful sequence. The name given this causal principle in ancient India was *karma*, and most who are familiar with the concept today know it by that name. According to the principle of karma, there are no true accidents in life. Even those events that appear to be without cause in fact have causes buried deep in the fabric of history. In revealing the lawful progression of cause and effect operating in our lives, karma embeds them in a larger natural order. While this natural order is not identical with the natural order of the physical universe, it shares with it the quality of lawfulness. Thus the concepts of karma and rebirth restore our sense of connectedness to the universe we live in. Through them our lives participate in the order and intelligence that surround us on Earth, and thus in the beauty as well.

Adopting a reincarnationist world view tends to change not just our abstract philosophical convictions but also how we meet the concrete challenges posed by our day-to-day lives. You can see this most easily by taking a moment to bring to mind any problem or task you might be wrestling with at the present time—perhaps a relationship, something at work, a financial problem, anything that is currently bothering you. Once you have one clearly in mind, consider how your experience of this situation would change if you saw it as something that did not just appear out of nowhere but came from somewhere definite, with specific purpose and potential for you. How could the adoption of such a posture fail to change your experience of whatever it is you are facing?

The shift is like watching a scene from a play in which suddenly a different and incongruous backdrop unrolls behind the actors. Behind Shakespeare, for example, unfurls the deck of the starship *Enterprise*. Your experience of the scene itself would necessarily change. Imagine yourself one of the actors in this play, speaking your lines, watching for your cues, when the backdrop changes. You try to continue the scene with the same delivery as before, but in your peripheral vision you see that the new backdrop is so different from the first that your lines are losing their meaningful placement in a larger context. Your sense of disparity grows until, good actor though you are, you can no longer continue. "What is going on?" you demand indignantly, your performance hopelessly interrupted.

What is going on, indeed? Adopting a reincarnationist world view can so change our perception of what we are and what we are involved in that it becomes impossible to continue playing the game by the old rules. We want to know what the "new rules" of a reincarnating universe are. How does reincarnation change our strategies for living our present life? One of the major objectives of this book is to answer these questions.

The longer I have lived within a reincarnationist philosophy, the more convinced I have become that knowing specifics about our former lives is unimportant and sometimes counterproductive. Therapeutically engaging our past can be psychologically liberating, but becoming preoccupied with our past, as so many believers in reincarnation tend to be, often constricts our perception of our present options. The past does not tell us who we are or what we might become if we put our minds to it. At the same time, knowing that our present does in fact emerge meaningfully out of our past has significant implications for how we engage our life as it unfolds around us.

As attractive as the theory of reincarnation may be in principle, it will remain just another speculative hypothesis unless we can find reliable data to support it. Fortunately, there are data, more data than at any other time in history. In times past we were forced to argue for or against rebirth on speculative or religious grounds. Today, however, we can examine a large and growing body of facts that are showing up in numerous disciplines, sometimes unexpectedly and uninvited. It is because of this body of evidence that I believe reincarnation is not fundamentally a religious question at all. Granted, it has religious implications, for it influences our perception of what is true about life in the larger sense, but in today's intellectual environment reincarnation has become essentially an empirical question. It is not something to be decided on faith but by the careful examination of cases.

The critical investigation of reincarnation has been under way for more than twenty-five years now. So much evidence has been amassed by skeptically minded professionals that secondary works are beginning to appear to guide the beginner through the evidence.[11] The next chapter will survey some of the types of evidence that have been collected for rebirth, but in the main I have not thought it worthwhile to duplicate arguments on behalf of reincarnation that are made well elsewhere. This book is therefore essentially descriptive rather than argumentative. For the most part, it assumes the reliability of the evidence for former lives and goes on to describe the broader *world view* that follows from this discovery.

I personally find the case for reincarnation compelling, and I believe that the majority of people who examine the research carefully and with an open mind will come to the same conclusion. Even so, I believe that something more than compelling data is needed at this

---

[11] Among them *Reincarnation: A New Horizon in Science, Religion, and Society* by Sylvia Cranston and Carey Williams.

juncture. Many of my university students find the data for rebirth provocative and even convincing on a case-by-case basis, but they stop short of accepting the concept because they do not have a comprehensive philosophy that can make sense of these data. They hold back because they do not understand what a world in which reincarnation occurs would look like. They require a vision of life that incorporates reincarnation while preserving the integrity of our individual lives as we experience them here and now. This book attempts to sketch such a vision. It describes what one sees when one looks at life convinced of the truth of rebirth.[12]

Many important questions about reincarnation will not be answered in this volume simply because we do not have reliable answers at this point in time. If the evidence can convince us that we live more than one life on Earth, it has not yet told us *how* this occurs. It does not explain the precise mechanisms through which one life flows into another. There is much that we want to know about the process but do not yet understand. Neither can the case histories by themselves tell us where our journey began or where it is going. Each answer seems to lead to new questions. The fact that our information is incomplete, however, should not cause us to draw back from accepting reincarnation as a fact of life. I do not need to know where the road in front of my house comes from or where it goes in order to know that there is indeed a road out my front door. Nor do I need to know everything about a particular phenomenon of nature to recognize that it is a natural phenomenon, and one deserving further study.

The works I draw upon in the following chapters represent a wide variety of sources. I consider the data in some of them very "hard," while in others they are considerably more tentative and exploratory. Some of them represent psychotherapies that are new and therefore unfamiliar to many readers. Some of them present ideas deriving from highly selective experiences that are quite rare, and therefore the concepts sound strange to our ears. For these reasons, I want to say at the outset that I have restricted myself in this study to sources that in my opinion represent sound methodologies carried out by investigators

---

[12] Philosophers of science tell us that the discovery of anomalous data is never by itself sufficient to cause careful thinkers to abandon an accepted theory. Before we will relinquish a working theory we need to see at least the outline of a new theory that will explain *both* what the previous theory explained *and* these new data as well. Thus, before we will be willing to let go of the familiar view that life is a one-shot affair, we need more than just reliable evidence of former lives.

of high personal integrity. Specialists will recognize the names of individuals who are pushing back the frontiers of consciousness research, but few of these will probably be familiar to the general reader. In general, I have not tried to explain why I think this particular researcher or that particular institute deserves to be taken seriously; this would have involved lengthy argumentation and long detours into justification. Instead, I have brought together what I consider significant pieces of information that are part of the current landscape in the study of consciousness and other selected disciplines and have organized them around the theme of rebirth. I encourage readers to examine the sources carefully and to decide for themselves whether they will stand the weight I place on them.

The religious philosophies of the East have cultivated a reincarnationist world view for thousands of years, of course, and we naturally turn there first to understand the broader implications of the data our Western research is uncovering. But reincarnation has never been simply an Eastern concept. Belief in rebirth was widespread in the ancient world, and even today its adherents circle the globe. The mystical traditions of even many Western religions have embraced reincarnation. What appears to determine whether a religious tradition accepts reincarnation is not whether it comes from an Eastern culture but how deeply its spiritual practices explore the psyche. Belief in reincarnation tends to show up whenever psychological exercises are employed that are capable of penetrating into the deeper levels of consciousness where memories of our former lives are stored. The real contrast, therefore, is not between Eastern and Western religions, but between what is often referred to as the *esoteric* and *exoteric* sides of religion. Since I will invoke this distinction often in the following chapters, let me explain it in some detail here.

THE EXOTERIC AND ESOTERIC LEVELS OF RELIGION

Religions are philosophies of life that engender many levels of participation. For some, religion is simply a weekly observance and a set of rituals that mark the major turning points in life. For others it is a set of values around which they organize their family life, their careers, their political activity, and so on. For still others it is a system of spiritual practices that propel them on a spiritual journey deep into their souls and initiate them into the inner workings of the universe. The *exoteric* or "public" side of religion is the more conventional side.

It is the "religion of the people" cradling the masses of humanity. It is that form of religion one finds at the local church, synagogue, or temple. Obviously it encompasses a wide range of observance and authenticity.

To find the *esoteric* or "secret" side of religion, one has to travel a bit. The mystical side of religion, it attracts those for whom belief alone is not sufficient, those who must actually experience the realities the doctrines describe. It calls for a more demanding life-style and draws only those who are willing to invest their entire life in a regimen of spiritual practice. Accordingly, the mystically inclined tend to withdraw from the cities into the mountains and behind monastic walls where they can practice their spiritual exercises with fewer distractions.

In the esoteric traditions one is not simply taught subtle concepts but is experientially initiated into the realities behind these concepts. Verbal theories become progressively less important as experience matures. Words literally lose their meaning without the experiences they assume. Nevertheless, over the centuries these explorers have left descriptions of their inner journeys and of the universe they have discovered along the way. As one might expect, these observations are as far removed from popular religious teachings as postgraduate physics is from what is taught in a high school classroom.

Because the quest for God and for transcendence is universal, each world religion has an esoteric as well as an exoteric side. Each religion serves both the larger populace for whom the simpler teachings suffice and those who must have this experiential knowledge. One might picture a religion as an ellipse, an oval in which all the points are equidistant from two centers. The two centers of religion are its exoteric and esoteric sides. As different as these two sides are, they are nevertheless part of the same tradition. They define different points on a continuum of religious experience and reflection. They are also often mutually interdependent—the esoteric few requiring the support of the populace to free them for their time-consuming practices, and the populace drawing intellectual and spiritual support from their spiritual elite.

Much of my professional work as a philosopher of religion has been focused on the esoteric side of religion. Along the way I have become convinced that there is a common philosophical thread running through the esoteric traditions of the world. Thus, I side with those scholars, such as Huston Smith and Frithjof Schuon, who believe they

FIGURE 1.1

can identify a consistent core set of teachings in the esoteric spiritual traditions, however different the exoteric sides of those same traditions may appear.[13]

To continue with the analogy of the ellipse, we might represent the interrelation of the various religions of the world as a series of overlapping ellipses (Figure 1.1). The outer circle of dots represents the exoteric dimension of the religions, the inner circle the esoteric. At the exoteric or popular level, what stands out are the differences in religious observance. Different religions celebrate different rituals, read from different holy books, follow different sacred calendars, name Ultimate Reality by different names, and so on. Yet at the esoteric or mystical level, there is a surprising convergence of views. Here the similarities stand out more.

The reason the esoteric levels of different religions tend to converge is really quite simple. Spiritual seekers around the globe are exploring the psychospiritual side of existence, and this reality is the same for all human beings. We may speak and think in many languages, but the anatomy of our brains is uniform for the species. Similarly, the more deeply we penetrate the spiritual fabric of existence, the more we exchange cultural diversities for common ground. Reincarnation has frequently been part of this common ground even within the Western religions.

Traditional rabbinic Judaism, for example, assumes a one-time-through metaphysics and emphasizes the prophetic tradition of strong social action in this life. Yet even here, the inward-facing mystics who formed Hasidic Judaism accepted reincarnation and incorporated it into their theology.[14] Similarly, mainstream Islam rejects the concept of rebirth and emphasizes the ancient Semitic idea of one God to Whom

---

[13] Huston Smith, *Forgotten Truth: The Primordial Tradition*; Frithjof Schuon, *The Transcendental Unity of Religion* and *Survey of Metaphysics and Esoterism*.

[14] For a convenient summary of the position of reincarnation in rabbinic Judaism, see Cranston and Williams, *Reincarnation*, Chapter 12.

we are ultimately responsible. This did not stop the Islamic mystics, the Sufis, from embracing reincarnation and from seeing humans as crystallizations of divinity in human disguises.[15] Within Christianity, the mystically oriented Gnostic Christians espoused reincarnation—as have several other Christian sects through history, all of whom were persecuted for their deviation from orthodoxy. The split among religions over reincarnation is therefore not primarily a division between East and West so much as a division between the exoteric and esoteric levels of religion.[16]

One of the exciting intellectual developments of our century is the fact that the vision of life that runs consistent through the world's esoteric spiritual traditions is beginning to be confirmed by contemporary research in multiple disciplines. Carl G. Jung, the Swiss psychiatrist, was the first Western intellectual to recognize this pattern, and the trend has continued to gather momentum since he wrote. Many people are by now aware, for example, of the similarities that exist between the descriptions of subatomic reality offered by quantum physics and the teachings of the Eastern masters of meditation. Books by Frijhof Capra, Gary Zukav, and Fred Wolf,[17] to name but a few, have demonstrated the surprising fact that those who have studied physical matter in greatest detail and those who have studied consciousness in greatest detail are saying remarkably similar things about how the world is constructed. In a similar vein, the contemporary study of consciousness has provided independent evidence for many elements of esoteric world view. The more deeply we explore consciousness using modern techniques, the more we are able to confirm many of the insights collected by these earlier explorers of the psyche. An excellent example of this

---

[15] See Cranston and Williams, *Reincarnation*, pp. 175–177, and MacGregor, *Reincarnation in Christianity*, pp. 45–46.

[16] The theological differences between the esoteric and exoteric sides of the same religion have sometimes made for strained relations between the two. In the West, for example, orthodoxy has tended to be defined by exoteric religion, which has not always been willing to countenance what its esoteric brethren have claimed on the basis of their spiritual experiences. Western mystics have handled the potential dissonance between their private experiences and public doctrine in different ways. Some have simply refused to accept as real any of their experiences that did not conform to existing Church dogma. Thus the famous seventeenth-century Catholic mystic St. John of the Cross wrote: "Since, then, there are no more articles of faith than those which have already been revealed to the Church, not only must anything new [that one experiences] be rejected, but it behooves the soul to be cautious and pay no heed to any novelties implied therein" (*Ascent of Mt. Carmel*, p. 325). One wonders what John might have seen in his raptures that he refused, out of deference to orthodoxy, to discuss.

[17] Frijhof Capra, *The Tao of Physics*; Gary Zukav, *The Dance of the Wu Li Masters*; Fred Wolf, *Star Wave*.

pattern can be found in Stanislav Grof's research in highly experiential psychotherapy.[18]

Because of this convergence of ancient and contemporary testimony, and because of the cross-cultural consistency of the esoteric perspective, I draw upon esoteric sources in this book without apology or lengthy defense. The vision of life I present in this volume, therefore, is an ancient world view that has been given fresh life by contemporary research. It is a spiritual vision of life, a vision that locates the physical universe in a larger and more fundamental spiritual universe. It sees the human journey as a cycling back and forth between these two dimensions, a journey that continues until we eventually complete what we came to Earth to accomplish.

In presenting this vision of life, I am keenly aware of walking a middle course between two alternative visions of reality that dominate the thinking of our culture. On one side is the traditional Judeo-Christian view that affirms the existence of a spiritual dimension but rejects reincarnation. On the other side is the materialist belief that matter is the only thing which exists at all—or, put more precisely, that it is the controlling core of everything that does exist. Since this philosophy denies the existence of an independent spiritual dimension altogether, it obviously has no room for reincarnation.

Because of Christianity's deep historical influence on Western thinking about the afterlife, I devote Chapter 6 to the question of whether there is room for reincarnation in Christian thought. I do not, however, allot similar space to materialism, and therefore wish to discuss that view briefly here. This is an important detour, for all of us who first learned to think in the twentieth century have been influenced by this vision of reality. It has directly and indirectly shaped what we consider possible and impossible.

IS MATTER THE CONTROLLING REALITY?

The view that only matter exists is called *materialism*. Under philosophical scrutiny materialism has shown itself to be untenable because our thoughts and feelings, to name but two examples, cannot be adequately described as material phenomena. They are not matter as we experience

---

[18] *Realms of the Human Unconscious, LSD Psychotherapy, Beyond the Brain, The Adventure of Self-Discovery, A Human Encounter with Death* (written with Joan Halifax), and *Beyond Death* (with Christina Grof). On this trend one might also consult *Dialogues with Scientists and Sages: The Search for Unity*, edited by Renée Weber, and *Ancient Wisdom and Modern Science*, edited by Stanislav Grof.

matter in other contexts, nor can they be reduced to matter in any meaningful sense. This flaw has led to a second formulation of the materialist hypothesis that goes by the name of *naturalism*. Naturalism is the view that (1) nothing that lacks a material component exists and that (2) in what does exist the physical component has the final say.[19] In essence, then, naturalism views everything that exists as rooted in matter. Matter is the ultimate foundation of reality, and everything must have a foothold in it. Our thoughts and feelings, therefore, are not exclusively material phenomena, but they have a material component—brain states—that is the decisive and controlling component. (The distinction between materialism and naturalism is often lost on the lay public, who correctly perceive that, in the final analysis, both views consider matter primary and "what truly counts.")

Metaphysical naturalism is the most powerful secular world view of our time.[20] It is the reigning "religion" of American intellectual circles even fifty years after quantum theory has begun to show us a more subtle universe than most metaphysical naturalists envision. How we came to this belief is a long story that combines a tale of severe disillusionment with Christianity (its irreconcilable factions, political interference, and suppression of knowledge) with the saga of science's extraordinary success in coming to understand and manipulate physical reality. So successful and dramatic were science's attempts to unravel the secrets of the physical world that step by step we came to believe we would eventually be able to explain everything in the universe in physical terms. That is, we came to the premature conclusion that the physical world is the foundation of everything that exists.

In the beginning, the scientific method existed alongside other methods for obtaining knowledge about reality. Science studied the material world; theology studied the spiritual world. As our confidence in the scientific method grew, along with our dreams of what we might accomplish with it, so did the conviction that science was studying something more *useful* than what theology studied. Theology's methods

---

[19] This definition is taken from Huston Smith, *Beyond the Post-Modern Mind*, p. 114. I am indebted to Dr. Smith for many of the points made here. For a fuller discussion of the role of science in shaping our current metaphysical assumptions and for a concise explanation of why neither science nor a philosophy based on science can *ever* develop an adequate philosophy of human existence, the reader should consult this illuminating book.

[20] I refer to this view as metaphysical naturalism to avoid confusing naturalism as it is defined here with other theories or movements that go by the same name. This will also help prevent positive associations we have for the word *natural* from being inappropriately transferred to this metaphysical theory of how the universe is constructed.

did not allow for the same precise verification or falsification that science's methods did. And was not scientific technology beginning to provide us many of the benefits we had previously tried to secure through religion, with much less success? The sentiment grew that we should not waste our time studying what we could not study well and should therefore restrict ourselves at this point in history to studying what we can study precisely and with clear results. This understandable and perhaps justifiable methodological preference, however, slowly turned into something quite different.

Given its dramatic successes, we began to feel that science was studying something more *real* than what theology studied. Eventually, we came to doubt that anything independent of physical reality even existed. It is a far cry from preferring the precision that working with physical reality makes possible to asserting that physical reality is the only thing that exists.

The latter view is often taken to be the "scientific" view of things, but this is a mistake—though scientists have played a large role in its development and wide acceptance. The "hard" sciences in the main restrict themselves to the study of physical reality, which they have investigated more successfully than has any other discipline yet developed in human history. By their self-imposed restraints, these sciences cannot offer an opinion on the existence of nonphysical domains or the laws that govern them. They obviously cannot legitimately pass judgment on issues their methods do not allow them to assess.[21] When scientists do so, they cease to represent true science and propound instead what Huston Smith calls scientism, or metaphysical naturalism masquerading as science. Scientism is bad science. It is a philosophy seldom adopted by the best research scientists today, though it is widely held by those who teach science as well as by those who seek the respect of science. While it may be sociologically true that many or even most persons trained in science affirm naturalism and do so with religious zeal, they have ceased to function as scientists when they do so. They have instead become philosophers, though usually offering no philosophical arguments for their assertions.

Under metaphysical naturalism's influence, social scientists have been telling us for many years that our intuitions and perceptions that something exists beyond the physical world are simply immature wishful

---

[21] Science can and has demonstrated, however, that certain events once thought to be governed by nonphysical laws are in fact governed by physical laws. Thus, science may legitimately "shrink" our estimate of the size and shape of the spiritual domain.

thinking, a cultural neurosis carried over from premodern times. Accordingly, they have taught us to dismiss such inner promptings as mere illusions created to protect ourselves from the harsh realities of a world without God and without eternal life. Impressed by the credentials of science and confusing science and scientism, we proceeded to cut ourselves off from the deepest part of our own being. In championing reason above all else, we ceased to attend to an even subtler voice that lay behind our reasoning minds. While science and its derived technologies have dramatically improved many areas of human life, albeit with mixed results of late, the spiritual sterility of naturalism has exacted a terrible price.

For better or worse, metaphysical naturalism has by now seeped deeply into our individual and collective bones. It has shaped how we measure our quality of life (standard of living) and how we explain our very consciousness to ourselves (brain states). It has led to heroic applications of medical technology to keep us breathing a few additional months because we have lost confidence in any existence other than physical existence. Our preoccupation with what science was giving us obscured what metaphysical naturalism was taking away from us and what science by itself was not giving us. In pursuing science, we allowed its extraordinary success at unlocking the secrets of the physical world to persuade us that we were in essence nothing more than physical creatures. But this is not true, nor does science demand that we come to this conclusion. *Metaphysical naturalism is not science's fault but our own.* It reflects a historical infatuation that has now largely run its course.

If the modern mind saw science and spirituality as being diametrically opposed to each other, the postmodern mind is reassessing the situation. This has occurred not from any lack of resolve but because of two important developments. First, major breakthroughs in the scientific disciplines themselves have overturned the Newtonian–Cartesian view of the universe as a gigantic physical machine. Quantum physics has challenged our assumptions about what matter itself is, while developments in information theory, consciousness research, cybernetics, systems theory, chemistry, and biology have combined to support the emergence of a new paradigm less hostile to spiritual realities. One cannot read the works of Gregory Bateson, Ilya Prigogine, Rupert Sheldrake, Stanislav Grof, and Arthur Young without recognizing that science is rapidly divorcing itself from metaphysical naturalism.

Second, the classical spiritual disciplines have experienced a dramatic revival in the West in recent years, allowing thousands of persons to experience firsthand the transcendental dimension of their own being.[22] Numerous masters of meditation have come to the United States over several decades and established centers where these disciplines are being taught. While the media have focused public attention on controversial and sometimes dubious representatives of Eastern spirituality, the more authentic teachers have labored quietly to transplant their traditions onto American soil. They have established institutes of learning and spiritual practice that are drawing tens of thousands of Americans to seminars and retreats each year. To these classical spiritual disciplines we should add the burgeoning number of highly experiential psychotherapies that have been responsible for introducing thousands more to the transcendental side of life. These developments have slowly begun to affect the intellectual community.[23]

Reincarnation research is only one of many fields of inquiry currently challenging metaphysical naturalism's vision of reality. If reincarnation is true, naturalism is false. If we live many lives on Earth, we do so by shifting back and forth between two domains, the physical and some nonphysical dimension, at least nonphysical in any classical sense. True science has no theoretical objection to the possible existence of such a dimension, though having a refined feeling for the rules of evidence, it will naturally scrutinize carefully the arguments given for it.[24]

WHAT LIES AHEAD?

All that remains in this introduction is to tell you what to expect in the chapters that follow. The plan of this book is simple. The early chapters present the core components of a theory of reincarnation while the later chapters explore some of the broader ramifications of this theory. The text is designed to be accessible to the beginner yet also stimulating

---

[22] In this context, *transcendental* means that which lies beyond ordinary physical reality.

[23] See, for example, Stanislav Grof, *Adventures in Self-Discovery*; Peter Francuch, *The Principles of Spiritual Hypnosis*; and Leonard Orr and Sandra Ray, *Rebirthing in the New Age*.

[24] The nonphysical domain might down the road turn out to be best conceived of as a highly rarefied form of physicality. On the other hand, perhaps the physical domain will eventually be best construed as a gross form of nonphysical "stuff." Certain discussions among quantum physicists sound suspiciously like this already. Regardless of what theoretical refinements might lie ahead, for now we can simply call these domains the domains of the physical and the nonphysical without committing ourselves to a strict metaphysical dualism. (I lean toward a metaphysical monism myself, seeing this dualism as functional and relative.) In the pages that follow I use the terms *nonphysical* and *spiritual* interchangeably, without intending any additional theological connotations for the latter term.

to those with more background in reincarnationist thought. It begins with the basics and quickly moves to more advanced levels of discussion.

We begin by surveying in Chapter 2 some of the types of evidence researchers have uncovered for reincarnation. The intention here is not to argue the complete case for rebirth but to give readers some idea of the range of evidence collected for it and to direct them to sources where they can assess this evidence for themselves. In Chapter 3 we examine the concept of karma and sketch some of the causal patterns connecting lives that have surfaced in various contemporary psychotherapies. From there we turn in Chapter 4 to explore reincarnation's impact on our understanding of our personal identity. (This was the most difficult chapter to write, and I suspect that many readers may find it the most difficult to come to terms with, for it invites us to expand dramatically our perception of what kind of being we are.) In Chapter 5 we reconsider the broader rhythms of human life from within a reincarnationist philosophy. We explore the idea that the human lifecycle should be thought of as running from birth to birth, with "death" being but a transitional midpoint. We also examine the notion of "soul age" and outline a map of the soul's evolution derived from Hindu chakra theory.

Chapter 6 asks whether the concept of reincarnation is compatible with the Christian faith. Does it compromise anything essential in the gospel message? I argue that it does not and outline both minimum and maximum options available to Christians today. (The related appendix criticizes the claim one sometimes hears that Jesus himself might have taught reincarnation, as reflected in either the Nag Hammadi sources or certain New Testament passages.)

If one adopts a reincarnationist world view, one is inevitably led to rethink the institution of the family, the focus of Chapter 7. Reincarnation invites us to look beyond the mechanisms of genetic coupling and spontaneous mutation to recognize a deeper logic and purpose to the gathering of individuals in a family. Chapter 8 extends this line of reflection beyond the family. Developing the metaphor of the web of life, it explores how the concepts of karma and rebirth can improve our ability to recognize, understand, and respond to the changing patterns of our *present* life.

Chapter 9 continues the discussion of the web of life in several directions. First, it presents a model for our interactions with the web that develops the idea that we are a self-selecting field of experience. It then uses this model to discuss a particularly striking phenomenon I call the "field effect." Namely, when major breakthroughs take place in psychotherapy they occasionally trigger dramatic and immediate changes in one's external environment in ways that appear not to be mediated by physical channels. Finally, this model is used to demonstrate how Buddhist meditation practices and Christian ethical practices interrupt the cycle of karma in different places but with similar end results.

Chapter 10 concludes the book by briefly examining how adopting a reincarnationist perspective might change our perception of the great religious teachers of history.

Because the question of our life expectancy is basic to so many other considerations, it is important that we not make a mistake on it. Just as it would be damaging to systematically underestimate our potential by underestimating our life expectancy, it would be equally damaging to overestimate it. Damaging and cruel. We do not want to torture ourselves with unrealistic dreams of what cannot be, nor do we want to labor under delusional perceptions of the life process. But how can we decide? Is the question of rebirth one we can solve empirically, or is it one of those hopelessly abstract contentions about which we can argue forever without a decisive result? This is where we should begin our inquiry.

2
About the Evidence

*I*n many cultures around the world reincarnation is taught as a basic truth of existence, where all of one's life from start to finish is cast against the backdrop of countless cycles moving across eternity. Such is not the way this idea is entering Western society, however. For better or worse, we are a culture that deeply values the weighing of evidence. We have taken to heart the guiding principle that the strength of our belief in a postulate should be proportionate to its evidence. If reincarnation is to take root in this postenlightenment culture of ours, therefore, it will have to do so on the merits of the available evidence.

Though many do not realize it, these are precisely the grounds on which Buddhism and Hinduism have recommended reincarnation from ancient times. If not among the masses, at least among the intellectually sophisticated rebirth has been viewed not as a theoretical postulate to be accepted on faith but as a law of nature capable of demonstration. If we have lived before, there should be traces of these lives somewhere within our consciousness. For twenty-five hundred years the philosophical traditions of India have insisted that these traces are there and that anyone who is prepared to give himself or herself over to the systematic study of his or her own consciousness through meditation can verify this fact personally. These memories are said to be memories like any other, except that they are stored considerably "further" from our present awareness than memories derived from our present life. To retrieve them is traditionally thought to be a lifetime undertaking. Fortunately, we do not need to wait that long today.

A former colleague and close friend of mine was fond of saying "Anyone who doesn't believe in reincarnation today is either uneducated or boneheaded." That is, either he or she is unaware of the research already published or is intransigently committed to an incompatible theory of life. I would not go quite so far as this, perhaps, but each year his case gets stronger. My personal opinion is that researchers have amassed sufficient evidence for reincarnation that if we are not already past the stage of reasonably "proving" rebirth, we soon will be. Put more cautiously, we might say that at this point sufficient data have been collected and assessed to move rebirth from a low-probability to a middle- or high-probability thesis.

It is not my intention to argue the case for reincarnation here; this would duplicate information available to the reader elsewhere. Yet it would be inappropriate to say nothing whatsoever about it. It seems high-handed to state that strong evidence exists but give no indication of its content or organization. The purpose of this chapter, therefore, is to speak about the evidence—to hold a preliminary hearing, as it were, in order to convince the judge that we have a good chance of winning our case if we go to trial. While not wanting to present all the evidence, we need to give some sense of what we have and how it bears on the case.

Whether we can know that we have lived lives previous to this one will be decided on essentially the same grounds as whether we can know where we were and what we were doing last month. The only way we have of determining anything about our past is to identify specific memories we have of doing something and to secure independent verification of at least some of those memories. The procedure for verifying the existence of former lives is essentially the same. The case for rebirth will stand or fall on whether or not we can (1) find within our psyche experiences from an earlier life that look, feel, and behave like genuine memories and (2) secure external verification of at least some of these experiences. Verifying former-life memories is more complicated than verifying present-life memories in two respects. First, because these memories lie deeper within the psyche than the memories we are used to dealing with, they are more difficult to retrieve intact and free of distortion. Second, because the events in question usually happened long ago, corroborating evidence is harder to come by. Nevertheless, verifying continuity of experience across multiple lives is in principle the same as verifying continuity of experience within one lifetime.

The former-life memories studied by researchers are of two types: spontaneous memories and evoked memories. That is, either they come to awareness spontaneously, usually as soon as a child is able to speak, or they are triggered by some consciousness-expanding technique. Each category raises different methodological questions and contributes a different kind of evidence to the case for rebirth. Let us consider them separately, beginning with spontaneous memories.

SPONTANEOUS MEMORIES

There are children in every culture who, shortly after they begin speaking, begin to mention matter-of-factly their "other life" in another place, with other people, in another body. These apparent memories surface spontaneously and unproblematically (for them at least) and blend into the flow of their present-life memories and experiences. Dr. Ian Stevenson is the foremost investigator of these children, and his many books and articles document many such cases. His painstaking and meticulous research constitutes the strongest evidence gathered for reincarnation to date, and his numerous books are required reading for any serious student on the subject. These include *Twenty Cases Suggestive of Reincarnation* (1974); *Cases of the Reincarnation Type*, Vols. I–IV (1975, 1977, 1980, 1983); *Unlearned Languages* (1984); and *Children Who Remember Previous Lives* (1987). Stevenson is the Carlson Professor of Psychiatry at the University of Virginia Medical School.

The thoroughness with which Stevenson researches and presents the cases he has published makes them difficult to summarize—and, indeed, they ought not be summarized. Their persuasive power lies in the cumulative effect of the hundreds of details that go into each case, and therefore each should be studied as originally presented. Nevertheless, as part of our pretrial hearing, let us review the highlights of a case presented in *Twenty Cases Suggestive of Reincarnation*.

Parmod Sharma was born on October 11, 1944, in Bisauli, India.[1] His father was Professor Bankeybehary Lal Sharma, a Sanskrit scholar at a nearby college. When Parmod was about two and a half he began

---

[1] For the complete case see *Twenty Cases*, pp. 109–127.

telling his mother not to cook his meals for him any longer because he had a wife in Moradabad who would cook for him. Moradabad is a town about ninety miles to the northeast of Bisauli. Between the ages of three and four he began to speak in detail of his life there. He described several businesses he had owned and operated with other members of his family. He particularly spoke of a shop that manufactured and sold biscuits (cookies) and soda-water, calling it Mohan Brothers. He insisted that he was one of the Mohan brothers and that he also had a business in Saharanpur, a town about a hundred miles north of Moradabad. Parmod tended not to play with the other children in Bisauli but preferred to play by himself, building models of shops complete with electrical wiring. He especially liked to make mud biscuits, which he served his family with tea or soda water. During this time he provided many details about his shop, including its size and location in Moradabad; what was sold there; and his activities connected to it, such as his business trips to Delhi. He even complained to his parents about the less prosperous financial condition of their home compared to what he was used to as a successful merchant.

Parmod had a strong distaste for curd, which is quite unusual for an Indian child, and on one occasion even advised his father against eating it, saying that it was dangerous. Parmod said that in his other life he had become seriously ill after eating too much curd one day. He had an equally strong dislike for being submerged in water, which might relate to his report that he had previously died in a bathtub. Parmod said that he had been married and had five children—four sons and one daughter. He was anxious to see his family again and frequently begged his parents to take him back to Moradabad to visit them. His family always refused his request, though his mother did get him to begin school by promising to take him to Moradabad when he had learned to read.

Parmod's parents never investigated or tried to verify their son's claims, perhaps because of an Indian folk belief that children who remember a previous life are fated to die early. News of Parmod's statements nevertheless eventually reached the ears of a family in Moradabad named Mehra, who fit many of the details of his story. The brothers of this family owned several businesses in Moradabad, including a biscuit and soda-water shop named Mohan Brothers.[2] The shop had been started and managed by Parmanand Mehra until his death on

---

[2] The shop had been named after the eldest brother, Mohan Mehra, and had originally been called Mohan and Brothers. This was later shortened to Mohan Brothers.

May 9, 1943, eighteen months before Parmod's birth. Parmanand had gorged himself on curd, one of his favorite foods, at a wedding feast, and had subsequently developed a chronic gastrointestinal illness, followed later by the appendicitis and peritonitis from which he died. Two or three days before his death he had insisted, against his family's advice, on eating more curd, saying that he might not have another chance to enjoy it. Parmanand had blamed his illness and impending death on overeating curd. As part of his therapy during his appendicitis, Parmanand had tried a series of naturopathic bath treatments. While he had not in fact died in a bathtub, he had been given a bath immediately prior to his death. Parmanand left a widow and five children: four sons and one daughter.[3]

In the summer of 1949, the Mehra family decided to make the trip to Bisauli to meet Parmod, who was a little under five years old at the time. When they arrived, however, Parmod was away with his family and no contact was made. Shortly thereafter Parmod's father responded to an invitation from the Mehra family and took him to Moradabad to explore his son's compelling remembrances firsthand.

Among those who met Parmod at the railway station was Parmanand's cousin, Sri Karam Chand Mehra. Parmod threw his arms around him weeping, calling him "older brother" and saying "I am Parmanand."[4] (It is common for Indians to call a cousin "brother" if the relationship is a close one, as it was between Parmanand and Karam.)[5] Parmod then proceeded to find his way to the Mohan Brothers shop on his own, giving instructions to the driver of the carriage that brought them from the station. Entering the shop, he complained that his special seat had been changed. It is customary in India for the owner of a business to have an enclosed seat—a *gaddi*—located near the front of the store where he can greet customers and direct business. The location of Parmanand's gaddi had in fact been changed some time after his death.

---

[3] Parmod's uncle had been temporarily stationed as a railroad employee in Moradabad while Parmod was very young. Because of Parmod's interest in biscuits, his uncle had brought him biscuits from the Mohan Brothers shop. The biscuits had the shop's name embossed on them, and although Parmod could not yet read, the biscuits might have stimulated associations for him. Interestingly enough, Parmod's mother says that Parmod did not recognize the biscuits. His uncle had not been in Moradabad when Parmanand was alive, nor did he have any personal acquaintance with any of the Mehra brothers. He was not familiar with the family's business affairs.

[4] Parmod had not used the name Parmanand before this meeting.

[5] Stevenson points out that the genuineness of the deep emotions such reunions generate is a piece of evidence just as important as verification of information about external objects and events.

Once inside, Parmod asked, "Who is looking after the bakery and soda-water factory?" (This had been Parmanand's responsibility.) The complicated machine that manufactured the soda water had been disabled in order to test Parmod. When shown it, Parmod knew exactly how it worked. Without any assistance he located the disconnected hose and gave instructions for its repair.

Later, at Parmanand's home, Parmod recognized the room where Parmanand had slept and commented on a room screen that he correctly observed had not been there in Parmanand's day. He also identified a particular cupboard that Parmanand had kept his things in as well as a special low table that had also been his. "This is the one I used to use for my meals," he said. When Parmanand's mother entered the room, he immediately recognized her and addressed her as "Mother" before anyone else present was able to say anything. He also correctly identified Parmanand's wife, acting somewhat embarrassed in front of her. She was, after all, a full-grown woman and he was only five, though apparently possessing at least some of the feelings of an adult husband. When they were alone he said to her, "I have come but you have not fixed bindi," referring to the red dot worn on the forehead by Hindu wives. He also reproached her for wearing a white sari, the appropriate dress for a Hindu widow, instead of the colored sari worn by wives.

Parmod correctly recognized Parmanand's daughter and the one son who was at the house when he had arrived. When Parmanand's youngest son—who had been at school—showed up later, Parmod correctly identified him as well, using his familiar name, Gordhan. In their conversation Parmod would not allow the older Gordhan to address him by his first name but insisted that he call him "Father.""I have only become small," he said. During this visit Parmod also correctly identified one of Parmanand's brothers and a nephew.

Parmod continued to show a striking knowledge of the details of Parmanand's world. While touring the hotel the Mehra brothers owned in Moradabad, the Victory Hotel, Parmod commented on the new sheds that had been built on the property. The Mehra family confirmed that these had indeed been added after Parmanand's death. Entering the hotel, Parmod pointed to some cupboards and said, "These are the almirahs I had constructed in Churchill House." Churchill House was the name of a second hotel the Mehra brothers owned in Saharanpur. Parmanand had, in fact, had these cupboards constructed for Churchill House during his life. Shortly after Parmanand's death, however, the family had decided to move them to the Victory Hotel.[6]

On a visit to Saharanpur later that fall, Parmod spontaneously identified a doctor known to Parmanand in that city. "He is a doctor and an old friend of mine," he said. During that visit he also recognized a man named Yasmin who, he insisted, owed him (Parmanand) money. "I have to get some money back from you," he said. At first Yasmin was reluctant to acknowledge the loan, but after being reassured that the Mehra family was not going to press for repayment, he admitted that Parmod was quite right about the debt.

Stevenson reports that he has collected more than three thousand such cases but has published only a small percentage of the cases investigated. He throws most out because they do not meet the highest criteria of credibility. For example, he dismisses cases where the family of the second personality has profited in any way from contact with the family of the first personality, either financially or in social prestige or attention. (Stevenson himself never pays his sources.) He also throws out cases where the two families are linked by a person who might inadvertently have transmitted information from one family to the other. Furthermore, some cases turn out to be explainable in terms of cryptomnesia ("hidden memory"). In these cases, someone acquires information through entirely natural means, such as overhearing a conversation or reading a novel, and then forgets the circumstances in which it was learned. Later something triggers the information, which subjectively appears to come "out of nowhere." Perhaps from a former life, we think. Yet in hypnotic regression, the true source of the information is revealed. Case dismissed. Cases in which testimony is inconsistent, where witnesses are of questionable character, or where there is even the slightest indication of possible fraud are also immediately dropped.

Stevenson has published only the strongest cases, those involving no gain, no evidence of ulterior motive, no previous connection between families, generous recall of details that can be confirmed by associates of the former personality, and ideally the opportunity to bring together the second personality with persons known by the first. His cautious skepticism and critical methods have earned him the attention even of

---

[6] The consistent pattern for these children is to know nothing about events that occur in the former personality's world after his or her death. This is an important point in deciding whether they are unconsciously reconstructing the details of this life by telepathically reading the minds of those who knew the deceased or possess these details as genuine memories.

quite conservative professional journals. In 1977, the distinguished *Journal of Nervous and Mental Disease* devoted almost an entire issue to his research. In an editorial justifying this attention, Dr. Eugene Brody wrote: "Our decision to publish this material recognizes the scientific and personal credibility of the authors, the legitimacy of their research methods, and the conformity of their reasoning to the usual canons of rational thought."[7] Two years earlier, in a review of the first volume of *Cases of the Reincarnation Type* in the *Journal of the American Medical Association*, Dr. Lester S. King concluded that Stevenson had "painstakingly and unemotionally collected a detailed series of cases in India, cases in which the evidence for reincarnation is difficult to understand on any other grounds. . . . [H]e has placed on record a large amount of data that cannot be ignored."[8]

Given the weight I am placing on Stevenson's research, it might be worthwhile to review a second case, also from *Twenty Cases Suggestive of Reincarnation*.

Swarnlata Mishra was born in Shahpur, India, on March 2, 1948.[9] She was a bright and pleasant child, much loved by her parents. When Swarnlata was between three and three and a half years old, her father, a lawyer, took her on a trip that took them through the city of Katni, about a hundred miles away from their current home in Panna. As they drove along, Swarnlata suddenly asked the driver to turn down a road she said led to "my house." Later, while stopped for tea, still in Katni, Swarnlata suggested that they could get better tea at "her" house nearby. Her father was perplexed by her strange suggestions but made note of them.

Over the next several years, Swarnlata spoke occasionally of a previous life she claimed to have lived in Katni, though more to her brothers and sisters than to her parents. She said her name had been Biya, that she had been born to a family by the name of Pathak and had later married and had two sons. She said that her house in Katni was white and that it had black doors fitted with iron bars. She described its interior as consisting of four stuccoed rooms with other rooms less finished and a front floor of stone slabs. From her house, she said, you could see a railway line and lime furnaces. Behind her house was a girls' school. She also said that the Pathak family had owned a car,

---

[7] *JNMD*, May 1977.

[8] *JAMA*, December 1, 1975, p. 978. Stevenson has also had his critics, of course. Foremost among these would be Paul Edwards, "The Case Against Reincarnation" (especially Part 4); Ian Wilson, *All in the Mind*; and D. Scott Rogo, *Search for Yesterday*.

[9] For the complete case see pp. 67–91.

something quite rare in India, especially before 1948. Swarnlata's father doubted the authenticity of his daughter's supposed memories and did not attempt any form of verification for more than six years.

In 1958, the Mishra family was living in Chhatarpur, where Mr. Mishra was an assistant in the office of the district inspector of schools. Swarnlata was almost ten years old. A professor in Chhatarpur, Mr. Agnihotri, learned of Swarnlata's claims to remember a previous life and invited her father to bring Swarnlata to his home to share her memories with a few friends. While there, Swarnlata learned that the professor's wife had come from the Katni area and asked to meet her. When she came out, Swarnlata immediately recognized her as a former acquaintance. Then Swarnlata reminded her of the wedding that she and Biya had attended at a village named Tilora and the difficulty they had had finding the bathroom there. An astonished Mrs. Agnihotri was able to confirm this and many of Swarnlata's other statements about Biya's life in Katni. Soon after this meeting, Mr. Mishra committed his daughter's claims to writing for possible subsequent verification.

Nine months later, in March 1959, Mr. Hemendra Banerjee arrived to investigate Swarnlata's case. He spent two days with the Mishra family and then traveled to Katni, where he was able to locate the Pathak house from Swarnlata's description and later met the Pathak family. They had never heard of Swarnlata or her family but were able to substantiate many of her observations. Swarnlata's memories fit the life of their daughter, Biya Pathak. Biya had been raised in Katni until she married a man named Chintamini Pandey and moved to Maihar, a town north of Katni. Biya had died of heart disease in 1939, almost ten years before Swarnlata was born. (We might mention that the Bathak family was quite Westernized as Indian families go.)

Later that summer, members of the Pathak and Pandey families traveled to Chhatarpur to meet Swarnlata. During this visit Swarnlata made numerous correct observations I shall describe below. Not long thereafter, Swarnlata and her family visited Katni and Maihar, where Biya had lived much of her married life. Swarnlata made additional recognitions of places and buildings during these trips.

Before outlining these recognitions, I should mention that the Mishra family never lived closer than a hundred miles to either Katni or Maihar. And while there was a distant contact connecting the two families,[10] Stevenson (who investigated the case in 1961) found no cause

---

[10] One of Biya's brothers had some acquaintance with a cousin of Swarnlata's mother in her mother's home town of Jabalpur.

to doubt both families' claims that they had not been acquainted with each other before Swarnlata's remembrances brought them together.

Swarnlata's recall of Biya's life proved to be thorough and subtle. All of the items already mentioned (the house, the car, the family names) were confirmed. Because the Mishra family had occasionally passed through Katni on trips and because the Pathak family was well known there, we might assume for caution's sake that Swarnlata could have come to learn some of the outer architectural details of the Pathaks' home through entirely normal means. The same cannot be said, however, for the interior. In addition, Swarnlata's knowledge of Biya's life continued to unfold as she visited the places Biya had lived. On her first visit to Katni, for example, she asked about the neem tree that had previously grown in the family compound. She also asked about a particular parapet located at the back of the house. On a visit to Maihar she recognized Biya's room and a road that led to a river used for bathing. On a visit to Tilora she recognized the room where Biya had died and observed that a veranda that used to be attached to the house where she had lived was now missing.

Swarnlata's ability to recognize persons from Biya's life was also striking. All in all, she recognized twenty persons. Many of these recognitions took place under somewhat formal conditions arranged by the family. Swarnlata would be presented with a crowd of people numbering anywhere from eleven to forty and asked if she was able to recognize anyone present. People who had known Biya were mixed in with strangers, and often family members tried to trick her with false identifications or refusing to acknowledge a correct identification. Through it all Swarnlata recognized a long list of family members including Biya's four brothers (calling one by his pet name, Babu, and placing the others in their correct birth order), four sisters-in-law, Biya's husband and two sons, and a cousin of Biya's husband. In addition she recognized various friends and acquaintances, including a female servant (saying "She is my servant."), a midwife, the family cowherd, a betel-nut salesman, and a husband and wife who were friends of the Pathak family.

Interesting nuances often marked Swarnlata's recognition of these people. For example, when Biya's husband and one son named Morli came to Chhatarpur to meet Swarnlata, they kept their identities secret, telling no one in Chhatarpur who they were. Swarnlata was nevertheless able to identify them in a crowd of eleven men. She acted appropriately bashful around her husband, as is typical of Indian wives. Morli did not at that time believe in reincarnation and insisted for almost twenty-four hours that he was not her son. Swarnlata held fast to her identification, however, and he eventually yielded. He had also brought along a stranger whom he tried to pass off to her as Biya's second son. Again, Swarnlata was not taken in and later correctly identified her second son on a visit to Maihar. (Morli was eventually persuaded that Swarnlata was the reincarnation of his mother.) The Pathak family considered the family cowherd as an especially difficult test of recognition, which Swarnlata passed despite the fact that one of Biya's brothers tried to persuade her that the cowherd had died. Finally, when she was identifying the husband-and-wife pair she spontaneously commented on the fact that he was now wearing glasses, which he had not done in Biya's time.

One final attempted deception. Biya's fourth brother suggested to Swarnlata that Biya had lost her front teeth, to which she replied that she had not but rather that she had gold fillings in her front teeth. The Pathak brothers were unable to remember whether this was true or not and asked their wives, who confirmed that it was in fact the case.

Stevenson points out that overall Swarnlata's emotional identification with Biya was not as strong as, for example, Prakash's identification with Nirmal. Nevertheless, certain subtleties in her behavior around Biya's family should be noted. At her home in Chhatarpur, Swarnlata behaved like the child she was, perhaps a little more serious and mature than most children her age. In Katni, surrounded by the Pathak family, however, she spontaneously adopted the manner of an older sister to men who were forty years or more her senior. Toward Biya's sons she behaved in a reserved manner if members of the Mishra family were present. Morli reported, however, that when she was alone with them, she relaxed and adopted a more intimate, maternal manner.

A few more details. Swarnlata correctly stated that her father had worn a turban, which was quite unusual for that part of India. She also knew that Biya had had a sister-in-law who died before Biya. When served a particular sweet in Katni, she said, "I used to eat this in my previous life." This sweet, bara, was not known to the Mishra family and Swarnlata had never eaten any. It was, however, Biya's favorite sweet. And finally, Swarnlata reminded Biya's husband of the time that he had taken 1200 rupees from a box in which she had kept money. Her husband confided that only Biya and he had known about this incident.

Swarnlata also had some misses, though some of them should perhaps be considered near-misses. She missed the name of the district her family had lived in and she gave only approximately correct names of Biya's two sons. She said that Biya had had a pain in her throat and that she had died of a throat disease. Biya had, in fact, had throat trouble three months before she died and had been treated for the condition. Her death, however, was due to heart disease, not her throat. On another point she gave as the head of her family of origin the name Hira Lal Pathak. Her answer seems to have been a blending of the names of two successive heads of the Pathak household. Her father had been named Chhikori *Lal Pathak*; her oldest brother, who subsequently took over this responsibility, was named *Hari* Prasad Pathak. Overall, not bad for someone who had died twenty years before.

One other feature makes Swarnlata's case particularly interesting. Swarnlata claimed that she also had a few fragmented memories of a second incarnation, one that took place *between* her life as Biya and her present life as Swarnlata. She was able to give a name, Kamlesh; the district she had lived in, the Sylhet district; and a few geographical details, but not enough for this life to be identified. However, she seemed to possess one particularly striking carry-over from this inter-mediate life. From the time she was five or six years old, she had been able to perform three very intricate dances combined with songs. She had demonstrated the dances repeatedly through the years and always executed them in exactly the same manner, without omission or addition. This skill had always perplexed her parents, who had not taught her these dances and who were quite sure that she had not been able to learn them from any outside source. Indian children, particularly girls, are extremely sheltered by their families, and it is highly unlikely that five-year-old Swarnlata could have had contact with an outside teacher without her parent's knowledge. Furthermore, the songs that accom-panied the dances were in Bengali, which no one in the Mishra family could speak. Swarnlata herself could not speak Bengali beyond reciting the words to these songs, which she herself did not understand. She claimed to remember having been taught the dances by a friend of hers in her life as Kamlesh.

I will not go into the detailed investigation Stevenson made into these dances except to note that an Indian associate of his, Professor Pal, was eventually able to identify the texts of the songs and the dances. Two of the songs derived from poems by the Indian poet Rabindranath Tagore and the third from an unknown poet. Two of them celebrated spring, the third was a harvest song. The dances were of the Santinektan style, which Professor Pal had observed in public performance. Around Sylhet, where Swarnlata said she had lived as Kamlesh, Bengali is the predominant language, making her account of their origin at least coherent with the historical possibilities. After an exhaustive study, Stevenson concluded that it was highly unlikely that Swarnlata had learned these dances through ordinary, nonparanormal channels.[11]

Why do some children remember their previous life while most do not? We are not certain, but it may have something to do with the circumstances of their death. Stevenson reports that the events these children remember most vividly are the events leading up to and surrounding the death of the previous personality. In addition, he has found that in a large percentage of these cases, the previous personality died violently, far more frequently than for the general population. Phobias for the objects or circumstances that caused their death are also quite common.[12] Does the shock of such a death create a link strong enough to overcome the usual amnesia, allowing memories from the previous personality to penetrate the conscious awareness of the next personality? Possibly, but we do not know. Furthermore, Stevenson has found that for cases of spontaneous recall of a former life, the time interval between the death of the first personality and the birth of the second is usually less than three years.[13] This represents a much faster "recycling time" than appears to hold for the general population.[14] Is this a factor? Again, it is too early to say with certainty. There is much we do not yet understand about the processes involved.

It would be a mistake to think that Stevenson's cases come only from cultures that accept a philosophy of life espousing reincarnation. He has collected cases from Western as well as Eastern countries, including Great Britain and the United States.[15] It must be conceded, however, that at this point in time the strongest and most complete

---

[11] The Mishra family, for example, owned neither a phonograph nor a radio until Swarnlata was eight years old. She had never been to a moving-picture theater.

[12] For example, Romy's fear of motorcycles and Parmod's aversion to curd. Swarnlata's case does not fit this pattern of violent or premature death.

[13] The median interval appears to vary from culture to culture. Stevenson reports that the median interval for 616 cases from ten different cultures was fifteen months (*Children Who Remember Previous Lives*, p. 117).

[14] Helen Wambach's research with hundreds of subjects suggests that *on average*, people return to Earth after an interval of approximately fifty years, with a range of four months to two hundred years (*Reliving Past Lives*, p. 126).

[15] See, for example, the cases of Gillian and Jennifer Pollock (England), Samuel Helander (Finland), Roberta Morgan, Michael Wright, and Erin Jackson (United States) in *Children Who Remember Previous Lives*, pp. 71–91. As provocative as these cases are, they are not as strong as the cases presented here, either because of lack of external verification or the possibility of contamination through ordinary channels of communication. Incomplete though they may be, the American cases resemble more complete cases in numerous important respects such as the age of first speaking about the previous life, the content of the statements made, and related unusual behavior. See Stevenson, "American Children Who Claim to Remember Previous Lives."

cases come from countries that accept the premise of rebirth.[16] We must therefore ask, this question: Is the belief in reincarnation creating the cases reported or is the cultural acceptance of rebirth in these countries allowing more cases to come to the attention of researchers?

The disbelieving critic armed with psychological slogans about self-fulfilling prophecies and wish-fulfilling fantasies and paternalistic attitudes about the supposed gullibility of nonindustrialized cultures may move to dismiss out of hand all cases from cultures that accept the premise of rebirth. This would be an unwarranted and hasty move, however. A more balanced approach would be to examine the cases on a individual basis, to watch carefully for indications of cultural bias, and to assess each case on its own merits.

Studying the individual cases, one finds that even Eastern parents are often quite ill-disposed to their children's remembrances from a previous life. The Indian folk belief that it is harmful and possibly fatal for children to remember their previous life has already been mentioned. In addition, the parents often do not like the specific things their children are remembering. A child of poor parents, for example, who is remembering a life spent in luxurious upper-class comfort often stirs up feelings of inadequacy and resentment in his or her current family. (On the other side, family members of the previous personality are sometimes worried that the child's family may wish to exploit them financially and are therefore reluctant to cooperate with the investigation of claimed memories.) Sometimes children's identification with their memories are so strong that they actually reject their present family, creating severe strains on even the most affectionate parents. And if a child remembers being a murderer or some similarly unsavory character in his previous life, his parents seldom wish to pursue the discussion.

The point is that even in cultures that accept reincarnation in principle, individuals often have many reasons for adopting a negative attitude toward specific instances of claimed rebirth. In fact, in one series of cases studied, 27 percent of the subject's mothers and 23 percent of their fathers took some measures to suppress the subject's memories, often violent measures.[17]

---

[16] The majority of Stevenson's cases have come from northern India, Sri Lanka, Burma, Thailand, south-central Turkey, Lebanon, Syria, West Africa, and the northwestern region of North America (*Children Who Remember Previous Lives*, p. 93).

[17] Doctoral thesis of Satwant Pasricha (National Institute of Mental Health and Neurosciences, Bangalore, India, 1978) cited by Stevenson in *Children Who Remember Previous Lives*, p. 119. For more on the attitudes and motives of the adults involved in these types of cases, see pp. 118–20, 151–153. Stevenson's presentation and discussion of his research methods in Chapters 6–8 of this book is very instructive.

If these considerations support taking Eastern cases seriously, we do not have to look far to explain why so few strong cases have yet surfaced in Western countries. Researchers can only study cases that are brought to their attention, and many cases must be sifted through to find the relatively few capable of documented verification. In a culture where neither the religious nor academic institutions sanction the belief in reincarnation, the parents of a young child who begins to speak of an "other life" has no legitimated frame of reference for taking these statements seriously. Such recollections will therefore tend to be seen either as a bizarre curiosity or, worse, as an indication of pathology. Neither interpretation is going to incline the parents to seek an outside evaluation of their child's behavior, especially when it is relatively easy to simply suppress the behavior.[18] As belief in reincarnation becomes more widespread in the West and as professionals become more aware of and more willing to refer cases to trained researchers, we should expect the number of strong Western cases to increase. History will tell.[19]

Children who have spontaneous memories of a previous life almost invariably lose these memories between the ages of five and eight as they leave their family circle and engage the larger outside world. Stevenson has done follow-up studies on these children and finds that as a group they fare no better or worse than the general population in social relationships, schoolwork, career success, or general happiness. On the whole, spontaneously remembering a former life appears to be neither an adjustment liability nor an asset. Nevertheless, the awareness of a previous existence may in rare instances complicate the next life's beginnings. Child psychotherapists are beginning to report cases of developmental or pathological disturbance in children which may derive from the carry-over of an adult awareness into childhood.

In her book *Reliving Past Lives*, Dr. Helen Wambach, a clinical psychologist, briefly reports two such cases. In one a severely withdrawn five-year-old named Linda had rejected all human contact, withdrawing

---

[18] Remember, too, that the "window" for spontaneous memories to be recorded is brief indeed, usually between two and five years of age. Unless parents set the wheels of research in motion quickly, the opportunity will be lost.

[19] Given the increasing number of people who believe in reincarnation in the West, Stevenson has suggested that something more than just acceptance of rebirth is necessary for cases to surface. He speculates that it might have something to do with other cultural variables that distinguish nonindustrialized from highly industrialized cultures. These would include a slower pace of living that permits a greater sensitivity to one's inner psychological processes, placing greater value on these inner processes, and a deeper feeling for the interconnectedness of events. See *Children Who Remember Previous Lives*, pp. 165–169.

deeper and deeper into childhood autism, a condition from which few children ever escape. Interestingly enough, she also demonstrated high mathematical and reading skills that no one had ever taught her. Over the course of therapy, Linda eventually revealed how much she hated the passivity and helplessness of infancy by repeatedly force-feeding Dr. Wambach from a baby bottle. In this play she assumed the role of the adult and Dr. Wambach was the helpless infant. Only after she had made her therapist experience her frustration and resentment of her infantile condition was she willing to make contact with her at all.

Shortly after this breakthrough, therapy progressed rapidly. Eventually Linda was able to enter normal kindergarten classes with her peers. She had lost her reading and mathematical abilities and had to learn to write her name from scratch just like the other children. Her family moved away shortly after this and contact was lost. Dr. Wambach speculates that for unknown reasons, Linda had held on to a previous adult identity and rejected her rebirth in a child's body. Somehow, through therapy she came to accept her new condition, lost her adult fixation and its accompanying skills, and became as other children— innocent of other existences.[20]

The second case involved an unruly child named Peter, brought to her for hyperactive behavior. After he was sure that Dr. Wambach would not scold him for it, he began to talk at length about his former life as a policeman. He described his resentment at not being allowed to do many of the things he had enjoyed doing before, like smoking and playing basketball. Apparently his bewildered parents had discouraged him from talking about the policeman. Peter's therapy did not progress as well as Linda's, however, and after three months his behavior showed no signs of improving. He was withdrawn from treatment and Dr. Wambach lost contact with him.

These types of cases are just beginning to be reported in the psychological literature, and it remains to be seen whether they will come to constitute a significant line of evidence for reincarnation. At this point all we can say is that if we have reasons for thinking reincarnation to be true on other grounds, we should not be surprised

---

[20] Another possibly similar case is that of Nadia, the autistic child who from a very early age demonstrated exceptional untaught artistic skill (*Nadia: A Case of Extraordinary Drawing in an Autistic Child* by Lorna Selfe). Children who possess exceptionally precocious talents from infancy are a possible source of evidence for reincarnation that we do not have space to explore here. If, however, one were to listen carefully to the concerto Mozart composed when he was only three years old while viewing the pictures Nadia drew between the ages of three and six, one cannot help but be moved.

if *some* cases of emotional disturbance or adjustment disorder in children turn out to reflect complications in making the transition back into a new life. Or perhaps it works the other way around. Perhaps a child facing difficulties in this life can in some instances resurrect memories from a previous life as part of a complex defensive strategy to arrest or redirect development. It's an area worth watching.[21]

EVOKED MEMORIES

While few persons spontaneously recall their former lives, it is not uncommon today for people to deliberately evoke these memories by using some technique of consciousness expansion. Today's psychotherapeutic arena includes a number of techniques that appear capable of bringing memories of one's previous lives to conscious awareness. Traditional psychology tends to disparage these techniques, of course, because according to the metaphysical assumptions it has adopted there *cannot* be memories of former lives in the psyche. Most contemporary theories of personality were formulated within a one-timer's world view; therefore they assume that the psyche can have within it no content that predates this particular body. Any technique which turns up personal memories that predate this body is therefore immediately suspect. To accept these memories as legitimate would require a major revision of psychology's basic philosophical tenets, and this most theorists are loath to do. Most psychologists are too busy trying to prove themselves true scientists to risk abandoning the "scientific" premise of metaphysical naturalism.

The most common method used to uncover memories of previous lives is probably hypnosis, a technique for selectively focusing one's attention. Where one focuses it and to what end is very much determined by the model of consciousness the therapist and client have adopted. Accordingly, the therapeutic use of hypnosis has evolved as our understanding of consciousness has evolved. Today it is being used to reach deeper into the psyche than was ever dreamed possible only a few decades ago.[22]

The most frequent criticism made of hypnosis as a source of evidence for reincarnation is that there is too much danger of the therapist contaminating the data through suggestion. The hypnotic state

---

[21] It appears that the best way to prevent spontaneously emerging former-life memories from becoming a problem for a child is to allow them to be discussed without ridicule or censure. What is in the open is much less likely to create difficulties.

[22] See, for example, Peter Francuch, *The Principles of Spiritual Hypnosis*.

is by definition a highly suggestible one, and it is all too easy for the therapist consciously or unconsciously to plant the seeds of the desired outcome. Thus, the argument goes, no evidence from hypnosis can be taken seriously.

While the skeptics have a point here, I think they overstate both the suggestibility of the hypnotic subject and the naivete of the therapist. Their critique is based on an outdated conception of the hypnotic state as one in which the subject surrenders complete control of his or her consciousness to another person. Furthermore, it does not explain how verifiable information about other lives sometimes does surface in hypnotic sessions. If it is all suggestion, how does suggestion unlock true information previously unknown to either therapist or client?[23]

It is not necessary, however, for us to debate at length the merits of hypnosis because former-life memories surface in many therapeutic contexts other than hypnotherapy. I believe that a strong case can be made for the integrity of at least some of the information that comes from the skilled application of hypnosis. An even stronger case, however, can be made by observing that memories of former lives surface in psychotherapies using quite different evocative techniques. (I shall return to this point shortly.)

Most evoked memories do not permit the same degree of external verification as Stevenson's cases. Stevenson's children are recalling their most immediate previous incarnation, whereas the memories that emerge in psychotherapeutic contexts often reflect lives from the distant past, making verification of historical details exceptionally difficult or impossible. For this reason if for no other, evoked memories must be taken as having less evidentiary value for rebirth than spontaneous memories.[24] Nevertheless, these cases do have something to contribute

---

[23] Perhaps the best introduction to past-life therapy is Roger Woolger's *Other Lives, Other Selves: A Jungian Discovers Past Lives Therapy*, which I came across only as I was finishing this book. Had I discovered it sooner, I might have drawn on it more.

[24] Occasionally, however, the use of hypnosis does turn up a case of former-life recall that can be historically verified. The interested reader will want to study carefully the case of Jane Evans presented in Jeffrey Iverson's book *More Lives Than One? The Evidence of the Remarkable Bloxham Tapes*. A second interesting case is that of Ray Bryant, reported by Colin Wilson in his book *Afterlife: An Investigation of the Evidence for Life after Death*, pp. 195–197. And of course there is always the famous Bridey Murphey case, which was reported by Morey Bernstein in *The Search for Bridey Murphey* after being serialized in the *Chicago Daily News*. The cautious reader will also want to study the "exposé" of this case published by the rival *Chicago American*, which had failed to secure the serial rights on Bernstein's book, and the exposé of the exposé reported subsequently in the *Denver Post*. (A new edition of *The Search for Bridey Murphey* published in 1989 by Doubleday reviews the complicated history surrounding this case and assesses its current status.)

to the argument for reincarnation. The evidentiary value of evoked memories lies primarily in what we might call their internal verifiability; that is, in how they behave as psychological events. If we survey the psychotherapeutic literature on past-life regressions, the following four points speak for considering at least some of these memories to be genuine instances of former-life recall.[25]

First, we should note that these memories are being elicited today by not just one but many different therapeutic techniques—including rebirthing,[26] sensory isolation,[27] holonomic integration,[28] and the psychotherapeutic use of certain consciousness-expanding drugs.[29] In addition, former-life memories sometimes surface in the various "body therapies"[30] as well as in traditional meditational contexts.[31] This tells us that these results are not probe-specific; they are not tied to one particular exploratory technique. If the ancient idea of a storehouse of such memories deep within the psyche is correct, the widespread appearance of these memories in different clinical settings is exactly what we would expect to occur. We would expect different exploratory methods sooner or later to tap into these memories if they have the ability to carry the exploration to these deep levels. The current clinical picture suggests, therefore, that whenever consciousness is probed with a technique capable of penetrating to particularly deep levels of the psyche, former-life memories may emerge.[32]

A second consideration is the fact that these memories often surface "voluntarily" in therapies that are not in any way aiming at past-life recall, often catching the therapist completely off guard. A number of therapists have reported that when these memories first emerged in their practice they were not interested in and were even hostile to the

---

[25] To argue the complete case for the legitimacy of evoked memories would require a detailed analysis of each of the therapeutic techniques responsible for eliciting them and an evaluation of how these techniques effect consciousness. Obviously our preliminary hearing will not permit such a lengthy investigation.

[26] Leonard Orr and Sondra Ray, *Rebirthing in the New Age*; Elizabeth Feher, *The Psychology of Birth*.

[27] John C. Lilly, *The Center of the Cyclone* and *The Deep Self*.

[28] Stanislav Grof, *The Adventure of Self-Discovery*.

[29] Stanislav Grof, *Realms of the Human Unconscious*, *LSD Psychotherapy*, *Beyond the Brain*, *A Human Encounter with Death* (with Joan Halifax).

[30] Ida Rolf, *Rolfing: The Integration of Human Structures*; Moshe Feldenkraise, *Awareness Through Movement*; Milton Trager, "Psychophysical Integration and Mentastics."

[31] Nyanaponika Thera, *The Heart of Buddhist Meditation*.

[32] This observation rebuts the criticism registered earlier that the "memories" of former lives are due to the suggestibility of the subject in hypnotic trance. While this may happen in individual cases, it cannot explain why the same phenomena appear in contexts where suggestions of this sort cannot be made, such as holonomic integration.

idea of reincarnation. Having been trained in graduate schools that dismissed the possibility of reincarnation, these clinicians were completely unprepared for what confronted them in the actual practice of therapy. Yet, like uninvited guests, these memories kept showing up, and as clinicians they had to learn how to work with them—often going through a painful expansion of their own philosophical world view as they did.

For example, Dr. Alexander Cannon (an Englishman awarded degrees by nine European universities) reports his struggle to resist the idea of reincarnation despite the mounting clinical evidence. In his book *The Power Within* he writes:

> For years the theory of reincarnation was a nightmare to me and I did my best to disprove it and even argued with my trance subjects to the effect that they were talking nonsense. Yet as the years went by one subject after another told me the same story in spite of different and varied conscious beliefs. Now well over a thousand cases have been so investigated and I have to admit that there is such a thing as reincarnation.[33]

According to the canons of research, when data surface that are unexpected given the theoretical assumptions of the participants, and especially when they show up unwelcomed, it is an encouraging indication of reliability. Not a proof, of course, but a healthy sign.

A third piece of evidence for these memories being genuine is the company they keep. That is, memories of previous lives surface in the company of memories from one's present life. If we are using a therapeutic technique that brings forward unresolved memories first from the recent past, then from adolescence and childhood, followed by infancy and even the womb, we are not surprised by the progression. We have become accustomed to thinking of the psyche, in some respects at least, as a multilayered phenomenon that sometimes gives up its secrets only one layer at a time. If we continue to apply the same technique, however, we are often confronted next by unresolved memories from a previous lifetime. Should we cavalierly dismiss these as false memories on a priori grounds? Should we discount them simply because our theory of human nature tells us that they should not be there? If we have a therapeutic technique that successfully facilitates healing on familiar levels of the psyche, would it not be more consistent

---

[33] Cited in Fisher, *The Case for Reincarnation*, p. 43.

to follow its healing wherever the technique takes us, modifying our theory of human nature as called for?

The connection between former-life and present-life memories is even more intimate than this. It is not simply that the repeated use of the same therapeutic technique will often elicit former-life memories after triggering present-life memories. In very powerful experiential therapies, such as holonomic therapy or LSD-assisted psychotherapy, unresolved memories from both the present life and previous lives often emerge *simultaneously and intertwined*. Stanislav Grof calls these psychological amalgams systems of condensed experience, or COEX systems. The more superficial layers of a COEX system usually date from one's present life, but its deeper layers often derive from events in a previous incarnation. The two sets of experiences are linked in the psyche by the common emotions they share. When these emotionally-charged memories come forward in therapeutic work, therefore, they often come forward simultaneously as part of a multilayered experiential mass. The case of Tanya discussed later in this chapter will illustrate this point.[34]

A final and important piece of evidence for these events being memories is how they behave. They not only look and feel like personal memories—subjectively distinguishable from psychological impressions that do not have the character of memories—but they have a *therapeutic impact* which parallels the therapeutic impact of more conventional memories that typically surface in therapy. Healing in psychotherapeutic settings results from the conscious appropriation of unconscious stresses in the system. Micro- or macro-traumas from the past are confronted, differentiated from the present, and integrated into the present personality. When the problematic memories that surface in therapy are from a former life, they behave in essentially the same manner as memories from the present life. They impact therapeutically upon the individual just as present life memories do, freeing the individual from hidden agendas by bringing the core problematic experiences into the open, where they can be dealt with consciously. Apparently it matters little to the psyche whether the forces causing conflict in our lives are rooted in our childhood or in a life from the seventeenth century.

Not only are the therapeutic dynamics of engaging former-life memories identical to engaging present-life memories, but it also turns out that former-life memories often have even greater therapeutic value

---

[34] For more on the structure and dynamics of COEX systems see Stanislav Grof, *Realms of the Human Unconscious*, Chapter 3.

than present-life memories. The evidence coming in from past-life therapies is that engaging unresolved memories from former lives appears to heal the deeper wounds of life. From a reincarnationist perspective, this phenomenon makes perfect sense. Our previous existences are said to contain seeds of experience that did not come to full fruition in those lives—desires that were not fulfilled, conflicts that were not resolved, traumas not fully absorbed, ambitions not realized. One of the reasons for our continued existence in this life is to complete what was left unfinished in those lives. Accordingly, these seeds of incompleteness often constitute the core themes of our present life. They determine our mission—the issues, the relationships, the ailments, and the conditions that will haunt us all our lives until we solve them. Thus a therapy that focuses on these seeds will address the true roots of our present conflicts.

To sum up this line of thought, the psychological events that emerge in these powerfully evocative therapies possess certain features that suggest they are genuine memories. They surface in the context of other memories, their therapeutic impact on the subject parallels that of other memories while being typically deeper, and they can be elicited by any one of several different techniques. Finally, they often emerge unexpectedly and unbidden by either therapist or client.

Let us turn from theory to cases. The following three cases will illustrate some of the points made here.

Heather Whiteholme is the fictitious name Dr. Joel Whitton gives to a forty-four-year-old woman whose case he reports in *Life Between Life*.[35] Heather came to Dr. Whitton, a psychiatrist in private practice in Toronto, in the spring of 1979 suffering from a number of disabling physical and psychological problems. She was severely allergic to a long list of common substances, which caused her ears to ring, her head to throb with headaches, and her skin to break out in rashes and blisters. She had such difficulty breathing outside her carefully controlled home environment that she felt she was practically "allergic to life itself." Her respiratory problems were compounded by repeated attacks of pneumonia and bronchitis that confined her to her bed most of every winter, spring, and fall. Heather had seen many specialists through the years but her condition continued to deteriorate. Every medication and therapy tried had been without benefit. Extensive medical tests ordered by Dr. Whitton once again confirmed that Heather was suffering from

---

[35] The following account is taken from Chapter 8 of that book. I discuss Dr. Whitton's provocative research further in the next chapter.

"severe, intractable allergies exacerbated by an unusually low resistance to bronchitis and pneumonia."

From a psychological perspective, Heather was suffering from a severe lack of self-esteem and an acute sense of personal inadequacy. She was exceptionally sensitive to criticism, and her fear of failure was blocking a promising career in jewelry design. In addition, she suffered from periodic black depressions that always struck when she was happiest. On the positive side, Heather was intelligent, talented, and supported by a strong marriage.

Heather proved to be a very good trance subject, quickly learning self-hypnosis. Together Heather and Dr. Whitton decided that she would explore the roots of her dilemma at home using self-hypnosis, and that they would discuss her findings in weekly therapy sessions. For six weeks Heather brought in copious notes that described a rich outpouring of her unconscious, but none of it seemed to get at the core of her problems. Then she discovered Isobel Drummond.

Heather met Isobel—whom she immediately "knew" to be a former life—not all at once but piecemeal, her story unfolding bit by bit over many weeks. She first saw Isobel sitting down to play the piano in a beautifully furnished English home. She played one of Chopin's piano *Études* and played it exquisitely. Without understanding why, Heather was terribly upset by the sight of Isobel and came out of trance crying bitterly. She was preoccupied with the memory of Isobel all day long, and later that night was suddenly propelled into reliving a horrible automobile accident. She was in Isobel's body, lying on the ground near a burning car that had just careened over a cliff. Her right side was on fire. It was 1931, four years before Heather's birth.

Though lasting only a few seconds, the traumatic recall propelled Heather into a state of collapse. She spent the night crying and shaking, unable to set aside the images she had seen. The shock continued for three sleepless days, which she spent crying and suffering from nausea and a harsh bronchial cough. When sleep finally came, she awoke twelve hours later to the startling realization that she was breathing comfortably *without her allergy medication*. In addition, her habitual headache and the ringing in her ears were gone, and her skin was clearer. Two days later she ventured out into the world and found that her allergies were indeed in full retreat.

Despite this promising sign, for the next three weeks Heather suffered from nightmares, depression, and more fits of crying. So intense was her inner struggle that she was not even able to meet with her therapist. When she finally did meet with Dr. Whitton, she once again returned in trance to the scene of the accident, this time recovering more of the surrounding details. Dr. Whitton summarizes her experience:

> Isobel and a man called Robert are driving hard toward the late afternoon sun that tilts splendidly against the Mediterranean horizon. They are both nursing hangovers and arguing ferociously. Isobel is pregnant with Robert's child and wants to marry him; Robert wants nothing of the kind. In his anger, Robert is scorning the danger of the hairpin bends along the sinuous coast road that flanks the Maritime Alps near Juan-les-Pins. At one of these bends the narrow road turns sharply northeast, but his Bugatti convertible is traveling too fast. The car crashes through a low roadside barrier, flies into the air, and bounces down the side of a cliff, uprooting small trees and shrubs. There is a loud explosion as the vehicle smashes into a rocky outcrop. Robert is pinned behind the steering wheel and killed instantly. Isobel is thrown from the passenger seat into a patch of sandy soil where she lies unconscious. There are more explosions. Smoke and flame engulf Isobel's right side. Her dress and then her hair catch fire, the flames licking the right side of her face.

Heather is coughing loudly in Dr. Whitton's office as Isobel's lungs are seared by the hot smoke from the fire. She watches as French firefighters arrive on the scene and carry Isobel off to a nearby hospital. Her condition is critical:

> Nurses in white uniforms are soaking large gauze bandages and placing them over parts of her red and blistered body. . . . She moans in pain. The entire right side of her body is badly burned. Her right eye and eyebrow disappear in swelling, oozing redness. The nurses keep applying sopping wet gauze, leaving it on for a few minutes, then carefully lifting it off. They are remarking that she must receive all the morphine she needs. They feel that their patient, whose embryonic child has been aborted in the accident, will die within twenty-four hours.

Heather's allergies seemed to have derived from Isobel's inhaling the noxious fumes in the accident, as reliving the event left her allergy-free. Her depression, however, deepened in the weeks that followed. Over several therapy sessions, Heather learned more about Isobel's life. Isobel had been a beautiful, charming, and talented but deeply troubled woman. Born into an affluent English home, she is orphaned at an early age and raised by a envious housekeeper who resents her wealth and beauty. Without real affection in her life, she grows up selfish, self-destructive, and incapable of deep feeling, let alone genuine love. When she is nineteen, she comes to New York City to study piano. Her manager, a Russian Jew named Nickolaus, has booked several recitals for her in America. But distracted by the glitter of New York's high society, which threw open its arms to such a talented beauty, she soon begins to drink heavily. Her dedication to her music suffers from too many parties and too many lovers.

Attempting to stabilize her life, she decides to return to England and to marry Nickolaus, who is more a father to her than a husband. The marriage cannot contain her, however, and she gets involved in a string of affairs both in England and on the Continent. She meets Robert at a Mediterranean yacht party, gets pregnant by him, and wants to run away with him. Now back in London, she and Nickolaus have a major fight over the affair. Isobel storms out of the house and leaves with Robert in the Bugatti. Only later does she learn that Nickolaus died from a massive heart attack triggered by their heated argument.

Isobel survives the accident but is maimed physically and emotionally. The following account is a condensation from several of Heather's diary entries:

> In the winter of 1933 Isobel is living with a nurse and two servants in a seaside cottage near the town of Rye in Sussex, England. She moves very slowly and with a great deal of pain. Her vocal expression is limited to painful whispers. I force myself to take a close look at her—what a mess! Her face is scarred and distorted; the right eye and mouth are pulled askew. She is wearing a long silk scarf of a pale peach color wound around her head and neck. Her right hand is covered with blisters and puckered skin and looks useless. There is a piano in the cottage, but Isobel's playing days are over. With her left hand she paints watercolors of flowers in a semi-realistic style.
>
> Several times Isobel has thought about ending her wretchedness, and these thoughts are inflamed by a visit from Eleanor, a fashionably overdressed "friend" from London. Eleanor sits on the couch sipping tea as she rubs her chatty conversation into Isobel's gaping wounds. "Everybody keeps talking about your looks and hands having been ruined, Isobel dear. Of course, whenever they say anything nasty about you, I tell them how wrong they are. I don't think I could live if I were in your place. How can you stand it, my dear? I mean, how can you bear to look at yourself?" And so on.
>
> Not long afterward, Isobel walks out of the cottage, into a howling winter's night. With sleet beating against her face, she crosses the field that separates her home from the shoreline and plods along beside a wrathful sea. Then she descends some slippery

wooden steps to a beach of pebbles. Slowly and deliberately, she walks into the frigid and turbulent water and keeps on walking. . . .

Heather's black depressions were directly related to Isobel's despairing suicide. After reexperiencing Isobel's grim death, the waves of depression never returned. After this session she also recalled having written a composition as a schoolgirl in which she had unwittingly described Isobel's death in great detail. (I should also mention that Heather had shown a remarkable talent for the piano as a child and had studied at the finest music school in Mexico, where she lived at the time.)

In the months that followed Heather identified nineteen other former lives. Many of them had been involved in arts and crafts of some kind, as she was again in her present life. Apart from Isobel, however, only one other life seemed to have contributed in a major way to her present struggle, and we need not explore this life here. From these two lives Heather had inherited the physical and emotional suffering that would drive her to seek greater health and wholeness.

Over the next three years, Heather worked with Dr. Whitton using conventional therapeutic methods (that is, without hypnosis) to heal the damage incurred in her early childhood. Gradually her self-image grew stronger, as did her ability to express herself artistically. Her therapy ended in 1983, the dark influences from her past successfully resolved. Dr. Whitton reports that she continues to remain free of allergies and that her gallery showings are attracting the attention of art dealers as well as private collectors.[36]

Our second case comes from Dr. Stanislav Grof's *Beyond the Brain*, published in 1985. Dr. Grof's therapeutic methods are quite complex and cannot be easily summarized. For our purposes here it is sufficient to say that they involve very powerful and cathartic experiential exercises that precipitate a very deep opening of the psyche. No hypnosis is involved. Dr. Grof's research does not focus on reincarnation, nor does his therapeutic method center on recovering former-life traumas. He cites this case simply as an example of one type of experience that tends to surface regularly in therapy once it reaches a certain advanced stage.

---

[36] Heather's attempts to verify the details of Isobel's life were unsuccessful. She tried to trace the registration of Robert's sports car through the license number she had "seen" in trance, but was unable to because the French had destroyed all such records before the German occupation. Her attempts to verify Isobel's attendance at the English music school also failed because the school had suffered a major fire in their administration building, which destroyed the records of their previous students. (Personal communication with Dr. Whitton.)

His client, Tanya, was thirty-four years old, a teacher and divorced mother of two children. She was undergoing psychotherapy for depressions, anxiety states, and a proneness to fatigue. One of her sessions brought about an unexpected solution to a severe physical problem that had been thought to be purely organic. Grof writes:

> . . . For the previous twelve years she had been suffering from chronic sinusitis with occasional acute flare-ups because of colds or allergies. The sinus troubles had started shortly after her wedding and represented a severe inconvenience in her life. The major manifestations were headaches and strong pains in her cheeks and teeth, low-grade fevers, heavy nasal discharge, and bouts of sneezing and wheezing. On many occasions she was awakened by a coughing attack; some mornings these symptoms lasted three to four hours. Tanya had numerous tests for allergies and was treated by many specialists with antihistamines, antibiotics, and flushing of the sinuses with disinfectant solutions. When all this failed to bring any therapeutic results, the doctors suggested an operation of the sinuses, which Tanya declined.
>
> [In one of her sessions,] Tanya was experiencing suffocation, congestion and pressure on her head in the context of the birth experience. She recognized that some of these sensations bore a close resemblance to the symptoms associated with her sinus problems; however, they were greatly amplified. After many sequences that were clearly of a perinatal nature, the experience opened fully into a reliving of what appeared to be a past-incarnation memory. In this context, the experiences of oppression, choking and congestion that had earlier been part of the birth trauma became symptoms of drowning. Tanya felt that she was tied to a slanted board and was slowly being pushed under water by a group of villagers. After dramatic emotional abreaction associated with screaming, violent choking, coughing, and profuse secretion of enormous amounts of thick, greenish nasal discharge, she was able to recognize the place, circumstances and protagonists.
>
> She was a young girl in a New England village who had been accused by her neighbors of witchcraft, because she was having unusual experiences of a spiritual nature. A group of villagers dragged her one night to a nearby birch-grove, fixed her to a board, and drowned her head-first in a cold pond. In the bright moonlight, she was able to recognize among her executioners the faces of her father and husband in her present life. At this point, Tanya could see many elements of her current existence as approximate replicas of the original karmic scene. Certain aspects of her life, including specific patterns of interaction with her husband and her father, suddenly appeared to make sense, down to the most specific details.

Grof goes on to comment that as convincing as Tanya's experiences were on the subjective level, they obviously do not by themselves constitute proof of reincarnation or of a causal link between the drowning event and her sinus problem. "However," he continues, "to the astonishment of everybody concerned, this experience cleared the chronic sinus condition that had plagued Tanya for a period of twelve years and had proved completely refractory to conventional medical treatment."[37]

Tanya's case demonstrates a common pattern that shows up in past-life therapies: that problems tend to move whole from life to life. That is, they often move from one life to another as a knot whose strands include physical trauma, emotional trauma, specific people, and even specific places. Accordingly, when healing occurs at the deepest levels, whole persons are healed, including their bodies, their psyches, and their relationships.

While most cases of evoked memories do not lend themselves to external verification, it would be a mistake to think that all such cases are unverifiable. Dr. Grof reports in *The Adventure of Self-Discovery* a case in which many of the details of an evoked memory were subsequently verified through unusual circumstances. This third case deserves to be quoted in full.

> During the time when Karl was reliving in primal therapy various aspects of his birth trauma, he started experiencing fragments of dramatic scenes that seemed to be happening in another century and in a foreign country. They involved powerful emotions and physical feelings and seemed to have some deep and intimate connection to his life; yet none of them made any sense in terms of his present life.
>
> He had visions of tunnels, underground storage spaces, military barracks, thick walls, and ramparts that all seemed to be parts of a fortress situated on a rock overlooking an ocean shore. This was interspersed with images of soldiers in a variety of situations. He felt puzzled, since the soldiers seemed to be Spanish, but the scenery looked more like Scotland or Ireland.
>
> As the process continued, the scenes were becoming more dramatic and involved, many of them representing fierce combat and bloody slaughter. Although surrounded by soldiers, Karl experienced himself as a priest and at one point had a very moving vision that involved a bible and a cross. At this point, he saw a seal ring on his hand and could clearly recognize the initials it bore.

---

[37]*Beyond the Brain*, pp. 288–289.

Being a talented artist, he decided to document this strange process, although he did not understand it at the time. He produced a series of drawings and very powerful and impulsive finger paintings. Some of these depicted different parts of the fortress, others scenes of slaughter, and a few his own experiences, including being gored by a sword, thrown over the ramparts of the fortress, and dying on the shore. Among these pictures was a drawing of the seal ring with the initials.

As he was recovering bits and pieces of this story, Karl was finding more and more meaningful connections with his present life. He was discovering that many emotional and psychosomatic feelings, as well as problems in interpersonal relationships that he had at that time in his everyday life, were clearly related to his inner process, involving the mysterious event in the past.

A turning point came when Karl suddenly decided on an impulse to spend his holiday in Ireland. After his return, he was showing for the first time the slides that he had shot on the Western coast of Ireland. He realized that he had taken eleven consecutive pictures of the same scenery that did not seem particularly interesting. He took the map and reconstructed where he stood at the time and in which direction he was shooting. He realized that the place which attracted his attention was the ruin of an old fortress called Dunanoir, or *Forte de Oro* (Golden fortress).

Suspecting a connection with his experiences from primal therapy, Karl decided to study the history of Dunanoir. He discovered, to his enormous surprise, that at the time of Walter Raleigh, the fortress was taken by the Spaniards and then besieged by the British. Walter Raleigh negotiated with the Spaniards and promised them free egress from the fortress, if they would open the gate and surrender to the British. The Spaniards agreed on these conditions, but the British did not hold their promise. Once inside the fortress, they slaughtered mercilessly all the Spaniards and threw them over the ramparts to die on the ocean beach.

In spite of this absolutely astonishing confirmation of the story that he laboriously reconstructed in his inner exploration, Karl was not satisfied. He continued his library research until he discovered a special document about the battle of Dunanoir. There he found that a priest accompanied the Spanish soldiers and was killed together with them. The initials of the name of the priest were identical with those that Karl had seen in his vision of the seal ring and had depicted in one of his drawings.[38]

This discussion of evoked memories should not end without at least mentioning Dr. Helen Wambach's research, since her work provides a useful counterpoint to the more typical study of individual clinical cases.

---

[38] Grof, *The Adventure of Self-Discovery*, pp. 92–93. Karl's drawings are reproduced on pp. 94–97.

In her book *Reliving Past Lives*, Dr. Wambach reports on two major research projects she carried out over several years in which she hypnotically regressed a total of 750 subjects, each at least several times. Instead of studying the causal relations connecting individual lives across time, she used these regressions to collect large quantities of detailed information about past historical periods. The typical pattern was for her to regress a group of ten to twelve back to former lives of their own choosing without giving specific instructions as to century or location. After the session she would immediately have them fill out detailed sociological questionnaires asking for information about themselves and the times in which they had lived. Were they male or female; what kind of work did they do; where did they fit in the social hierarchy of the period? What country were they in and what date was it? How were they dressed; what were their clothes made of? What kind of food did they eat; what kind of utensils were used? What kind of currency was exchanged? What form of government was operating, what type of priesthood? How did people make their living, worship, and so on? After collecting tens of thousands of such observations, she went to the history books to determine how the data obtained from her subjects compared with what historians were able to tell us about these various places and periods. Would the "memories" of her subjects square with our historical reconstruction of the past? Would this comparison support or disprove her subjects' subjective sense of having actually lived in the historical periods on which they reported?

Time and again, in category after category, the data reported by Wambach's subjects were confirmed by the historians. Both in small details of dress, coin, crockery, diet, social relationships, etc., and in larger patterns such as the percentages of persons in upper, middle, and lower classes, Wambach's subjects turned out to be accurate observers of history, sometimes adding interesting nuances to well-established historical information.

Amid the many fascinating patterns Dr. Wambach plots in her book, one of the most telling is also one of the simplest—the balance of males and females in each period of history. With fascinating consistency, Dr. Wambach's subjects found themselves evenly divided into males and females for each historical period reported on—50/50 +/− 1%. That is to say, regardless of the percentage of males and females among the subjects who regressed to a given century, the lives they reported going back to were evenly divided between men and women, thus following nature's uncanny balancing of the sexes in each generation. Disparities as high as 70/30 in the present were consistently reduced to 50/50

$+/-$ 1% for the past. The only exceptions to this pattern were for countries that were at war in a given century, and here too history was accurately mirrored with women being more numerous than men. At this point we must ask what factor could be responsible for producing this striking result if it is not to be explained in terms of reincarnation?

Wambach's research refutes the widespread belief that hypnotically regressed persons frequently go back to lives as Napoleon, Cleopatra, or other famous personalities. Because only one person living now could have been Napoleon, this redundancy would suggest that hypnotic regressions merely trigger our pet fantasies about our past, not genuine memories. Similarly, many people think that hypnotized subjects usually recall "former lives" as knights and princesses, generals and revolutionaries, or whatever romantic images of the past they have collected from television and books. However this conception got started, it does not appear to be accurate. Wambach reports that the vast majority of the lives remembered by her subjects were burdensome lives of poverty, boring and devoid of color. In not a single instance did one of her many subjects regress back to a life as a historically famous person.

This chapter has not been intended to convince the skeptic, but rather to invite readers to investigate the rich and fascinating literature on the evidence for reincarnation for themselves and to offer a few observations on patterns in the research that become visible if one takes an overview of the field. The cases mentioned here are but a small sampling of the hundreds of cases in print. I personally believe that the evidence for reincarnation today is compelling. It is strong enough at the very least that, as Stevenson puts it, one need not apologize intellectually for believing in rebirth.[39]

Questions and Answers

Q: Isn't reincarnation contradicted by the experiences reported in near-death episode (NDE) research? This research indicates that persons who are conscious during an NDE often report having experienced a heavenly existence to which they would have gone if they had not chosen, or had not been ordered, to

---

[39] To repeat something said in Chapter 1, the evidence gathered to date does not explain *how* rebirth occus. As much as we would like to have the answer to this question, we do not have to have it before accepting the evidence that rebirth does in fact occur. The premise that we live on Earth more than once is not an endpoint of investigation but a new starting point.

return to Earth. Doesn't this description of a heavenly existence contradict the idea of rebirth here on Earth?

A: Not at all. NDE research reports on the conditions surrounding the transition from the physical plane to the nonphysical plane of existence. It does not give us detailed knowledge of what lies down the road after this transition takes place. In fact, Dr. Kenneth Ring (past president of the International Association for Near-Death Studies and author of two books on the subject) reports that it is not uncommon for persons who have had a near-death experience subsequently to adopt a belief in reincarnation. It is not that reincarnation is an intrinsic part of the NDE experience itself, although Ring has come across cases in which the experience itself was highly suggestive of reincarnation, but rather that people often become familiar with the concept and are attracted to it from studies they undertake after their NDE.[40] As a group they apparently do not feel any contradiction between their experience of transcendence in the NDE and the notion of being reborn. We might add here that the description of death that appears in *The Tibetan Book of the Dead* follows closely the descriptions of dying reported in NDE research. This book later goes on to describe in similar detail the counterbalancing process of taking rebirth.[41])

Q: Isn't reincarnation contradicted by the ever-enlarging population of earth?

A: Only if we make a number of additional assumptions that are unwarranted. Reincarnation would be contradicted if, for example, we assumed that the number of souls is finite and that all of them were present on earth at or near the time Homo sapiens first emerged. Yet we have no reason for making these assumptions.

---

[40] See Ring, "Near-Death Experiences: Implications for Human Evolution and Planetary Transformation," p. 80. P. H. M. Atwater, herself an NDE survivor and someone who has interviewed many NDE survivors, puts the belief among survivors much higher. In her book *Coming Back to Life* she observes: "[Survivors] talk about reincarnation as if it were an established fact and, almost to a person, mention a *life plan* and speak of how our lives follow rhythmic cycles of development" (p. 101). In *Heading Toward Omega* Ring does mention one individual, Belle, whose life review covered several past lives in addition to her present life and another, Janis, who claimed to have learned a great deal about the "mechanics" of reincarnation during her NDE.

[41] *The Tibetan Book of the Dead* is an important eighth-century Buddhist text that is a guide for the dying and the dead. It describes the dying process and the stages of the intermediate state between the death of one body and rebirth into another. For more on this work see pp. 00–00 below.

Cultures that have traditionally taught reincarnation have generally held that our lives on Earth function as a lengthy but temporary school for the perfection of our souls. We will eventually graduate from this school, they say, to a more fulfilling spiritual existence. Thus they see humanity as a stream from which some individuals are leaving (permanently), while others are just entering and most are somewhere in between. Where these beings come from and where they subsequently go are questions that take us beyond the limits of knowing. Beginner souls are frequently thought to come from higher animals finally ready to make the quantum jump to the next level of awareness. This idea situates reincarnation in the larger context of evolution and has a certain elegance to it. It also ensures an endless supply of beings ready to swell our human ranks.

Robert Monroe describes a different scenario in his book *Far Journeys*. Monroe's experiences in the out-of-body state have convinced him that beings from nonphysical energy systems completely unknown to Earth are always entering the Earth school to take advantage of the curriculum here. As the number of available bodies grows, an even larger number of spiritual beings waits to incarnate in them. (Monroe also credits the traditional view that at least some humans come from higher animals.)

The point is that there are a number of ways to explain the growing number of humans on earth within a reincarnationist framework.

Q: Is belief in reincarnation always tied to the notion of being reborn as an animal?

A: No. In fact, sophisticated theories of rebirth usually reject the possibility of humans being reborn as animals. Having been around for at least three thousand years, reincarnation is an extremely old notion. During this time it has often kept company with many primitive folk beliefs, including the notion that humans can and will return to Earth as animals—immoral persons as lower, unpopular animals and good persons as noble animals. Some cultures even constructed an elaborate system that tied specific moral failings to specific animal incarnations. This may be an effective method for teaching moral behavior to children and for reinforcing it in adults, but it is not a philosophically adequate concept of reincarnation. Even in India, where rebirth as an animal is a common folk belief, Indian philosophers have often rejected the notion, for example, Sri Aurobindo.

In the course of the evolution of consciousness across many lives there are certain thresholds. Once you cross one of these thresholds, you can never drop back to the previous level. One such threshold is said to be the transition from animal to human consciousness. Once one is operating within the context and resources of human consciousness, all of one's lessons will take place in that context. A graduate student in physics would no longer benefit from taking courses in arithmetic; likewise, a human being no longer has anything to learn from the lower animal kingdoms. Among the philosophically sophisticated, therefore, the rule is: Once a human, only a human—or better. (This does not imply, however, that all human beings were once animals.)

Q: Are we always reincarnated as the same sex?

A: Apparently not. The evidence from many different sources suggests that while people tend to track as either males or females, it is not uncommon to change one's sex. We may change not only our sex but also our religion, race, and nationality.

Q: If people have always possessed memories of their former lives, why are these memories starting to surface now after remaining dormant for so many centuries?

A: Several factors seem to be converging to produce this result. The most important, perhaps, is the fact that the therapies identified in this chapter constitute much more powerful methods for exploring the psyche than were commonly available even a few decades ago. As long as psychoanalysis dominated Western psychiatry, verbal free association was the principal technique used to investigate the psyche. The basic idea was that by relaxing in a reclining position and allowing one's thoughts to associate freely and without editing by the ego, one could, with professional assistance, learn something about the way one's psyche functioned in the shadows of awareness. This technique, however, is simply not a very powerful instrument of exploration by today's standards.

The direction of psychotherapy in recent decades has been away from "talking therapies" and toward more "experiential therapies" that deliberately sidestep the verbal, cognizing ego. Following Fritz Perls's dictum, "Lose your mind and come to your senses," these very powerful therapies have carried the founder of Gestalt psychology's suggestion further than he ever envisioned. Together they are uncovering parts of the psyche that have never been systematically studied in the West before now. The more one familiarizes oneself with these innovative therapies, the more one cannot help but conclude, I think, that the clinical textbooks of the future will look quite different from those in current use.[42]

Skeptics, of course, offer an alternative explanation for the increased number of cases of "former-life recall." Reincarnation, they say, is simply a fantasy that has recently come into vogue. From the front pages of tabloids sold in supermarkets to best-selling paperbacks to popular music we are collectively fascinated with the notion of perpetual existence through the recycling of life. It tempers our fear of extinction and inflates our value in the cosmos. Little wonder, therefore, that such so-called memories should be coming up in therapeutic contexts today, for people in therapy belong to this society and are influenced by this collective flirtation with reincarnation. They are simply giving expression to psychodynamic problems acquired in this life in a form that reflects this societal infatuation.

This is an interesting hypothesis requiring careful consideration. It is an interpretation that needs to be taken to the specific cases reported in the literature and examined in that context. Is it the most plausible interpretation of the individuals involved, of their attitudes toward and previous contact with reincarnationist thinking? Does it do justice to the specific techniques that have elicited the purported memories? If readers examine the individual cases carefully, I think they will find this interpretation unconvincing, but people must decide the matter for themselves. However, by itself this argument offers no explanation for the accuracy of the information Dr. Stevenson's subjects have generated. Nor does it explain Dr. Wambach's subjects' accurate reporting on conditions in previous centuries.

Having said this, it is also clear that we live at a time when increasing numbers of people are beginning to take reincarnation seriously and that this in itself is influencing the data becoming available. According to a Gallup poll published in *Adventures in*

---

[42] For a particularly interesting and important attempt at such a textbook, see Grof, *Beyond the Brain.* For more in this area, consult back issues of *Revision* and *The Journal of Transpersonal Psychology.*

Immortality, almost one quarter of the adults polled in the United States in 1981 believed in reincarnation (23 percent). People are beginning to ask questions about themselves they had not previously asked and to consider answers they would not have previously entertained. This increasing interest in rebirth does more than follow the rise in information on rebirth. It actualy seems to be feeding into it in some way, contributing to a snowball effect.

The important question here is: Is the increased interest in reincarnation creating false data or simply permitting certain aspects of reality to emerge into our awareness? Is the belief in reincarnation fabricating "memories" of previous existences or is it making it easier for genuine memories to come forward in our consciousness? Probably both, but the latter is more interesting phenomenon than the former.

I do not believe our increasing acceptance of reincarnation is itself capable of producing the full range of data being reported in the serious literature on the subject. It may, however, be allowing people to have easier access to those portions of their consciousness where memories of their former lives are stored. Access to these memories can, of course, be facilitated by immature belief as well as by mature belief. Reincarnation's popular acceptance among the poorly informed can have the same effect of lowering our resistance to these memories as its critical acceptance among the well-informed.

There is every reason to believe that as more persons become familiar with the high quality of critical evidence for rebirth, belief in reincarnation will continue to grow and access to these dimensions of consciousness will become even easier. These trends hold fascinating implications for the direction of social evolution as we enter the twenty-first century.[43]

---

[43] If we introduce Rupert Sheldrake's concept of morphogenetic fields into the discussion, we have perhaps an even deeper way of understanding how the breakthroughs of individuals impact on the capacity of an entire species to subsequently effect similar breakthroughs. The concept of morphogenetic field suggests that when a critical number of individuals in a species possess a certain talent or insight, that talent or insight suddenly becomes more easily learned by other members of the species. For more on this revolutionary idea see Sheldrake. *A New Science of Life: The Hypothesis of Formative Causation.*

3
Karma and Rebirth

_____

The fact that we incarnate many times on Earth does not in itself
mean that these lives are meaningfully connected to one another.
Perhaps reincarnation is a completely random process, a cosmic
lottery in which we simply take our chances. Or perhaps we do choose
our lives but guided by nothing more than whimsy. Perhaps in selecting
our incarnations we are like a child standing before a display case
bulging with different-colored candies—choosing some of these and
some of those and dumping them all together into our sack. There is
nothing illogical with either of these scenarios, and yet most of the
spiritual traditions that embrace reincarnation have held that life does
not work this way. Our lives, they contend, do not follow one another
either randomly or whimsically, but causally. The continuity that connects them is causal. In India, the name given to this causality is _karma_.[1]

Practically everyone today is familiar with the concept of karma. It
shows up regularly in popular music, talk shows, and situation comedies.

_____

[1] In _Children Who Remember Previous Lives_, Ian Stevenson lists three groups who affirm
reincarnation but not karma: the Shiite Moslem sects of western Asia, the peoples of
West Africa, and the Tlingit of southeastern Alaska (p. 36).

By now everybody understands the principle of receiving back what we give, of having done to us what we do to others. It is an idea deeply rooted even in Western religions: As you sow, so shall you reap. He who lives by the sword shall die by the sword. In our hearts, too, we know that there is no escaping the consequences of our actions and even our private intentions. Our doctors are now telling us that our bodies register our attitudes and beliefs in a thousand subtle ways. Everything we say, do, or think seems first to impact on us before it affects anyone else. If our bodies let us get away with so little, is life going to be a worse accountant?

Karma is a simple concept at one level and extraordinarily complex at another. As a maxim that counsels us always to treat others with the same care and attention we wish for ourselves, karma is quite simple. When we begin to ask exactly *how* karma works, however, it quickly stops being simple. If we try to fathom how actions, or even thoughts never put into action, can influence events hundreds of years distant, karma moves into the mists of deep mystery. Furthermore, karma is not something we can stand outside while examining. It is the current within which our lives exist. To explore karma is to look into the entrails of our own being, for we are personified karma. To seek to understand it is to seek to understand how human life works at its core.

In this chapter I draw upon two bodies of knowledge to discuss karma. Though coming from different periods of history and different cultures, their perspectives on karma and rebirth are mutually consistent and complementary. The first is the description of karma found in the world's esoteric spiritual traditions. While the Eastern religions will obviously figure largely here, Western religions are represented as well. Hasidic Judaism, Islamic Sufism, and Gnostic Christianity have all taught reincarnation and karma. In addition, the American theosophical movement of the last two centuries has added its own insights to those received from abroad. The second source is case histories from past-life therapy. These cases are used not to argue for reincarnation but to illustrate some of the causal processes operating between lives. The esoteric traditions will place karma within a larger theoretical context while the case histories will provide insights into specific karmic patterns. Finally, I give special attention to Joel Whitton and Joe Fisher's fascinating book *Life Between Life* because of its innovative attempt to explore that phase of life which takes place between death and rebirth, where the karma of one life is actually translated into the conditions of the next.

THE ESOTERIC TEACHING

Karma refers collectively to the many principles of cause and effect that govern the evolution of human consciousness. *Karma* literally means "act" or "deed."[2] Since its linkage to reincarnation in the Hindu Upanishads (in approximately the sixth century B.C.), karma has meant "action which causes [rebirth]." According to the philosophies of karma, our evolution through many lifecycles is guided by the interaction of making choices and experiencing the consequences of these choices. This is how all learning takes place. We make choices and then we experience conditions that result from these choices. In this new context we make new choices, which then generate new conditions, and so on. It is not a deterministic system because it begins with and constantly recycles through our own choosing, which is to varying degrees free.[3]

The esoteric spiritual traditions teach that we incarnate on Earth in order to develop ourselves through specific challenges. As one subject of past-life therapy put it, "I know we have to be given obstacles in order to overcome those obstacles—to become stronger, more aware, more evolved, more responsible."[4] Thus Earth can be thought of in certain respects as a school we enter for the development and perfection of our souls.

With repeated incarnations, however, our choices in this school tend to become increasingly conditioned by our previous choices. Our perception of events becomes less neutral and more colored by our experience here. Each life adds another layer to our conditioning, further eroding our capacity to make genuinely free choices. Eventually we come to exist in a maze of self-programming, unaware of who and what we are outside this programming. We can spiral so deeply into

---

[2] *Karma* (cause) generates *vipaka* (effect). The word *karma* is often incorrectly used to mean both cause and effect. Thus, people often speak of inheriting "good karma," when technically one inherits "good vipaka." This generalized usage is by now so deeply entrenched in our language, however, it is probably impossible to reverse. I will not, therefore, press the distinction.

[3] According to the yogic tradition of psychology, all of our actions leave residues in the psyche called *samskaras*. Samskaras are latent tendencies in the unconscious mind. They are likened to "seeds" from which sprout the conditions of our life. The samskaras are the roots of all the conditions of our present experience, both the inner conditions we experience as our personality and the outer conditions we experience as our historical circumstances. These seeds resurface in our experience in order that "what is unfinished and important can be completed and thereby transcended" (Ajaya, *Psychotherapy East and West*, p. 67).

[4] *Life Between Life*, p. 41.

this conditioning that we may not fully escape its effects even after separating from our physical bodies at death.

Karma and vipaka. Cause and effect. Making choices and inheriting the consequences of these choices. We have chosen our way step by step into this labyrinth of conditioning and we can choose our way back out again. Choices that weaken or neutralize conditioning are described as generating "wholesome" karma, while choices that reinforce or deepen our conditioning are said to create "unwholesome" karma.

The esoteric spiritual traditions view human beings as *embodied spirits* trapped in repetitive cycles of human existence, struggling to extricate themselves from the conditioning they have created for themselves. They view the religions of the world as beacons on Earth, calling souls back to their spiritual home and back to the freedom of spiritual existence. It is not that earthly existence is inherently evil, but it is limited and should not become permanent. We do not want to be trapped here indefinitely. Thus the esoteric teaching on karma is largely a teaching of *return*. It is a teaching designed to help us extricate ourselves from entanglements that do not reflect our deepest nature. It is a teaching that refocuses us on our ultimate objective.

Most frequently, karma is described as the principle of moral reciprocity: "Whatever you give is what you will get back." How you treat others is how the Universe will treat you. If you steal from them, you will sooner or later find the Universe stealing from you. If you are generous to others, you will sooner or later find the Universe being generous to you. The ethical recommendation that follows from this principle is universally represented in the world's religions: "Do unto others as you would have them do unto you." Though self-sacrifice is recommended as an antidote to chronic self-interest, at a broader level we are recommended to value all persons as equals, including ourselves, and to act accordingly.

Each religious tradition has a word for this kind of spiritually grounded egalitarianism. The Christians call it *agape*, the Taoists *tz'u*, the Jews *hesed*. In a word, it is love in its highest form. It is compassion, to "feel with" someone, to crawl inside that person's experience of a situation and choose your course of action taking both your interests into account. The Taoists call acting in such a selfless but not self-deprecating manner *wu wei*. Sometimes mistakenly translated "non-action," it is rather "non-self-motivated action."

As we shall see below, karma actually encompasses a much broader range of cause-and-effect relationships than just moral reciprocity. Nevertheless, this emphasis on moral reciprocity is perhaps justified because the principle of moral reciprocity is central to our efforts to return to spirit. To understand why this is so, we must introduce a second belief that runs through the esoteric traditions.

These traditions teach that the innermost essence of every human being is nothing less than the Divine Essence itself. Beneath our different surface identities, we all participate in a single Divine Identity. We were all formed not only *by* God but *from* God. We are all crystallizations of the Divine Field. The appearance of separateness is said to be an illusion created by the conditions of time/space.

Moral reciprocity in this context takes on a new significance. We are encouraged to treat other persons as we ourselves wish to be treated because, in point of fact, they and we are different manifestations of a single, underlying Reality. By treating others as we wish to be treated, we gradually weaken the bonds that tie us to this illusion of separateness and strengthen our awareness of the underlying oneness. We are advised, therefore, to follow the Golden Rule not for idealistic reasons but because through it we can rediscover the primary truth of our existence.

Now, from the physical perspective, the claim that we are all one is obviously false. In the physical world, we exist as distinct and separate entities. We are born separately, we squabble for our daily bread separately, and we die separately. If anything is clearly true about us, it is that we are not all one, however much we are encouraged to behave as if it were so. Because of this separateness, I can pursue my individual well-being at your expense. I can undermine your career to advance my own, and my net result is that my life is genuinely enhanced. I will make more money and move into a more satisfying position at the office, and these improvements are real despite the fact that I've crippled your career. Idealism notwithstanding, pursuing my individual good at the expense of others appears to work.

From a spiritual perspective, however, this sense of separateness is an illusion, not ultimate reality. Not only is all of life interconnected, it is all a manifestation of a single reality. In those moments when life splits open to reveal its most profound truths, we consistently discover that our deepest and truest identity is an identity we share equally with all beings. In this identity, there are not two of us but always One. For this reason I can never advance myself for long by excluding you from my heart. It will not work because my actions run against the grain of reality. This truth no one can teach another. Each of us must learn it for ourselves—through karma and rebirth.

An analogy frequently used for this paradoxical state of being

Physical
plane

Spiritual
plane

FIGURE 3.1

separate in appearance yet one in actuality is the ocean. Imagine a series of waves traveling across the surface of the ocean. The waves are separate from one another yet they are not. Imagine further a horizontal plane dividing the waves halfway down their height, separating the top half from the underlying ocean. The resulting picture would look something like Figure 3.1. Above the line is reality as it manifests on the physical plane while below it is reality as it manifests on the spiritual. The perception that the waves are separate and independent of one another is a trick of the physical senses and belies the deeper truth of oneness. No wave is truly separate from the ocean, because the ocean is throwing out and reabsorbing each wave from moment to moment. Because all the waves derive their substance, form, and energy from the same source, they are simply different manifestations of the same reality.

While Christianity has not officially adopted reincarnation, this idea of an underlying or encompassing reality that unites us all into a larger whole is an important Christian theme. Jesus used metaphors derived from family life to describe these matters. He taught that this reality, God, was our Father, the source of each of our lives. Because we all come from this common divine source, we are all brothers and sisters in one spiritual family, despite our different biological parents. Thus we must care for each other as brothers and sisters care for one another. Paul pressed this point even further when he said that all Christians were one in the body of Christ (I Cor. 12:12–30). Each part of the body depends upon all the other parts for its own well-being. There is no health for individual parts separate from the health of the whole.

According to the esoteric traditions, the illusion of separateness is actually created by the conditions of material existence itself. To exist on Earth is to exist in separateness; there is no other way aboard. Yet while we exist here as separate beings, we are learning oneness. By systematically inheriting the consequences of choices made on the assumption of separateness, we are led step by step to penetrate this illusion and to discover the Divine Identity that binds us all into a single Being. We inherit our treatment of others because when we injure someone out of self-interest, we are in fact injuring ourselves. Likewise, when we help someone, we are helping ourselves. Life reflects back to us our treatment of others in order to teach us that we and these others, though physically distinct, are of one essence.

The drama generated by this feedback process unfolds across many centuries. The principle of karma teaches that our present is not an independent moment in time but part of a causal chain that has its roots deep in history and its completion in tomorrow. Karma is a conditioning set in motion through countless choices we have made. It is the momentum of these choices in our lives. Energy started in motion must complete itself. What we gather to ourselves must eventually express itself. At any point in time, history has a momentum so large that it must project itself into tomorrow. This is true at all levels of existence. History is the intertwined momentum of individuals, families, communities, nations, races, and planets, all meaningfully, causally connected. Choice and the effects of choice, all for our awakening.

So much for generalities. When we press for specifics as to exactly how one life impinges upon a subsequent life, we find we have more questions than answers. The lines of causality are so diverse and so complex that our attempts to catalogue them have barely begun to skim the surface. The Hindu Upanishads taught reincarnation as an empirical fact of life, yet they cautioned us against ever hoping to understand it all:

> What is one's thought, that he becomes;
> This is the eternal mystery.

Nevertheless, ever since karma was first recognized as a law of nature we have tried to understand how it worked, and our understanding has evolved through several phases.

Early on, for example, karma was usually described in terms of *retributive justice*, an eye for an eye and a tooth for a tooth. If you killed someone, in another life he would kill you; if you stole from, cheated, belittled, or demeaned someone, in time you would find yourself receiving the same treatment from the same person. Later, this principle was supplemented by the principle of *compensation*. You might not later be killed by those you killed, but you must eventually compensate them in some way for their loss. If you stole their life in one place, for example, you must restore it to them elsewhere.

In time karma came to be thought of less in terms of a strict balancing of accounts and more in terms of *learning*, allowing the principle of compensation to be applied more broadly. If you do not end up compensating your original victim, you may compensate other victims of similar crimes. If you kill someone, you may in a subsequent life work on behalf of the families of murder victims, thus confronting indirectly the consequences of your act. The point is to learn from your mistakes. While we often learn our lessons in the company of our original partners, we can also learn from surrogates.

Sometimes karmic learning does not require the involvement of another person at all. Sometimes karma operates through the simple transfer of a particular attitude, emotion, or habit intact from one lifecycle to another. Whereas it may have been appropriate to the circumstances of the first life, it only causes pain in the second. Deserved guilt rejected in one life, for example, may be carried over intact into a subsequent life, undermining that life's self-esteem and wreaking all manner of psychological havoc until it is resolved.

The trend in contemporary descriptions of karma is to emphasize the necessity of learning from one's previous experiences and to recognize that this learning can take many different forms. It is important, therefore, that we break our habit of thinking of karma strictly in terms of retributive justice. The ties that connect our lives are too subtle and too ingenious to be captured by such a narrow concept. All the forms of learning listed above show up in the case histories taken from past-life therapy, and surely there are many causal patterns that we have yet to discover.

As important as the principle of moral reciprocity is for our spiritual evolution, our lives are linked by many causalities other than moral reciprocity, and all of these are karma. Chronic hunger in one life may result in compulsive eating in a later life. Death by a fall may lead to a phobia of heights. Years of practice at the piano may emerge as a "natural aptitude" for the instrument in a different century. Karma includes the full range of cause-and-effect relationships that orchestrate human experience, and that range is broad indeed. In fact, *everything* that we commonly take to be innately "us" has roots somewhere in our history.[5]

Contemporary discussions of karma are being influenced by the

---

[5] In *Psychotherapy East and West*, Swami Ajaya defines karma somewhat classically as the law of action and reaction, a law which posits that "every imbalanced action—that is, action which springs from identification with one side of a polarity—creates an equal and opposite reaction" (p. 67). As useful as the notion of polarities is for describing many karmic causalities, I am not convinced that it is broad enough to do justice to the diverse causal patterns showing up in psychotherapeutic contexts. I find it difficult, for example, to conceive of a transmitted musical talent as resulting from identifying with one side of a polarity, but perhaps there are ways of conceptualizing it so.

many case histories of past-life recall being reported in the psycho-therapeutic literature. There are hundreds of cases in print in which individuals have recalled experiences ostensively from another time in history with dramatic therapeutic results. By studying these cases, we can identify patterns of karmic inheritance and slowly deepen our understanding of how effects are tied to causes across lives. The three case histories that follow, therefore, will illustrate a few of the patterns showing up in the literature. As most of us have a tendency to think of karma in terms of moral reciprocity, these cases will present, as a counterpoint, examples of nonmoral karmic inheritance.

CASE HISTORIES FROM PAST-LIFE THERAPY

One problem that arises from using case histories is that not all of them can be counted on to contain genuine memories of former lives. Here, however, we are helped by the sheer volume of cases being reported by reputable and conscientious therapists. Even if not every case can be taken as a genuine instance of former-life recall, there is some safety in numbers. By restricting ourselves to patterns of inheritance that occur in many cases and not just a few we are more likely to be tracking actual karmic patterns, not just spurious psychological artifacts. The three cases that follow, therefore, represent a larger body of evidence. Each case represents a class of cases, any one of which might have served equally well to demonstrate its particular karmic pattern.

In Chapter 7 of *You Have Been Here Before*, Dr. Edith Fiore reports the case of Joe, a man in his midthirties who came to her suffering from severe insomnia. Under hypnosis Joe returned to a life on the American Western frontier as Dale. When Dale is seventeen, his father, a marshal, is gunned down in a shootout. Three years later Dale (who is himself quite handy with a gun) joins a wagon train and heads for California to seek his fortune. One day the wagon train is ambushed by Crow Indians, forcing the settlers to take shelter in some nearby trees. Dale is the only competent fighter among them. Many are killed. They spend the moonless night in complete darkness, watching and waiting, hoping to steal away one by one before light. They are stalked all night and more die screaming. Dale kills two Indians in hand-to-hand combat. Unable to help the group any more, he slips away a few hours before dawn, but is pursued. For three days he runs for his life, forced to stay alert each night, catching quick catnaps during the day only when he is sure those trailing him are far behind.

Dale is quick and resourceful, and he eventually escapes his pursuers unharmed. After a brief flirtation with being an outlaw, his ability with a gun earns him a living as a guard. Eventually he follows in his father's footsteps and takes a job as a sheriff in Kansas. The lawlessness of the times and his reputation with a gun force him to kill many men through the years. He does so with regret but resignation. Later he moves on to a larger town in Colorado, where he is marshal. Here as before, most of his work is at night when most crimes are committed and most drunks get rowdy. Thus his job requires him to spend his nights alert and on edge. He keeps to the shadows as he walks the streets and checks around each corner before showing himself. There is always someone looking for a quick reputation at his expense.

Eventually Dale is gunned down while playing pool with friends in the local pool hall. Caught by surprise by a shotgun blast through an open window, he immediately knows he is dying. He is angry for letting himself get caught off guard in a lighted room with the blinds up. Years of relentless attention to such details had saved his life, until tonight. He was careless for an hour and look what it got him.

After reexperiencing Dale's life in great detail, Joe's insomnia disappeared. Had it actually been caused by all those years of life-threatening, nighttime tension so long ago, or was Dale simply a projected fantasy Joe's mind created to (somehow) free him of his problem? As we ponder the possibilities, we should note that after his regression Joe recognized a few other traits he shared with Dale. Like Dale, Joe was basically a loner who did not let people get close and who also had a knack for spotting people's weaknesses. Finally, it turns out that shooting has been Joe's favorite hobby ever since he was a kid. "And I'm damn good at it!", he reports.

In this example, the karmic inheritance from Dale's life appears to be morally neutral. Fiore's report of the case is brief, but Joe's insomnia does not appear to result from any moral debt incurred in Dale's life. Dale does not appear to feel guilty either for the settlers he could not save or for the men he had to kill while a law officer. The problem carried over appears to revolve around the stress of constant vigilance, and especially from the conviction emblazoned in his memory during his last waking minutes.[6] Joe's insomnia reflects the fact that Dale did not appear to learn to manage the stress created by his chosen life-style. He never learned how to take advantage of or create opportunities to

---

[6] One's thoughts at the moment of death have a powerful effect on mediating the inheritance from one life to another. In these moments we either make our peace with our life as it was or carry our lack of peace forward to work out later. Dale could not forgive himself for letting down his guard for even one night.

truly relax. Instead, he keeps himself always "on," always alert. Such an approach to living is unhealthy and counterproductive. It appears to have created an imbalance that had to be redressed in a later existence.[7]

Joe's talent with guns demonstrates another common karmic pattern. Talents developed in one life are frequently passed along as "natural aptitudes" in another. Sometimes a skill is carried over and refined through many lives. It makes intuitive sense that a great statesman, philosopher, military tactician, or artist does not simply pop into existence overnight, but develops the required skills slowly and with considerable practice. Indeed, in some case histories we find instances of people setting out to accomplish great things in a particular life but failing because they are unprepared for the task.[8]

The second case comes from the files of Dr. Morris Netherton and can be found in his book *Past Lives Therapy*, written with Nancy Shiffrin. One point that should be made at the outset is that while his patients often enter deeply experiential states as they relive events from their previous lives, Dr. Netherton does not use hypnosis in his work. Instead, he identifies key phrases patients use in presenting their problems and then asks them to lie down, close their eyes, and repeat these phrases until some sort of mental picture emerges. Once begun, the scenarios that come forward unfold according to their own inner logic and resist attempts to alter their content in any way.

Carl Parsons was in his midthirties when he came to Dr. Netherton suffering from an incipient stomach ulcer.[9] He was in charge of a failing electronics/engineering firm and obsessed with the prospect of losing everything. For several months he had been bothered by loss of sleep, constant indigestion, and a pain just below his solar plexus that he described as feeling "like a hot poker being run right through me." In addition, he was frequently impotent, a symptom that did not fit Carl's otherwise typical ulcer profile.

Using the "hot poker" phrase as a starting point, Carl[10] found

---

[7] To determine whether the karmic carryover in this case is completely morally neutral, we would have to investigate the karmic roots of Dale's life as well.

[8] See, for example, Michael Gallander's life as Hildebrandt von Wesel in *Life Between Life*, pp. 85–92.

[9] *Past Lives Therapy*, Chapter 4. In other chapters Netherton presents cases involving claustrophobia, epilepsy, male and female sexual problems, relationships, alcoholism, migraines, hyperactivity, and incipient cancer.

[10] For now we will allow ourselves the ambiguity of referring to these previous lives as Carl, though this is inaccurate and misleading. This simplification will be remedied in Chapter 4 when we discuss the Oversoul.

himself in a primitive village, possibly somewhere in Africa or South America. The following is an edited transcript of his experience:

> I had been trying to win this girl, a thirteen- or fourteen-year-old girl . . . for a wife, but my . . . rival, my sworn enemy, he took her instead. The tribal fathers decided. He took her and they have a hut near mine. I hear them moaning in the night, whining and insulting me with their . . . noise. But now he's off . . . to the hunt? To a war? I really don't know. He's not here and I've lifted up the flap to the door and she's in there. . . . We don't wear any clothes, I guess, at least we don't wear any at the moment. She's not . . . I guess she doesn't know how to object . . . women just don't here. I'm, uh, mounting her and we're rocking back and forth on some skins on the floor. But now . . . the light! Someone's opened the door—the flap—and I'm being pulled off. He's come back! With his spear, his hunting spear. He is shouting, "You son of a bitch!" in the . . . it's a different language but that's the exact phrase! "You son of a bitch, you'll never make love to another man's woman!" And he . . . he pushes me across the room. He hurls the spear right—!
>
> . . . He's got me, right here in the gut, right here, and I'm . . . it went right through and I'm pinned to a post holding up the hut. Now he's reaching down and, oh my God, he's cutting it off. My penis, he's . . . but I can't feel it, I'm . . . I guess it's shock. Oh, I'm paralyzed. The pain is all in the gut. I can't feel anything below. I'm slumping now and I can't feel, I . . . I guess . . . death is coming now. It's . . . I'm so surprised by everything. I've lost the pain.

This session established the connection between Carl's sexual impotence and his stabbing stomach pain, a tie that was repeated in a subsequent session that uncovered a life with strikingly similar themes. In this life Carl was a fetus. From within the womb he experienced his mother having extramarital sex with another man when they were suddenly discovered by his father. Enraged, his father pulled the man off his mother, stabbed him, and than ran his mother through with a sword, killing both the mother and her fetus. As she lay dying, she heard her husband scream "You'll never do that to me again!"[11]

---

[11] This is not the place to delve into the complex problems concerning the self-awareness and identity of the developing fetus. It must suffice here to note that Dr. Netherton's cases as well as many cases from Dr. Stanislav Grof provide us with striking evidence (from present as well as past lives) that the fetus is quite aware, though its awareness is essentially "through the mother." It appears to be cognizant of her thoughts, feelings, and perceptions—which it indiscriminately accepts as its own. The line between *her* and *me* in utero is apparently quite vague. Whether this type of awareness is sufficient to describe the fetus as being self-aware or as possessing a separate identity is a question that must be addressed elsewhere. However the philosophers decide this one, the clinical evidence suggests that these experiences, brief and partial though they may be, become part of the fabric of the soul's ongoing experience.

Still missing from the picture, however, was the connection between these two symptoms and Carl's business and financial problems. This piece of the puzzle was added in yet another session in which Carl found himself living as an aristocrat in an English mansion. He was sneaking up the back stairs away from a costume party to engage in illicit sex with another man's wife.

> Now we're in my bedroom and she makes me watch her get undressed, earring by earring, it takes so long. . . . Women wore . . . so much clothing, layers and layers of crinkly stuff beneath her dress. Now we're in bed and I'm on top of her; I'm naked too . . . and she says something in my ear . . . "What does it feel like to screw another man's wife?" And, God, suddenly, I'm doubled up on myself, like a knife going in. That's my first instinct—she's stabbed me—but it's not true, it's just me. The pain, the pain.

Dr. Netherton suggests that this is a case in which a past life is itself controlled by an even more remote past life. His lover's question in the English mansion appears to have been answered quite literally by the unconscious replaying of the experience internalized from Carl's earlier tribal misadventure—as if to say "This is how it feels to screw another man's wife." Carl's English life pivots around this event and quickly goes downhill. The woman leaves, not wanting to get caught with Carl. A doctor is called and diagnoses Carl as having a perforated stomach and a mild heart attack. He remains bedridden for a long time and is unable to control his financial affairs during a critical period. By the time he is out of his sickbed he is close to ruin. He becomes obsessed with rebuilding his wealth and consumes increasingly large doses of belladonna, which his doctor had prescribed for him. His mental health deteriorates, as does his estate. Large portions of his mansion are eventually closed off to avoid heating costs, and only one servant remains. In the end, he commits suicide by drug overdose.

As Carl worked these events through in therapy, his sleep improved and his stomach pain eased. Despite the connections he had uncovered between his sex life, his business affairs, and the stomach pains, final resolution of his difficulties continued to elude him. He continued to be stressed by the perilous financial condition of his electronics firm and was increasingly haunted by a feeling that someone was "coming to get me." This phrase eventually unfolded into a story that Dr. Netherton notes was one of the most detailed and complete ever told him by one of his patients. Dr. Netherton summarizes it as follows:

He described a Mexican plain, where he had lived for many years as a foreign-born national. Through a life of nearly ceaseless industry he had built up enormous ranch holdings and had become very powerful. He described an elaborate, teasing courtship with a woman who seemed to love him obsessively. They were married, and suddenly she turned cold, refusing to have sex with him, closeting herself with her brother for long periods of time. Carl became instantly suspicious of this woman, but he took no action, except to look for sexual satisfaction elsewhere. He found himself with a prostitute in an expensive hotel somewhere in an urban area. As he engaged in the sex act, he realized that his wife had somehow followed him or arranged to be present.

"My wife knows, doesn't she?" he asked the woman. The response was silence, a turning away of the head. At this moment Carl experienced a sharp pain in his upper abdomen identical to the one he had suffered in England in his aristocratic past life. He made no connection between the two as he described the experience in Mexico, but I pointed out that he was describing similar patterns. . . .

His infidelity in Mexico proved just as disastrous as it had been in his English lifetime; his wife and her brother rushed into the room following his painful attack and, finding Carl in an adulterous sex act, had him taken to prison. Eventually, by bribing government officials, they arranged for his transfer to a mental hospital. In the process, they managed to take over all of Carl's holdings, and he was left destitute.

Carl spent years in this institution, the days blending meaninglessly into each other, with only his death standing out distinctly. This event he recounts in his own words:

I'm in a room, a dark little concrete cell and the dawn comes. There's a man, he brings me food and water. He opens the door this morning, like any other morning. He sets the stuff down—he gives me a horrible look. I haven't seen myself in God knows how long, there's no mirror or anything and I can't. . . . I don't even know what I look like . . . but he screams, "Oh, my God . . . the plague!" and slams the door. I don't know what's happened, I feel all right, but I sit thinking . . . they've done this to me, they'll come to get me yet, to finish me off. I know this isn't over . . . they're coming to get me. . . . I'm blinded by the light! It's midday and the door swings open. They're stuffing hay into my cubicle—unbaled, loose hay keeps coming in, and I know . . . they're doing this to me. My wife and her brother. Someone says, "We have to, you know . . . it's plague." And they touch a match to it and close the door.

As he died, Carl's mind was fixed on one thing—how he had lost everything through the intrigue surrounding his sexual infidelity. This death-thought had profoundly shaped the configuration of his current life. As Carl processed and integrated these and other similar events into his conscious awareness in the following weeks, he began to realize that he did not even want to own a business. He began to see that he had created for himself the tension-filled life of owning his own business simply because he had needed to repeat these deeply ingrained patterns of worry and loss, hopefully bringing about a better resolution this time around. As he finished his therapy, Carl sold his firm and took a less stressful position with a large corporation. His health improved and his potential ulcer never developed. The cycle had finally been broken. The juxtaposed experiences from his earlier lives—illicit sex, stomach pain, and financial ruin—that his consciousness had internalized together as an unconscious script had finally been separated from one another.

In the two cases presented thus far, the karmic problems pressing for resolution have primarily affected only the individual concerned. As the next case demonstrates, however, many karmic carryovers involve relationships. This case is taken from Chapter 9 of *Life Between Life* by Joel Whitton and Joe Fisher.

Gary Pennington was a successful forensic psychologist, the proud father of two children, and an exceedingly happily married man. His relationship with his wife, Elizabeth, had begun when they were teenagers and had only deepened and intensified through sixteen years of marriage. Their warm home and rich family life was the envy of many of their friends, and Gary had never been seriously tempted by outside sexual adventures. Never, that is, until he met Caroline at a Christmas party in 1982. Gary and Caroline's immediate and overwhelming attraction to each other quickly developed into an intense and passionate affair. "It was like being welcomed home," Gary said.

From the start Gary informed his wife about Caroline, expecting her to tolerate his obsession. She did her best for three months but eventually could no longer handle the continuing erosion of her marriage. She tried to commit suicide. Though the attempt failed, Gary was so badly shaken that he immediately ended the affair with Caroline. Devastated, Caroline jumped into another relationship. When this relationship did not develop as she had hoped, she attempted suicide but was discovered and thwarted. Those around her knew that the true cause of her desperation was her doomed relationship with Gary.

Meanwhile, Gary's marriage, though badly shaken, was on the

mend. He had truly returned to Elizabeth, and trust between them was slowly being restored. Gary was able to forgive himself for what he had done and for the chain of events he had triggered, but he was at a complete loss to understand what had come over him. Why had Caroline been so irresistible to him that he had been willing to jeopardize everything he held dear in life just to satisfy his yearning to be with her? It was to answer this question that he eventually came to Dr. Whitton.

In hypnotic trance, Gary returned to 1944 and the life of Pilot Officer Peter Hargreaves, an RAF intelligence officer stationed near Salerno, Italy. Though trained to fly, he is not officially a pilot. Yet today he is going to fly an unarmed P–51 Mustang low over enemy territory. Aerial photographs have indicated the possibility of German preparations for a counterattack nearby, and he wants personally to inspect the area involved. Some of his fellow officers are trying to talk him out of going on what they see as a reckless and foolhardy mission, insisting that he should let air reconnaissance do their own work. But Hargreaves disregards their warnings and takes off. His plane is intercepted by German fighters behind enemy lines, and he is badly wounded in his left leg. Unable to control his plane, he crash-lands in a field, is captured and taken to an SS interrogation center. There he is repeatedly beaten in the attempt to extract intelligence information from him. Though deprived of food, sleep, and medical attention, he holds out. In a final attempt to break him, his interrogators pull out his fingernails. He dies a terrible but heroic death.

Several things fell into place for Gary after the recall of his life as Peter Hargreaves. Though born and raised in Canada, as a young child Gary used to speak with a convincing British accent, fooling more than one teacher into thinking he was adopted. He also had a lifelong phobia about breaking his leg which had kept him off ski slopes. He was similarly anxious about traveling anywhere by plane. He had once considered taking flying lessons to overcome this fear but then thought better of it. Though he felt instinctively that he already knew how to fly a small plane, he had stopped himself out of fear of being reckless, a curious reaction he never understood until now. In addition, he saw Hargreaves' work in intelligence as quite similar to his work in forensic psychology. And perhaps now he had an explanation for his almost perverse fascination with torture.

In a subsequent hypnotic session, Gary's relationship with Caroline was added to this list of missing pieces in his life. Because Hargreaves is fluent in Italian, he is called upon to work with the local resistance movement when the Allies enter Italy. In Salerno, where he is stationed, his principal contact with the resistance is a young woman named Elena Bocchi, Caroline's previous incarnation. While working together under extremely dangerous conditions, they fall in love. Elena's father has been recently killed in combat, and Hargreaves does what he can to provide for her family. Their love is deep, and he promises to marry her as soon as the war is over—a promise he is not to keep. Soon after learning of Hargreaves's death through her connections in the underground, Elena commits suicide by jumping off a cliff. Gary learned that Hargreaves continued to feel terribly guilty even after his death for not being able to keep his promise to Elena and was tormented by his inability to prevent her from committing suicide (which he witnessed in his spirit form).

Gary and Caroline's love, however, reached back even farther than World War II. In still another session, Gary uncovered a life as Sevastjan Umnov, an emissary of Czarina Elizabeth Petrovna to the court of Louis XV in the eighteenth century. Given the unstable relationship between Russia and France at this time, his major responsibility is counterintelligence. Caroline is Sevastjan's younger sister, Lisenka, with whom he has a loving, incestuous relationship. Lisenka worries constantly during Sevastjan's long diplomatic travels abroad that he is taking up with other women. Her fear is groundless, however, because Sevastjan's love for her is as deep as hers is for him. Nevertheless, disturbed by a rumor about her brother's behavior, she impulsively marries a suitor. Several weeks later, regretting terribly having ended the one relationship she truly treasures in life, she hangs herself. When Sevastjan learns of her death, he is devastated and never again returns to Russia. He eventually dies of natural causes, alone and unhappy.

In addition to adding a deeper layer to Gary and Caroline's relationship, this session brought forward two other interesting bits of information. Once again, Sevastjan's professional skills and interests are similar to Gary's. Second, Caroline has a history of using suicide to deal with her problems.

If Gary had a previous history with Caroline that helps explain their attraction, what of his ties to Elizabeth, with whom he shares an even stronger bond in this life? Was their love similarly rooted in previous lives together? Not surprisingly, the answer was yes. Subsequent sessions revealed that they too had shared several lives as lovers. Their pattern was to find themselves in situations where their love was forbidden and thus carried out in secret. In their most recent life together, Gary had been Jeremy, a mathematics lecturer at Oxford University in the nineteenth century.

Jeremy leads a double life. His weekends are spent with his wife and family in the countryside outside Oxford, while his weeks are spent in town in the company of his mistress—who is Elizabeth in this life. Jeremy cares deeply for his mistress and illegitimate children and repeatedly promises to take good care of them. Unfortunately, he dies unexpectedly of pneumonia in his late thirties, his promise unfulfilled. His wife is well taken care of from Jeremy's estate, but his mistress is penniless and falls on hard times. Though well-intentioned, Jeremy lacked the foresight to plan adequately for this eventuality. (Now Gary finally understood his exaggerated anxiety over the financial security of his family, and why he had felt compelled to take out large amounts of life insurance just in case he should die unexpectedly.)

While Gary and Elizabeth had loved each other in many lives, their present life was the first time their love was lived openly and with public sanction. After so many centuries of clandestine meetings, no wonder their marriage was so fulfilling to them. Their life together had been carefully planned before their births, while Gary and Caroline's had not. This planning, it turned out, was the key to their enduring relationship, and why, despite its intensity, Gary and Caroline's relationship had no real future in this life. "It felt," Gary said, "as though we were two actors who simply ran out of lines."

Both these relationships demonstrate a recurring karmic pattern. Deep love relationships more often than not have roots in previous lives together. The relationship between a man and a woman is potentially so rich and inevitably so complex that it typically takes many lifetimes to develop fully. When we see couples absorbed in overpowering infatuations, or embittered conflicts, or mutually supportive co-creativity, we are probably witnessing pairs of souls at different stages of love's long journey. This journey can be lengthened, and made more interesting, if the couple chooses to switch sex roles at various points in order to experience both sides of the partnership.

A PERSONAL PHILOSOPHICAL INTERLUDE

When I was first learning about karma and rebirth, the sources I was reading stressed the impersonality of karma. There was no judge keeping track of us and handing out rewards or punishments in subsequent lives. Karma was simply an impersonal principle of nature operating to restore the harmony disturbed by our choices. The metaphor of equilibrium figured largely in these accounts, just as it had in Freud's theory of the psyche. But just as the concept of equilibrium could not explain the psyche's penchant for taking on new challenges, neither could it explain our constant drive to transcend our limitations across many lifecycles. Karma is not merely balancing the cosmic scales or returning the psychospiritual system to a tensionless zero state. It is a spiritual cybernetic system that advances our growth by giving us constant feedback on the choices we are making. And it does this absolutely impersonally, or so I thought.

In these early days, I used to think of karma as a massive, impersonal, organic machine that collected the energies inherent in all our thoughts and actions, digested them, and translated them automatically into the conditions and circumstances of a subsequent life. Then over time I came to realize two things. First, the creativity and wisdom of karma's translation of past choices into future lives was far too great to be suitably described by the metaphor of a machine. The dynamics of karma showed an intelligence that was not merely thorough but also exceptionally creative. It was the kind of intelligence we associate with living beings, not machines, even in today's world of computerized mechanical intelligence. Therefore I had to drop the machine metaphor in favor of a metaphor of living intelligence, or the intelligence of a living being or beings.

The second thing I realized was that while karma and rebirth explained many of the mysteries I had sought answers to, they did not explain themselves. Karma and reincarnation are principles governing the evolution of human consciousness in the Earth school. Taken by themselves, however, they cannot explain their own existence. To put it simplistically, we are left asking "Who created this system? Who designed such an exquisite masterpiece?" (Again, since the system itself is intelligent, it is more appropriate to ask *who* than *what*.)

Those who think reductionistically, who believe that we can always explain the greater from the lesser, the presence of genius from the random association of inanimate molecules, will not be able to appreciate either the logic or the power of this question. Karma and rebirth had taken over for me many of the duties traditionally ascribed to God. Order replaced the caprice of a deity who permitted, or willed, His supposedly beloved creations to suffer inexplicably. In karma and rebirth, suffering found meaning and mercy. It found purpose and goal. The Universe was compassionate after all. In the end, however, karma and rebirth required something even greater than themselves to explain themselves.

At that point, the magnitude of the intelligence involved, to say nothing of the power, so far exceeded my own that I had no choice but to surrender to this larger force that surrounded me and defined the rules of my existence. Without name or precise concept, the existence of this "something greater" was demanded by the evidence. This was not simply another trip around the circular logic of the medieval argument from design, but something different. It was part inference and part experience, part hypothesis and part obvious. I simply had no choice but to embrace this encompassing Reality.

When I dropped the machine metaphor for karma, it opened up two possibilities. Either the entire karmic system for all of us was orchestrated by one mega-intelligence, one mega-being, or it was managed by many intelligent beings. My original impulse was to choose the first option. My monotheistic background had left me with the habit of thinking of the spiritual domain as utterly simple, unified, One. Diversity, I had thought, existed here in the physical universe; on the other side was only God (or some single Intelligence). There were human souls too, of course, but God did not need them to carry out the actual work of the universe. God was by definition omniscient and omnipotent and therefore could take care of all the details Himself. Even after I had abandoned this concept of God, the idea of an essentially homogenous and unified spirit domain persisted.

Eventually, however, this option collapsed under the weight of its many responsibilities and its unquestioned assumptions. It seemed to me increasingly necessary to think in terms of many coordinated intelligences rather than a single mega-intelligence. The tasks were simply too many and too diversified to be economically handled by a single intelligence. Furthermore, I was encountering too many responsible reports of contact with spiritual guides for this concept to be dismissed out of hand. In time, systems theory helped me understand how I might conceptualize the simultaneous operation of many distinct intelligences within a single, all-encompassing Intelligence.[12] This theory's vision of systems nested within ever larger systems opened for me new ways of thinking about the One and its relationship to the Many. It gave me permission to revive the ancient idea of emanation and to

---

[12] See, for example, Gregory Bateson, *Steps to an Ecology of Mind* and *Mind and Nature*.

think of the Universe in terms of an organic hierarchy of intelligences. Not a hierarchy of value, for all is divine, but a hierarchy of awareness, of responsibilities, of discrete beings.

This new way of seeing things also helped me work out a rough solution to a problem I was having with karma. Ever since I had felt obliged to introduce living intelligence, however conceived, into the lifecycling process, I did not know how to reconcile it with the presumably impersonal character of karma. Wise and trusted sources insisted that the cycles of cause and effect were absolutely impersonal, as constant and inevitable as gravity. Yet other respected sources mentioned spirit guides who assist us in the structuring of our next life. How was guidance, with all that the concept implied, to be reconciled with an impersonal chain of causation? Systems theory helped me think more flexibly and creatively about these things, and I slowly began to find ways of integrating both aspects into an expanded picture of karma. This is currently for me more a picture of the possibilities than a clear vision of how things actually work.

As far as it goes, this picture assumes the existence of beings who oversee and organize many aspects of the reincarnation process. Their responsibilities include mediating, as it were, between the individual and his or her karma. For its part, karma can indeed be thought of as an impersonal momentum moving through our lives, even carrying our lives along. While both inevitable and inexorable, this momentum is actually quite flexible in expression. Its impact can be delayed, temporarily suspended, or hurried forward. It can express itself in one's life either as something physical, emotional, or mental, as a confrontation with another or with oneself. It is an energy amassed from our previous choices, a living record, if you will, of what we have learned and not learned. Karma itself, however, does not write the next lesson plan. Rather, it *defines the limits* within which this plan can be constructed. We draw up this plan in consultation with the spirit beings who oversee our education.[13] They help us plan the lessons that will help us complete our unfinished learning and move on to new possibilities. If in some instances a lesson plan is largely of their design, we still retain full responsibility for our lives, because we are always free to reject their proposal.

The prospect of spiritual guides overseeing and assisting us in our spiritual evolution is an ancient and uplifting thought, yet it is also one

---

[13] In the Hindu tradition these beings are called the Lords of Karma.

many of us have a particularly hard time accepting. Because I fought this concept for a long time myself, I appreciate the difficulties it poses, both philosophically and emotionally. Nevertheless, there is a mounting body of evidence coming from several quarters that, if it does not prove the existence of spirit guides, at least it raises provocative possibilities.

For example, encounters with these guides are frequently reported at institutes that teach various consciousness-raising techniques, such as the Monroe Institute of Applied Science in Faber, Virginia. (The Monroe Institute publicly reports these encounters without taking a stand on their legitimacy.) Channeling represents another area of possible evidence. Though channeling is notoriously easy to fake, some channelers present us with data that is not easily explained.[14] In yet another area, contact with spirit guides is occasionally reported in advanced transpersonal therapy sessions. Dr. Stanislav Grof, for example, gives the following description of various spirit guides that have surfaced in the context of his holonomic therapy:

> Experiences of encounters with guides, teachers, and protectors from the spiritual world belong to the most valuable and rewarding phenomena of the transpersonal domain. The subjects perceive these beings as suprahuman entities existing on higher planes of consciousness and higher energy levels. Sometimes they appear quite spontaneously at a certain stage of the spiritual development of the individual; other times they suddenly emerge during an inner crisis, responding to an urgent call for help. In many instances, they continue appearing to the subject either on their own terms or at the request of their protege.[15]

Past-life hypnotherapy provides us yet another possible source of evidence for the existence of spirit guides. Several therapists have reported that some of their clients, while in the hypnotic state, have been able to recall making contact with their spiritual guides between their lives on Earth. One of these books, *Life Between Life* by Dr. Joel Whitton and Joe Fisher, reports extensively on one therapist's attempts to explore through hypnotherapy what occurs between death and rebirth. Because of its general relevance to many of the themes of this chapter, this book deserves attention here.

---

[14] For a recent study of this phenomenon, see Jon Klimo, *Channeling: Investigations on Receiving Information from Paranormal Sources.*

[15] *The Adventure of Self-Discovery*, p. 121.

LIFE BETWEEN LIFE

Dr. Whitton is a Toronto psychiatrist who conducted research for many years to determine whether hypnosis might yield reliable evidence for reincarnation. One day in 1974 he inadvertently discovered that while in hypnotic trance his research subject was able to explore much more than just her former lives on Earth. Given an ambiguously phrased command, she took the opportunity accidently offered her to explore her life *between* Earth lives. This surprised and stunned Whitton, who had never even considered such a possibility. This fortunate accident opened up a new line of research and eventually a new form of therapeutic intervention—which he developed for over ten years, withholding publication of his results until co-authoring *Life Between Life* with Joe Fisher, a newspaper reporter and author of *The Case for Reincarnation*.[16] By then he had escorted more than thirty people across the line separating physical and nonphysical existence, exploring in detail the events that transpired in their lives between incarnations. His study of these events might offer us a rare glimpse into how a new life emerges from its past karma.

When taken through the death experience of one of their previous lives, Whitton's clients experience the same things reported in the literature on near-death episodes—separation from the body, witnessing activities around the body and in neighboring vicinities, the tunnel, the encounter with the white light, life review, and the like. But where those who almost die are instructed to return to complete their current life, his clients continue on to explore what comes next in the *bardo*, as this dimension is called in *The Tibetan Book of the Dead*. Whitton calls this state of consciousness between earthly lives metaconsciousness.[17] It is a heightened state of awareness unlike anything we usually experience on earth. It is beyond time as we know it, for linear time apparently operates only within and near physical reality, including the period just after death and before birth. Beyond that, everything happens all at once, with causal sequence dissolved in simultaneity. Initially it is a quite

---

[16] Though the book was authored jointly, I shall refer in these pages only to Dr. Whitton, on whose research the book is based. This is not intended to minimize Fisher's contribution.

[17] The parallels between the intermediate state described in *The Tibetan Book of the Dead*, or *Bardo Thodol* as it is more properly called, and Whitton's research into metaconsciousness are numerous and intimate. One cannot help but be struck, even stunned, when concepts of the afterlife from an ancient esoteric literature of a distant culture are confirmed by contemporary investigations carried out with "naive" and often disbelieving subjects. I will elaborate on the *Bardo Thodol* in Chapter 5.

confusing experience, and Whitton had to teach his clients to isolate individual pieces from the holographic panorama that surrounded them. Presenting the events summarized here as a sequence, therefore, is a literary fabrication that translates metaconsciousness into something we can more easily recognize.

Metaconsciousness is experienced as being more "real" than earthly existence. Repeatedly it is recognized as our true home. There, not on Earth, is where we belong. Upon reawaking in Whitton's office, one subject said, "You've woken me up in an unreal world. . . . Now I know where the true reality lies" (p. 51). Another observed, "It's so bright, so beautiful, so serene. It's like going into the sun and being absorbed without any sensation of heat. You go back to the wholeness of everything. I didn't want to come back" (p. 31). Whitton's clients always have difficulty finding words to convey the richness, the intensity, and the saturated quality of the *bardo*. Their descriptions are filled with highly symbolic, archetypal images, and always express the disclaimer that they are not doing justice to the reality experienced.

Though we all experience this rapture after each life, apparently it catches us completely by surprise each time. In taking up our life on Earth, we forget. At death, our amnesia is suddenly lifted and we recover our place in the larger cosmic drama unfolding around us. One social worker who had experienced seven of her lives between incarnations described the experience in this way:

> I feel a definite physical change in trance after passing through a previous death. My body expands and fills the entire room. Then I'm flooded with the most euphoric feelings I have ever known. These feelings are accompanied by total awareness and understanding of who I truly am, my reason for being, and my place in the universe. Everything makes sense; everything is perfectly just. It's wonderful to know that love is really in control. Coming back to normal consciousness, you have to leave behind that all-encompassing love, that knowledge, that reassurance. When I'm at a low ebb, when life is particularly unpleasant, I almost wish for death because I know it would mean my return to a marvelous state of being. I used to be frightened of dying. Now I have no fear of death whatsoever. [p. 31]

As the *Bardo Thodol* reported twelve centuries ago, one's environment in the disembodied state is largely a reflection of each person's thought-forms and expectations. Sometimes individuals find themselves receiving illumination on topics they have been interested in all their lives. Underlying the individual imagery reported, however, is a consistent description of beauty beyond description, of rapturous reunion, and of restored wholeness. "Everything makes sense." How magnificent must be the experience that lies behind this simple observation. Finally to understand what our life has been about, and what Life itself is about![18]

In the *bardo* the soul comes to understand that the true purpose of the lifecycling process is to develop and purify the soul and return it to God. One woman described it as follows:

> We are created in God's image and the idea is that we have to become Godlike, to get back to Him. There are many higher planes and to get back to God, to reach the plane where His spirit resides, you have to drop your garment each time until your spirit is truly free. The learning process never stops. . . . Sometimes we are allowed glimpses of the higher planes—each one is lighter and brighter than the one before. [pp. 45–46]

Another woman saw a vision of her soul symbolized as a large cabbage of light with a dark mass of primeval sadness at its core. With each incarnation the cabbage unfolded a new leaf of light in order to release a portion of the darkness and shed some of the pain. After many leaves had been grown in this way, the cabbage was free of all its pain and filled completely with light.

The length of Earth time one spends in the *bardo* varies widely. The shortest stay Whitton has encountered was ten months, the longest about eight hundred years. The average, he says, is about forty years, though this appears to have been getting shorter over the past three centuries. People spend this time doing different things. At one extreme are those who are unambitious or indifferent to their spiritual development. They spend most of it "asleep," in something like a state of suspended animation, until they are roused for their next incarnation. At the other extreme are those souls who are deeply committed to their

---

[18] One's religious expectations appear to be able to structure to a degree one's experience in the *bardo*. One client relived a life in Spain as a devout Roman Catholic. At her death her religious expectations were gratified with "visions of cherubim and seraphim against a purple background, a full-throated choir, and the figure of Jesus Christ welcoming her with open arms" (p. 32). However, our beliefs cannot completely control or define our experience in the *bardo*. Dr. Whitton reports that persons with narrow, fundamentalist expectations have discovered that "the complex and protracted course of personal evolution cannot be supplanted by the simplistic notion of being 'saved' " (p. 34).

evolutionary progress, who spend their time in study of various kinds, preparing for their next life.[19]

The identity one assumes in the *bardo* appears to be that of the Oversoul with the most recent life emphasized.[20] It is this identity that, shortly after one's arrival in the *bardo*, is brought before a "Board of Judgment." Here the soul must confront the complete truth of the life just lived. Most of Whitton's clients report that they find themselves before a group of wise, elderly, archetypal beings whose job it was to assist them in learning the lessons from their current life and in planning their next incarnation. These beings sometimes take the form of figures from the individual's religious heritage, but to others they appear simply as very wise and loving beings charged with this responsibility. Sometimes they are beings who have themselves already completed the Earth curriculum. Some individuals are simply aware of a judging presence and see no one.

Before this "Tribunal" Whitton's clients reexperience the life just completed. "It's like climbing right inside a movie of your life," one client reported. "Every moment from every year of your life is played back in complete sensory detail. Total, total recall" (p. 39). In this review they do much more than simply reexperience the particular details of their life; they also discover the meaning of every person and every event in it. They discover the potential that existed in their life and how well they realized it. All the hidden turning points, successes, and failures come fully into view. Here in one mind-shattering instant they confront the full truth of their existence. None of the psychological defenses we use to buffer ourselves from truth on Earth operate here. If there is a private hell, reports Whitton, it takes place at this time of inner confrontation:

> This is when remorse, guilt, and self-recrimination for failings in the last incarnation are vented with a visceral intensity that produces anguish and bitter tears on a scale that can be quite unsettling to witness. . . . Any emotional suffering that was inflicted on others is

---

[19] Numerous sources, both contemporary and ancient, describe the *bardo* as consisting of many planes, the higher planes being more saturated with God-consciousness and therefore more blissful and the lower planes less so. Between lives one rises, so to speak, and exists on the plane that reflects one's level of spiritual development. For a particularly rich description of this concept, see Robert Monroe, *Far Journeys*.

[20] As used here, the Oversoul is the larger consciousness that incorporates and integrates all the experiences gathered in our many incarnations. This concept is discussed in the next chapter.

felt as keenly as if it were inflicted on oneself. But perhaps most distressing of all is the realization that the time for changing attitudes and rectifying mistakes is well and truly past. The door of the last life is locked and bolted, and the consequences of actions and evasions must be faced in the ultimate showdown which calls to account precisely who we are and what we stand for. [pp. 37–38]

Whitton's description of this encounter emphasizes its negative side. Yet for those who have met or exceeded their karmic challenges, this must also be a time of congratulations and deep personal satisfaction. How rewarding it must be for those who have labored long and hard in their lives to be told at the end that they have done everything asked of them, and more. The tilt toward the negative in Whitton's cases results from the fact that his clients are not a representative sample of the population at large. His clients have been brought to him by their pain, pain that derived from problems left unresolved in previous lifetimes. One might expect, therefore, that as the former lives of these individuals faced the Board of Judgment, their failings would dominate their experience. As always, therapeutic case histories necessarily tend to teach us more about pathology than health—in this case spiritual pathology. This is a general problem we must be sensitive to when using case histories from past-life therapy to study karma and rebirth. Given the population they reflect, these histories tend to skew our perception of things in a negative direction. We must constantly remind ourselves that for every person who is working to overcome debts inherited from a previous life, there is someone else who is building on the assets of a life well invested.

Whitton's clients report that in this moment of truth we, not the elders or God, are our own judge and jury. We condemn ourselves, while they bring forgiveness.[21] As one woman reported, "My whole anima is convulsing with pain, remorse, sadness, guilt, mourning. . . . I cannot look up at the Three for sheer shame. Yet all around me there is a glowing warmth of blue rays and peace, a peace I am unable to fathom" (p. 38). Eventually, each person who faces the Board is gradually led away from their pain to the love and forgiveness that surrounds them. Rather than condemn them, the judges radiate a healing energy that dissolves all guilt and opens the way to peace. They frequently initiate discussion of key episodes in the last life, offering retrospective counsel and reassuring the soul that even unsavory experiences can

---

[21] The parallels with near-death episodes on this particular point is striking. See, for example, *Heading Toward Omega* by Kenneth Ring, p. 70.

promote personal development. In these and many other ways they assist the soul in objectively understanding its actions. By viewing the present life against the background of its many lives, the soul gains insights into its karmic patterns and trends, and learns where it is in its spiritual evolution.

Later the soul brings this heightened awareness to the task of planning the next life. The soul does not undertake this work alone but is guided in it by the Board. They are aware of the soul's full karmic history and thus are able to make recommendations that exceed the individual's wisdom, a fact obvious to the soul involved. One person described it this way:

> I am being helped to work out the next life so that I can face whatever difficulties come my way. I don't want to take the responsibility because I feel that I don't have the strength. But I know we have to be given obstacles in order to overcome those obstacles—to become stronger, more aware, more evolved, more responsible. [p. 41][22]

Because the recommendations of the Board are based on what the individual needs and not on what it wants, they are often received with mixed feelings. The soul may not like the life recommended to it, but from its heightened perspective it recognizes its value as a learning device. The soul may be returning to a life in which it will be surrounded by old enemies or suffer great trials, but each ingredient in the life plan is carefully selected to create conditions that will help it grow beyond its current limitations. According to Whitton, each of us sees what we are getting into before we are reborn, and each of us understands and accepts its purpose. Said one client, for example:

> There are people I didn't treat too well in my last life, and I have to go back to the Earth plane again and work off the debt. This

---

[22] Traditions differ as to exactly how much of a hand we have in the construction of our next life. Some authorities attribute very little role to us, reserving most of the work to the guides, as Whitton does. There are so many variables and so much about the processes involved that we do not understand, how could we be entrusted with the responsibility? This is the position taken by Kalu Rinpoche speaking for Tibetan Buddhism in his book *The Dharma*, pp. 16–24. He sees the forces of karma as too powerful to permit much latitude on these things. Other persons, such as Robert Monroe in *Far Journeys*, credit us with greater say in the when, where, and what of our next life. Perhaps these differences reflect differences in the "age" and experience of the individual soul doing the planning. Perhaps the more trips we have under our belt, the more input we can have on specifics. (The concept of "soul age" is discussed in Chapter 5.)

time, if they hurt me in return, I'm going to forgive them because all I really want to do is to go back home. This is home. [p. 42]

Another reported the following:

> I chose my mother knowing there was a high incidence of Alzheimer's disease in her family and that there was every chance that I, too, would suffer from it. But my karmic links with my mother were much more important than any genetic deficiency. There was another reason for choosing my mother. The judges told me that I should undergo the experience of being raised without a father in this life and I was aware that my parents would soon be divorced. I also knew that my choice of parents would put me in the ideal geographical location for meeting the man I was destined to marry. [p. 42][23]

To advance we must be challenged, and these karmic challenges come in the form of every anxiety, confrontation, disorder, and frustration known to humankind. As Whitton observes:

> Physical and psychological tragedies of all kinds can be attributed to karma. . . . [M]oral deficiency and unresolved and repressed emotions are conferred on future incarnations in the form of disease, trauma, phobias, and various other manifestations of difficulty. [p. 75]

A hard life, however, is not necessarily a sign of making amends for past failings. It may also be part of a training plan for future endeavors. Souls who are particularly interested in their spiritual development sometimes plan several lives at a time, using a series of trials in the first lives to develop strengths and sensitivities which will be needed to underwrite great accomplishments in a later life. (Thus a folk tale tells the story of a soul who was preparing itself to be king of a given land. Wanting to be a good king, it chose to prepare itself by first taking three lives among the poorest people in the land. After incarnating as a penniless beggar, a drought-stricken peasant, and a

---

[23] This woman's observations caution us against assuming, as all too many do, that every single condition or incident in our lives is filled with karmic significance for us. Reincarnation enthusiasts often seem, in my opinion, to overwork both karma and themselves trying to figure out what they are "supposed to learn" from every detail of their lives. In this woman's case, she was simply willing to risk getting Alzheimer's disease in order to secure the other things she wanted in this lifecycle. There are many lines of causality operating on Earth, and we apparently must pick and choose among the possibilities available at any given time or wait until a more suitable set emerge.

diseased child, he finally became king. Spurred on by the compassion he had acquired in these difficult lives, he brought about great social reform.)

Most of us have a tendency to equate hardship with punishment, and yet there is simply no justification for this formula. If we suffer greatly in this life, or if we see someone else suffering, we cannot infer that we or they must have committed some great crime or heinous act in a previous life. In the first place, as mentioned above, this suffering may be preparing the individual for a future undertaking. In the second place, as a soul draws nearer the completion of its sojourns on Earth, it comes to understand better what is going on and often seeks to accelerate the process as much as possible. Thus these souls tend to undertake more ambitious lives. Whitton observes that people's lives tend to become more difficult as they advance through the curriculum. The great difficulties they incorporate into these lives sometimes represent great challenges designed to promote great inner growth. Sometimes they represent the summing of bits and pieces of unresolved karma collected from many lives and grouped into intense learning experiences. When one sees the good suffering, therefore, we may be seeing a soul in a hurry to complete its course of study. Because we can never know the whys and wherefores of a person's misfortunes in this life, the best course is always to offer no judgments at all.

The *karmic scripts* proposed by the spirit guides are developed in consultation with all the other souls who will participate in them. A great deal of planning is required for these souls to come together on Earth under the proper circumstances. The choice of one's parents is critical to establishing the themes of one's life. If reunions between people are to be ensured down the road, the timing and place of each person's birth is vitally important.

As an aside, Whitton's information on planning our next life in consultation with spirit guides parallels findings Dr. Helen Wambach reported in *Life Before Life*, published in 1979. In this book Dr. Wambach summarizes information gathered from over 750 subjects who had been hypnotically regressed to explore the conditions leading up to their present life. She reports that 81 percent of her subjects were conscious of having chosen to reincarnate, although 67 percent were apparently reluctant to do so. Most of the 81 percent report being helped in planning their life, though they tend to report a broader range of figures who advised them than do Whitton's subjects. They describe an assortment of beings variously referred to as counselors, guides, teachers, soul guardians, and personal friends. Often some kind of gathering accompanies the planning: "a council of many in a circle," "a group of loved ones who supported me," "a board or committee," or "a council of souls." Interspersed in this group may be figures with whom the subject has a special relationship: "a wise old man whom I respected, obeyed, and loved," "some old mentors of mine," "a complete friend." Approximately 10 percent of Wambach's subjects report planning their lives in concert with significant persons from their present life—parents, children, husbands and wives, relatives or friends. A large number, 41 percent, were aware of receiving instructions and counseling but could not discern individual figures doing the advising or could not identify the vague presences they felt. Interestingly, only one-tenth of one percent described the power that guided them in their rebirth as God.[24]

Creating a karmic script does not guarantee that the planned outcome will be realized. We are dealing here with probabilities and conditionalities, not predestined necessities. Whitton likens the process to planning a large fresco. In the *bardo*, only a rough sketch of the life is executed. We create the actual painting on Earth, filling in the details and making the final choices there. Only when we return to the *bardo* after our death do we learn how our actual painting compares to the original outline. It may fall short or exceed what had been projected.[25]

Whitton reports that his clients have occasionally been allowed to see a upcoming event in their current karmic script. They may learn specific points or only a general hint of future developments. Interestingly enough, the psyche exercises complete control over whether they will be allowed to remember any of what is seen when they return to normal consciousness. Sometimes the amnesia is spontaneous; on other occasions, clients have asked Whitton to make sure that they are not allowed to recall specific future events they have seen lest they be tempted to tamper with their karma. Whitton reports that in those

---

[24] For more details, see *Life Before Life*, Chapter 3.

[25] Does God foreknow or predestine what we will actually do on Earth? In lieu of the extended discussion this question deserves, let me only register two brief points. First, from the point of view developed in this chapter, God is not outside these activities looking on, but rather is the larger whole within which these activities are taking place. We are the extension of God's freedom in this particular place and time. As such we *are* God's potential experimenting with the possibilities, not the mere passive recipients of a divinely ordained fate. Second, having said this, I also wonder whether the awareness of outcomes varies according to the level of consciousness doing the observing. The future might look more open-ended from one level of consciousness than from a more encompassing level. If it is true that the farther one moves beyond physical reality, the less time behaves linearly, what looks like foreknowledge here may look like present knowledge elsewhere.

instances where knowledge of the future involved events close enough in time to be verified, they have proved accurate.

Apparently, our karmic scripts are often designed with considerable room for improvisation. One of the interesting details Whitton reports is that less-developed or "younger" souls seem to benefit more from very detailed karmic blueprints, while more developed "older" souls prefer more room for improvisation in order to respond more creatively to challenging situations.

Even within a planned necessity we often have options. One of Whitton's clients was a thirty-seven-year-old woman who had been lured into the bush and raped. For a long time she struggled with why she had been victimized in this way. In trance she learned her answer:

> My plan was that I would pick a tragic event which would cause me to change my entire soul complexion during my thirties. By focusing on this event, I would search with whatever means were at my disposal to find deeper meaning in my life. This is exactly what happened. [p. 47]

Another client, who had almost died from a disease, discovered that his illness had not been part of his original karmic script. "I gathered it was something that I brought about in order to fulfill my plan" (p. 153).

Implicit in both these examples is the idea that each of us exercises great control over the unfolding events in our lives even after we take birth. How we actually do this is largely beyond our sight. If we exercise this kind of influence over what happens to us while earthbound, it must be done from the spiritual dimension. Out-of-body research suggests that we go out-of-body almost nightly. Perhaps during these sojourns we work out the details of our script as we go along. Alternatively, this may be accomplished through the agency of some superordinate level of awareness (see the next chapter, on the Oversoul). The bottom line is that we understand very little about how plans drafted in the *bardo*, either before or after our birth, actually influence physical events on Earth.

The metaphysical literature repeatedly asserts that the spiritual domain is the realm of cause and the physical domain the realm of effect. It teaches that the cause-and-effect relationships we see operating in the physical domain are subject to a higher causality in ways that escape physical perception. Whitton's clients support this metaphysical claim, for in trance they occasionally witness these higher causalities operating. Sometimes, in planning their next life, they experience in highly symbolic forms the mechanisms they are working with. For example, one person saw

> a sort of clockwork instrument into which you could insert certain parts in order for specific consequences to follow. I deduced that I was working on something that I wanted to change. And I was setting up this change by working with this machinery, making the necessary alterations to the interlife plan in order that they might transpire in my forthcoming life on earth. [p. 43]

While visions of this sort may be experientially compelling for those who have them and suggestive for us who later read about them, they do not give us specific information on the actual causal mechanisms involved. We are still left wanting to know more than we are told.

Our karmic scripts sometimes include *karmic tests* hidden at key points in our lives. Depending on how we respond to a given test, our life may subsequently take different courses. Steve Logan found this to be true in his life. Steve had just cause to feel extremely hostile toward his father and therefore seldom visited him in the nursing home where he lay extremely ill. One day, however, he felt moved to visit him, "feeling that something important was at stake." When he entered the room he noticed that his father was having difficulty breathing. He quickly saw that the air line had become dislodged and he was not getting the oxygen he needed. Steve knew he could walk away and let his father die. After a moment's reflection, he called a nurse instead. Several years later Steve was in a serious bicycle accident. Broadsided by a truck, he miraculously escaped with just a fractured femur. More than ten years after that, when Steve was in his early forties, he learned in his work with Dr. Whitton that these two events in his life were causally connected:

> My karmic script clearly stated that the life-or-death incident with my father was most definitely a very important test that I had set myself. If I could forgive him his transgressions against me—which appeared to extend over several lifetimes—I would not be killed in the bicycle accident. The expectation was there in the plan that because of my past conduct I would allow my father to die. But I passed the test and, after my accident, the plan was at an end! I

learned that sketchy plans for future lives had been brought forward
to operate in the current life. [p. 45]

Steve's last observation makes a fascinating point. If we engage our
life tasks with courage and resolve, we can actually complete our allotted
karmic assignment and then have the option of moving plans tentatively
scheduled for our next life into our current life. For those who are
deeply committed to their own evolutionary progress, it is possible to
accomplish many lifetimes of work in a single lifecycle.[26]

Ben Garonzi represents another instance of embedding a test in
one's karmic script. Through a long succession of lives as different men
and women, Ben had consistently responded to abuse with violence,
killing those who treated him badly. In this life he was severely brutalized
as a child by his father. Understandably, he came to hate his father
intensely. When he was eighteen, he was given the opportunity to act
on that hatred. One night when his father was drunk and unconscious,
Ben got a knife from the kitchen intending to cut his father's throat,
once again reinforcing the cycle of violence. Suddenly an inner voice
rose to discourage this act. Ben listened to it and put the knife back.
This decision marked a major turning point in his life. From that point
on, his life slowly began to improve. Aimlessness was replaced with
ambition. He became more outgoing and went on to pursue a successful
career. In metaconsciousness, Ben learned that he had chosen this
difficult childhood with his father, who had been a major antagonist in
a series of previous lives. The conditions of his life were designed to
teach him to withstand extreme provocation without resorting to violence. By putting away the knife he had passed a major karmic test,
thus extricating himself from a long pattern of self-defeating mistakes.
Before his birth, a voice in the *bardo* had told him "If you do it right
this time, things will work out all right. If not, you will require a learning
environment of even greater intensity" (p. 72).

Not all tests are successfully navigated. In the case of Heather
Whiteholme presented in Chapter 2, Isobel Drummond failed to actualize the life she had planned. In metaconsciousness Heather learned
that had Isobel continued her music diligently and resisted the temp-
tations of debauchery, she could have had a brilliant musical career. "I
picked up from the interlife," she observed, "that Isobel would have
died just recently as a happy, successful lady and great grandmother.

---

[26] One of the six detailed histories presented in *Life Between Life* represents such a
case—Chapter 7, the case of Michael Gallander.

If only she had been patient and persevering, she could have had it all" (p. 113).[27]

While it would be foolish to do so, we are always free to reject the life proposed by the Board of Judgment. To do so results in reincarnating without a "ratified plan." There is no penalty for rejecting the Board's counsel other than living what will most probably be a wasted life. With no inner compass guiding us through life, we become extremely susceptible to the historical currents of the moment. Whitton reports that the discovery in hypnotic trance that one has returned to Earth without a plan is invariably communicated in great fear. On the other hand, a planned life filled even with great hardship is typically reported calmly and without anxiety. Apparently, nothing is worse than to have no course charted for yourself in life. Without an inner script to follow, we are forced to extemporize too much. There is no feedback from within telling us how we are doing.[28]

If we do have a plan, how do we know whether we are fulfilling it? As one might expect, it's a matter of sensing whether one is properly aligned with one's inner being and with Life itself. "Those who are living out their karmic scripts, or have even exceeded them," says Whitton, "have an inner sense that life is unfolding as it should. Those who have strayed from their blueprint feel, instead, that everything is out of control. Chaos rules" (p. 46).

It is no small thing to be *intellectually* convinced of reincarnation and of the existence of a spiritual domain which is our true home, but it is another thing entirely to *experience* that domain. Experiencing the encounters in the *bardo* and the decisions made there had a powerful effect on Whitton's clients. It is good for readers to remember that what they read here is a summary of another person's summary of still another person's private experience. It is therefore several times diluted. If we want to appreciate fully the impact these experiences have on a person and if we want to gauge their true experiential credibility as memories of a previous existence, we must give back to them something of what the telling has taken away. We must transpose words back into

---

[27] The irony in this particular case is that if Isobel had not squandered her talent, Heather would not have existed. Her life had been "hastily assembled as an emergency measure" shortly after Isobel's death. "She was almost wrenched into being," writes Dr. Whitton, "to cope with the karmic repercussions of Isobel's misspent and prematurely curtailed existence" (pp. 112–113).

[28] Dr. Wambach reports that approximately 3 percent of her subjects reported rejecting the advice of their guides. The usual reason given was impatience and being in a hurry to "get on with it," thus leading them to be less selective than they should have been in choosing their point of reentry (*Life Before Life*, Chapter 3).

experience. These people insist that they come to *know*, not just believe, that life is eternal and that the ultimate purpose of earthly existence is learning to love. Here as in most things, only those who have had similar experiences will be able fully to appreciate the distinctive epistemological power of these experiences.[29]

Those who have experienced the planning of their lives in the *bardo* all return with the same insistent message for us: We are solely responsible for who we are and for the circumstances in which we find ourselves at every point in our lives. We have created the karmic momentum in our lives and we have chosen how this momentum is even now moving toward resolution. No matter how difficult or seemingly inexplicable our lives may be, everything in them is there for our own benefit. When we feel beaten down by life and tempted by our pain to reject the possibility of there being any logic to it all, we can take encouragement from those who have seen more than we.

Karma is the causality that gives our lives their logic and project. It is what weaves the many threads of our many lives into a unified tapestry. In the end, our learning does not serve simply our individual development but is tied to the evolution of other persons. Through them it becomes part of a larger web of evolutionary development we can only catch glimpses of here on Earth. More than anything else, perhaps, it is these fleeting impressions of the grandeur of the immensely complex, majestic processes we are part of that lifts us above our pain and restores to us our willingness to go on. Who could resist the opportunity to be part of such undertakings? Who would not do all they could to see them through to completion?

Questions and Answers

Q: It seems that the concept of karma would lead to social passivity. Why bother trying to help those who suffer if it is their karma to be born into such disadvantaged lives? Would this not be to interfere with karma?

A: If it is someone's karma to be born into suffering, it is also the karmic responsibility of those who witness this suffering to try to alleviate it. The concept of karma cannot be used as a justification for social apathy—or rather it is abused when used in this way. If

---

[29] There are interesting parallels between the long-term aftereffects on values and personality of touching the *bardo* state in hypnosis and touching it as a result of a near-death episode. For a description of the long-term impact of the near-death experience, see Charles Flynn's book *After the Beyond* and Kenneth Ring's *Heading Toward Omega*.

karma and rebirth give us some insight into the processes through which we keep meeting each other on Earth, they do not dissolve the responsibilities that arise within each individual lifecycle. Karma is not fatalistic or deterministic. It defines conditions, not how things "must be." Karma is also interdependent. One person's karmic burden is another person's karmic opportunity. We do not interfere in others' karma when we assist them, but rather we operate from within the karmic context of our juxtaposition in life.

Q: Do the notions of karma and karmic script mean that chance plays no role whatsoever in our lives on Earth? And if chance does play a role, does this not contradict the idea that the circumstances we face in life are karmically intentional for us?

A: The fact that *some* of the basic conditions and events that shape our lives may be planned from the start does not mean that *everything* about our lives is predetermined. If the outcome of our lives were inevitable, what would be the point of incarnating at all? We would just be going through the paces, mechanically actualizing in the physical plane a plan drafted elsewhere. Furthermore, if human beings have the capacity to make choices that are at least relatively free, as most spiritual traditions insist, then the outcome of events on Earth must remain indeterminate, thereby keeping some degree of randomness in the system.

Karma says that our choices generate consequences. This does not necessarily exclude chance from the arena in which these consequences manifest. We make certain choices before we are born that define our general course through life, our karmic script. We are born into these restricted options and then make more choices which further define our options as we go along. There is no reason to assume that chance plays absolutely no role within these broad guidelines. In living organisms, a certain measure of randomness increases the probability of novelty and creativity, and this would seem a desirable feature to build into the system. Moreover, if randomness compromises strict determinacy at one level of the system, we could easily imagine ways in which it might be recouped at higher levels.

If it is not too silly a comparison, we might draw an analogy to playing putt-putt golf on one of those multicourse complexes one finds at large amusement parks. Imagine that there are five courses ranging from novice to advanced levels of play. Once you choose your course, your options are defined by the conditions of that course, but you still must choose how to play each hole. The more advanced the course, the more complex its holes and thus the more choices it affords. The eventual destination for all players of one course, the eighteenth hole, is the same, but the outcome (one's individual score) is not.

Let us imagine further that the course is designed so that chance plays a larger role in the more advanced courses. There are little hidden trapdoors that randomly open up on the greens, suddenly taking your ball off one and dumping it onto another. (One particular trapdoor on course #4 might even result in your sudden "transfer" to course #5.) The point is that chance has been consciously built into the more advanced courses and presumably constitutes a major part of their attraction. The laws of cause and effect still hold, but the increased role of chance requires a much more sophisticated understanding of how they would apply.

The point of this analogy is that karma does not exclude chance, but chance does exclude simplistic conceptualizations of how karma works in life. Chance does not threaten the notion that we can trust the circumstances we find ourselves in at any given point in our lives to constitute a *meaningful* challenge for us. Perhaps a particular situation was not intended, in the sense that it was not part of our original karmic script, yet it can still be karmically meaningful to us if our response to it will be incorporated into the system and advance our game. Perhaps chance on the Earth plane functions like wild cards in poker; it can only improve our hand, not make it worse. It requires only a little imagination to come up with any number of ways to integrate chance and karmic necessity.

The real question, therefore, is not whether chance exists here on Earth or whether its presence undermines karma, but rather: Can we can trust Life to blend cause and chance in a manner that protects and advances our best interests? Is chance compatible with care? The next question will sharpen this question further.

Q: The suffering of individuals may make karmic sense on a case-by-case basis, but how are we to understand instances of mass suffering? Are we to suppose, for example, that it was planned for specifically these six million Jews to die in Hitler's concentration camps and no others?

A: The notion that there is a logic to human suffering is most taxed not by the suffering of individuals, as difficult as that in itself is to comprehend, but by the suffering of large numbers of people.

When one learns of a busload of children killed in a traffic accident, or of twenty-five thousand killed in an earthquake, or when one ponders the fate of the six million Jews, the enormity of the suffering mocks our attempt to fathom the logic of it by whatever theory. Though I accept the principle of karmic self-determination, I confess that I am often brought out of my chair in anger when I hear the facile "explanations" reincarnationists sometimes give these human tragedies. "They all chose their lives" is too superficial a response to the thousands of children who are starving to death in the wake of African droughts. Such callous sentiment seems designed more to insulate us from the enormous suffering involved than to offer genuine insight into its possible purpose.

It is more honest, I think, to admit that suffering of this magnitude brings us to our philosophical knees. We have no recourse but to confess our inability to understand the karmic causalities underlying these events. Here we must make a choice that at this point in time no argument can compel. Does such collective human suffering reflect meaningful purpose? In the face of such inscrutable pain, how can we dare suggest that the Universe plays fairly with us?

Despite the fact that our evidence is incomplete, two considerations lead me to believe that human suffering is meaningful and that there is a logic to it, even when I cannot demonstrate its logic.

In the first place, when working with individuals in past-life therapy we can use various techniques, with notable consistency, to uncover and reconstruct the events that have brought them step by step to their present position. We can identify the causal principles operating across their lives. We may not succeed with every individual, but we will with most of them, enough at any rate to justifiably conclude that within this small group of individuals, human suffering appears to make sense. There is a logic to it. The question now becomes: Should we generalize from this small sample to the entire human race? (I am talking, of course, not just of the few cases reported here but of the hundreds of cases in print they represent.) Should we assume that these principles of cause and effect hold not just for these few but for all human beings? If we have reasonable grounds for believing that at least some human beings live within a meaningful fabric of events, should we project these results and conclude that all human beings, however great their collective suffering, live within the same intentional fabric.

Despite the enigma presented by mass suffering, it is not unreasonable to think that we should generalize our results. When we find nature consistently behaving in a certain manner in one corner of a garden where we've been digging, it is not unreasonable to expect it to be operating in a similar manner where we have not yet dug. When we find that the riddle of an individual's suffering can be penetrated by expanding our insight into that person's history, and when this process can be repeated in case after case with illumination and healing the result, the most reasonable conjecture would be that similar insight could be gathered for any human being in any situation, at least in principle. Thus it is not unreasonable to hypothesize on the basis of our investigation of a small sample that all human suffering is meaningful, even mass suffering. If karmic causalities are in fact natural causalities, then, like the laws of physical nature, they are reasonably conceptualized as universally binding principles. Our confidence in this generalization, of course, will reflect our level of confidence that we have in fact identified lawful causalities operating in our small sample.

And yet if chance plays a part in the Earth experience, as suggested in the answer given to the preceding question, we must qualify this result. If chance is part of the system, it would seem that we have two options at this point. First, we could hold that the influence of chance on human events does not include major human suffering. This would be a "restricted chance" option. It would allow chance into the system but restrict it to minor events that may disturb us but which do not constitute major life challenges to us. In this view, the existentially important human suffering, including mass suffering, would be strictly governed by karmic necessities.

The second option would be to allow chance to play a role in even major suffering, but to preserve meaning by holding fast to care. The real burden of chance is that it seems to reflect a callous disregard of our aspirations and efforts. It tells us that our sweat and tears are not important in the larger scheme of things, that we do not count for much in the final analysis. And yet, if chance is part of a larger system that mindfully and benevolently incorporates all our responses to life into our larger evolutionary development, then chance is subordinate to care. If this system preserves our consciousness even as our bodies die, and folds each life's accomplishments (whether achieved by design or through encounter with chance) into our personal evolution, then the sting is taken out of chance. Chance becomes simply one of the risks we take on in participating in this accelerated curriculum we call the human experience.

Of the two options, I am inclined toward the second. The first seems arbitrary and contrived. The second, however, still taxes our credulity. The suffering of humanity surrounds us daily and is easy to see. The care behind the system that would permit this suffering in order to hasten the evolution of us all is hard to see. Why should we think it is there? Why should we believe that Life blends cause and chance in a way that protects and advances our best interests? Even if we admit that reincarnation is a fact of life, why should we not conclude that random chance can wreak havoc even in a reincarnating universe? This brings us to the second consideration.

The second consideration is an argument from experience, experiences that are intensely personal and therefore private but show up in numerous contexts and are replicable to a degree. In metaconsciousness, for example, Dr. Whitton's clients sometimes have deep experiences of the meaningfulness of the flow of existence, a meaningfulness that fills them with wonder and lifts their vision beyond the horizon of their individual sagas. As one of Whitton's clients put it:

> I have been allowed the barest glimpse of levels of creation that are far above anything I can even begin to put into words. I was made to feel that everything that we do has meaning at the highest level. Our sufferings are not random; they are merely part of an eternal plan more complex and awe-inspiring than we are capable of imagining. [p. 98]

Those who come close to death but are revived with the assistance of advanced medical technology often report similar experiences of gaining profound insights into the purpose and trustworthiness of Life. One of the things that makes the survivors of a near-death episode interesting to study is that they are naive. That is to say, they did not in any way cultivate their experiences but had them thrust upon them by their brush with death. One such experience is reported in Kenneth Ring's *Heading Toward Omega*:

> By my side there was a Being with a magnificent presence. I could not see an exact form, but instead, a radiation of light that lit up everything about me and spoke with a voice that held the deepest tenderness one can ever imagine . . . as this loving yet powerful

Being spoke to me, I understood vast meanings, much beyond my ability to explain. I understood life and death, and instantly any fear I had, ended. . . .

For what seemed to be endless time, I experienced this Presence. The Light Being, pure, powerful, all-expansive, was without a form and it could be said that great waves of awareness flowed to me and into my mind.

As I responded to these revelations, I knew them to be so. Of course, it didn't matter if one lived or died, it was all so clear. There was a complete trust and greater understanding of what these words meant.

It seemed whole *Truths* revealed themselves to me. Waves of thought—ideas greater and purer than I had ever tried to figure out came to me. Thoughts, clear without effort revealed themselves in total wholeness, although not in logical sequence. I, of course, being in that magnificent Presence, understood it all. I realized that consciousness is life. We will live in and through much, but this consciousness we know that is behind our personality will continue. I knew now that the purpose of life does not depend on me; it has its own purpose. I realized that the flow of it will continue even as I will continue. New serenity entered my being.

As this occurred, an intensity of feeling rushed through me, as if the light that surrounded that Being was bathing me, penetrating every part of me. As I absorbed the energy, I sensed what I can only describe as bliss. That is such a little word, but the feeling was dynamic, rolling, magnificent, expanding, ecstatic—*Bliss*. It swirled around me and, entering my chest, flowed through me, and I was immersed in love and awareness for ineffable time. [pp. 74–75]

While this woman's experience does not directly address the problem of human suffering, I think it safe to speculate that she would agree with Whitton's client that all human suffering is part of a plan "more complex and awe-inspiring than we are capable of imagining." If we were to ask her "Given the horrible things that happen to people on Earth, can we trust life?," I have no doubt that she would answer yes. And she would do so not necessarily because she had discovered the answer to the riddle of all human suffering, but because she had had intimate contact with some essence underlying the life process and had felt only love, serenity, and wisdom flowing from it.[30]

When one has a profound experience of this sort, or when one experiences the meaningful, coordinated orchestration of one's life events extending across hundreds of years, this experience carries an

---

[30] Those who participate in highly experiential forms of psychotherapy often have similar transformative experiences at advanced levels of work. The interested reader will find many examples in Stanislav Grof's books.

epistemic weight at least equal to, if not greater than, many rational arguments. Philosophers will tell you that getting philosophical mileage out of experience is a complex task, and this is quite true. And yet actually to *experience* the meaningful placement of one's life in a larger web of events moves one to affirm that meaning pervades the *entire* universe, even those parts where one's vision cannot penetrate. How could meaning soak one portion of existence so thoroughly and leave another portion high and dry? Such an inconsistency in the fabric of reality seems unfathomable.

No doubt some would suggest that this experience of the flow of one's life being saturated with meaning is a complete hallucination, but those who say this are consistently people who have not had such experiences. Those thousands, even millions,[31] who have had this kind of experience insist that their state of mind during it was much clearer and sharper than their ordinary consciousness. Far from being a hallucination, they insist that they were seeing and knowing more accurately and more deeply than they ever did in their sensebound mode of perception. The only thing that causes the skeptics to doubt their word is the fact that our current, postenlightenment worldview cannot at present accommodate their testimony, and so he has no other recourse than to dismiss it, usually as wish-fulfilling projections. The world they are describing is simply too good to be true.

Having had this sort of experience myself, however, I know that it is not a hallucination, and I am sensitive to the experience in others. One recognizes a kindred spirit, someone who has seen something similar to what you have seen and who is struggling to put into words an experience that cannot be squeezed into language. Yet at the same time I know that such confessions will have limited impact on those who have not had anything approximating this experience themselves. There is not much that one can do at this point except point out the diverse contexts in which these experiences occur, outline the long-term impact they have on those who have them, and let it go at that. In the end, experience is a reasonable grounds for belief, but probably not rationally compelling grounds for those who have not had comparable experiences. When combined with the first consideration, however, it strengthens the argument, though exactly how much I would not want to try to calculate.

---

[31] A Gallup poll taken in 1981 estimated that approximately eight million Americans had had a concious near-death episode experience, in which this type of experience is not uncommon.

4
The Oversoul

It is not particularly difficult to imagine ourselves living multiple lives, each the causal extension of lives preceding it and itself the cause of lives following it. This is simply to multiply the self through history and represents no great intellectual hurdle. It is more difficult, however, to see our present being as part of a larger being. The theory of reincarnation suggests that behind our present identity is a collective identity, as unique as our smaller identity but vast in depth and scope. Stretching our minds to grasp the concept of such a being and our relation to it is perhaps the greatest challenge raised by shifting to a reincarnationist world view.

Let's begin our inquiry with a few basic questions that seem to follow naturally from the picture of reincarnation painted in the previous chapters. If I have lived many lives before this one, what has happened to all the experiences I have collected in these lives? Do they somehow all reside inside me, reflected in my current interests and aptitudes? No doubt this is part of it, and yet can it be only this? For example, if I have lived many lives before this one, then I have probably experienced growing old a number of times. Let's assume for the sake of discussion that I have lived to be an old man or woman at least ten times. What exactly has happened to those experiences of aging? If I have more than once watched my children take over the work I used to do and watched their children become young adults, where have these experiences gone? If I have watched death approach many times, drawing slowly closer to me day by day, what has become of the courage, wisdom, and insight these encounters probably aroused in me? In short, as I live today as a young man or woman, where are "my" experiences of old age? Do I have access to them? Can they assist me in the task of growing old as I experience this again in this life?

In essence, these questions are asking "What is the present status of my former lives now that a new 'I' has taken their place on Earth?" Do they continue to exist somewhere as active life forms even now, or have they in some way been folded into me and therefore exist today only as memories, as mental echoes of a once-living being? These are important questions, as they inquire into our own fate. Obviously the fate of my former lives will eventually be the fate of my present identity, for in the long run we are no different from each other. What will happen to me after "my" next life has picked up where I left off? Do I simply cease to exist after passing on my karmic inheritance to the next in line? Do I somehow live through that next life? Without our bodies we become purely beings of consciousness, centers of awareness that hold and integrate all the experiences collected during our sojourn on Earth. Will we still function as intact centers of awareness after the torch of embodied learning has been passed?

One way to approach these questions is to construct a fantasy of a long series of lives for ourselves, developing each as completely and richly as we can. We should give each of them a full share of the triumphs and tragedies that come to every life—the joys and disappointments, the loves and broken hearts, the separations and reunions. After creating only a few such lives, it should become clear that it is impossible for all of their experiences to fit inside me, as it were. One often reads in reincarnationist literature that "You are the extension of everything that has gone before." This exercise should convince us, however, that if I am in some sense an extension of my former lives, I am not a summation of their experiences. My wisdom is too small to have incorporated their collective wisdom; my capacity for joy is not the sum of their capacities for joy. If my life moves beyond theirs in some progressive development, it also repeats the human experience afresh with each birth, at least in certain respects. And so we return to our original question. If I do not collect and integrate all the experiences of all my former lives, where are these experiences being collected? To put it simply, who has them?

THE OVERSOUL

Reflections of this kind have led many reincarnationists to speak of an Oversoul.[1] If the term *soul* is used for the consciousness that collects and integrates the experiences of a single incarnation, the term *Oversoul* is the name given to the larger consciousness that is collecting and integrating the experiences of both my life and all the lives that precede and follow mine.[2] All these lives are thought to be alive within the Oversoul, somehow maintaining their integrity while joining themselves into a larger consciousness, perhaps as the memory of one day joins itself to the memory of the next while still remaining distinct. My present life is an extension of the Oversoul; it is one cycle within its vastly larger lifecycle. Thus the Oversoul is a deeper identity to me than the identity I have assumed in this birth. Through the Oversoul I am rooted into a deeper history.

It was the Oversoul who actually created the form that I now am. I did not choose the components of my present life, for my personality did not exist until after those choices were made. Neither were these choices made simply by the life immediately preceding mine. My "whole identity" made those choices, the integrated sum total of all of the experiences of my lineage, a lineage reaching back beyond the horizon of time itself. The Oversoul chose the particular components of my life to advance and enrich its own life. Strictly speaking, it is not I who incarnate many times, but It.

When I first began to understand the nature of the Oversoul I was intrigued but also agitated, even angry. Agitated because I was used to experiencing myself as a primary reality and did not want to surrender that position. By this I mean that I had grown accustomed to the primacy of my current identity. I had grown used to thinking of myself in terms of this body and this personality. Whatever came before and whatever would come after, at least this was what I am now. Yet if behind my current personality-self lurked a larger identity, not a celestial identity of universal God-consciousness but a particular identity tied to a particular lineage of experience, then my present short-term identity felt displaced in some way. The concept of the Oversoul made me feel like I was simply one arm on a many-armed creature reaching out for more and more life. Because of its vastness, the life of the Oversoul

---

[1] For example, Jane Roberts in her novels *The Education of Oversoul-7, The Further Education of Oversoul-7,* and *Oversoul-7 and the Museum of Time.*

[2] Because of its integrating function, Denys Kelsey and Joan Grant in *Many Lifetimes* call it the Integral.

was superior to mine. Its knowledge was greater, its power, its depth of insight beyond anything I could muster. What was I to it? I did not want to surrender the primacy of my life. I was angry.

But I was also curious, and this curiosity led me to explore the Oversoul further, both conceptually and experientially. I read more of the literature on it and began a series of meditational exercises designed to open channels of communication with it. In time my anger and resentment fell away and I became more comfortable with the idea that my identity is nested in this larger identity. I discovered that rather than diminishing the value of my life, its existence augmented my life's value. The richness of my particular existence began to stand out more clearly against the background of infinite time and infinite development. In the end I could not resist the appeal of being part of something so vast.

Before I came to this point of reconciliation, however, I struggled for a long time with how to understand the Oversoul and its relation to my life. How could I think of this larger life in a way that did not diminish the integrity of my own life? At one point during this long struggle I had a dream in which I saw a long snake form itself into a line of coils. Each coil was a single lifecycle, while the snake was the mega-being whose experience bound the individual loops into a coherent whole. Each atom, molecule, and cell of each coil belonged simultaneously to that coil and to the snake as a whole. This simple image triggered in me a deep experience of my inclusion in the Oversoul, but it did not answer all my questions. From one perspective I am only part of this being, a single coil among many, while from another I am fully this being. How was I to make sense of this?

As I was wrestling with this problem, I happened upon something that triggered a second "Aha!" experience for me. It too did not actually add anything to my conceptual understanding of the Oversoul, but it demonstrated to me how nature often combines multiplicity with oneness.

I was poking around a shop at the seashore and happened upon a large chambered nautilus. It had been carefully sliced open and mounted so as to display both the inner and outer sides of the same shell side by side. On one side, I saw a succession of chambers that began very small and grew evenly as they followed the graceful arch of the shell's unfolding spiral. To me, each chamber represented a human life, a finite stage in a larger development, always followed by another larger than it. Round and round the lives unfolded, spinning the archetypal

FIGURE 4.1

spiral of cyclic yet infinite development. In this particular shell there were twenty-nine chambers, each connected to the next by a small, delicate hole in the chamber wall.

Next to this spiral of chambers was mounted the outer wall of the same shell. This side spoke of wholeness, for it showed a colorful pattern of strong brown lines that integrated and unified the twenty-nine chambers within. The design was so masterfully executed that it looked as though an artist had picked up a fully grown shell and painted it with a few bold strokes. The brown streaks cut smoothly across the shell's inner chambers as if they weren't there (see Figure 4.1).

Seeing both sides of the shell side by side jolted me into putting together at an intuitive level what my linear mind had been unable to join. What was divided into segmented stages from one side was from the other a single life form expressing a single intentionality. Neither side existed without the other. Thus the chambered nautilus became for me a metaphor of how individual lives can be beautifully integrated into a larger whole. It also convinced me of the necessity of thinking of the smaller self and the Oversoul as existing in two distinct though interpenetrating realities. The natural environment of the Oversoul is the spiritual world, which is not bound by the same laws of time and linear causality that govern the physical world. If I was going to understand the Oversoul (insofar as this is possible from this side of existence), I was going to have to learn to detach my thinking from the rules that govern life on the physical plane. In particular, I was going to have to learn to think atemporally, alinearly, and holographically. This exercise still continues.[3]

If our ego-self is our natural identity in the physical world, the Oversoul is our natural identity in the spiritual. As Dr. Whitton's subjects have testified, when we leave our physical bodies behind at "death" and return to the spiritual domain, we (ideally) exchange our ego-identities for the larger identity of the Oversoul. This larger identity consists of all the lives we have ever lived. To be reunited with the Oversoul, therefore, is to experience simultaneously a profound expansion of our being and a coming home to a deeper identity.[4]

I know of no better description of this process than the one Robert Monroe gives in his book *Far Journeys*.[5] His account describes an actual experience that he had not at the end of his life but while in the out-of-body state. Many years of consciousness-expanding work laid the foundation for the exceptional experience reported here. Monroe writes:

> I am in a bright white tunnel and moving rapidly. No, it is not a tunnel, but a transparent, radiating tube. I am bathed in the radiation which courses through all of me, and the intensity and recognition of it envelop my consciousness and I laugh with great joy. . . . The radiation flow is two-directional in the tube. The flow moving past me in the direction from which I came [Earth] is smooth, even, and undiluted. The flow that I am is moving in the opposite direction and appears much different. It is organized in a more complex form. It is the same as the wave moving past me, but

---

[3] The concept of rebirth presented in this volume is linear and therefore necessarily one-sided. From the Oversoul's perspective "reincarnation" might look less like a long succession of incarnations and more like multiple incarnations going on all at once. Indeed, several authors have suggested that a better way to conceptualize what is actually taking place is to imagine that all our lives are being lived simultaneously, that our "former lives" are even now existing in their time/space slot while we exist in ours. From this perspective, karma would have to be reconceptualized away from linear causality and in the direction of holographic interactions arching across simultaneous lives. While I am attracted to this model and while I am moving in this direction myself, I have nevertheless presented a linear description of reincarnation in this volume because it is a more manageable approach given my present level of competence in these matters. Shifting to a transtemporal model of reincarnation would add a dimension to what is presented here, but would not, I think, subtract anything essential. Such a move would preserve the basic insights developed here while translating them into a different metaphysical perspective.

[4] A word of caution. If the Oversoul is a larger and truer self than our present self, it is *not* what the mystics are referring to when they speak of discovering their "true Self." That Self is the Atman, the Divine SELF, which is the innermost essence of our being. I will return to this point later.

[5] Monroe is also the author of the widely read *Journeys Out of the Body* and founder of the Monroe Institute of Applied Science in Faber, Virginia.

it contains a multitude of small waves impressed upon the basic. I am both the basic and the small waveforms, moving back to the source. The movement is steady and unhurried, impelled by a desire I know but cannot express. I vibrate with joyous ecstasy just by the knowing.

The tube seems to become larger as another joins it from one side, and another waveform melds into me and we become one. I recognize the other immediately, as it does me, and there is the great excitement of reunion, this other I and I. How could I have forgotten this! We move along together, happily exploring the adventures, experience, and knowledge of the other. The tube widens again, and another I joins us, and the process repeats itself. Our waveforms are remarkably identical and our pattern grows stronger as they move in phase. There are variegations in each which, when combined with another related anomaly, create a new and important modification of the total that we are.

The tube expands again and I am no longer concerned with its walls as still another I enters the waveform flow. This is particularly exciting as it is the first I perceive as returning from a completely nonhuman sojourn. Yet the intermesh was near-perfect and we became so much more. Now we know that, somewhere, a consciously controlled physical tail, much like a monkey's, is useful in ways for more than balance and acting as a third hand for holding things. It can be a very efficient means of communication far beyond a super sign language just as eloquent as the spoken word.

Steadily and surely, one I after another joins us. With each, we become more aware and remember more of the total. How many does not seem important. Our knowledge and ability is so great that we do not bother to contemplate it. It is not important. We are one. [pp. 120–121]

For Monroe to have continued in the tube to the source of the energy which had created all the lives he experienced himself as being, he would have needed to have been "complete," as he says elsewhere. But he was not yet complete and thus was not able to continue beyond a certain point.

If the Oversoul has within it all the capacities and knowledge collected over many thousands of years of living, we must flex our minds considerably to imagine what the consciousness of this being might be like. Monroe goes on to describe this larger collective identity he now was experiencing himself to be:

Flowing through all of us is a coherent energy that is our creation, that displays immensely the reality of the whole as far greater than the sum of the parts. Our ability and knowledge seem without limit, yet we know at this point such is valid only within the

energy systems of our experience. We can create time as we wish
or the need arises. . . . We can create matter from other energy
patterns, or change the structure thereof to any degree desired,
including reversion to original form. We can create, enhance, alter,
modulate, or eradicate any percept [insight or knowing] within the
energy fields of our experience. We can transform any such energy
fields one into another or others except for that which we are. We
cannot create or comprehend our prime energy until we are
complete.

We can create physical patterns such as your sun and solar
system, yet we do not. It has been done. We can adjust the environs
of your planet Earth, yet we do not. It is not our design. We can
and do monitor, supplement, and enhance the flow of the human
learning experience, as well as other learning experiences of similar
content throughout time-space. This we perform continuously at all
levels of human awareness so as to prepare properly those entraining
units of our prime energy [i.e., humans] for entry and meld into
the totality that we are becoming. It is the essence of our growth to
do so. Such assistance and preparation is forthcoming from us only
by request from one or more levels of consciousness within the
entraining unit. Thereafter, a bonding is in effect through which
many forms of communication pass between us until the ultimate
transformation occurs. [P. 122][6]

As one would imagine, merging with this higher, collective identity
was an extremely powerful and moving experience for Monroe. The
awesome knowledge which was temporarily his in this experience
strongly reminded me of a similar feature of near-death experiences.
People who undergo a near-death episode sometimes report coming
for a few brief moments into possession of extraordinary knowledge.
The transformative effect of having touched this knowledge even once
continues long after the knowledge itself has been lost. In *After the
Beyond*, Charles Flynn reports two such incidents. Quoting others, he
writes:

(1) Feeling myself enveloped in that love, feeling myself surrounded with the knowledge that came off of it, I felt like I knew
the secrets of everything from the very beginning of time to infinity,
and I realized that there was no end. I realized that we are but a
very small part of something that's gigantic, but as people we inter-
lock into each other's lives like puzzle pieces, and that we are just
an infinitely small part of the universe. But we're also very special.

(2) During the experience I knew that I would lose practically

---

[6] Monroe's term for the Oversoul is Inspect, short for "Intelligent Species."

everything but a splinter of this essential knowledge, this absolute knowledge. But one of the things I discovered is that a great deal of what is essential to understanding we already possess. All you have to do is find it within yourself. In this sense, we have a phenomenal amount of information in us. [p. 12]

I suspect that the knowledge these people touched in almost dying might be the knowledge they had accumulated through their many previous lives. If so, it would be part of their own deeper identity as the Oversoul, which for a brief moment they again became.[7]

While the Oversoul's knowledge and power seem extraordinary, it appears to focus its attention on helping us learn what we have come to Earth to learn. We are the means through which it is now learning what it must learn to complete itself. It completes itself by helping us complete ourselves. We are its current student in the Earth school, a part of itself sent off to work for the good of the whole, yet obliged to forget its tie to the whole as part of the conditions of learning.

And yet this forgetfulness can be penetrated to a degree even while we are in the Earth school. Once we know of the existence of the Oversoul and of our connection to it, we can begin to open ourselves to it in a deeper way. We can, to a degree, make an unconscious re-lationship conscious.

As Monroe states above, the Oversoul can only really begin to help us if we ask for assistance. This appears to be a general principle governing the spiritual domain—the more conscious dimension of our being is not allowed to help the less conscious dimension unless the latter asks for help. Until we ask for assistance, we are more or less left alone to try to work things out by ourselves as best we can. Because we will sooner or later encounter challenges that exceed our limited means, the system ensures that eventually, this life or next, we will discover for ourselves the reality of this larger identity and our proper relation to it. But it is not necessary for us to come to the end of our rope before we take advantage of the extraordinary resources of the Oversoul and what lies behind it. We can work from a positive base as well as a negative one. With the Oversoul's support, we can live our lives perfectly balanced and without strain, instead of from crisis to crisis.

---

[7] At least this, perhaps more. In *Heading Toward Omega*, Kenneth Ring discusses several cases in which persons acquired extraordinary knowledge during their NDE and the source of this knowledge was the Being of Light itself (see Chapter 3, especially pp. 58–60).

OPENING TO THE POSSIBILITIES

As long as we look at life from the perspective of having only one brief life to live, we can only conceive of a purpose and place for ourselves in the larger order of things in terms that fit into these few years. Whatever is going on in the universe, our role in it cannot be larger than our years permit. From the one-timer's perspective, we are all necessarily reduced to bit parts in life. If the physical universe is approximately fifteen billion years old, then from this perspective we are reduced to cameo appearances and can have no significant share in the universe's adventure. This fundamental constriction does not seem to me to be alleviated by adding an eternity of reward or punishment after only a few decisive years of action and learning.

When we open to the truth of rebirth, however, this artificial constraint on our years falls away. If we pulse in and out of physical existence, this demonstrates that we are not merely the physical beings our scientistic, rationalist culture has told us we are. Reincarnation does not answer all our questions about ourselves, but it lifts a key restriction in our self-concept. It all hinges on time. We cannot become more than we have time to become. We cannot play a greater part than we have time to learn. Reincarnation gives us reason to ask larger questions about what we are and what our place in the scheme of things is. It also gives us cause to expect larger answers to these questions. When we begin to glimpse our true longevity, when we begin to appreciate the true scope of our lives, we can no longer see ourselves as simply the citizens of one country or one century. We must instead come to see ourselves as time travelers with unrestricted passports.

It is not our present ego-personality that reaches this far across time, but the Oversoul. The Oversoul is our bridge into the cosmos. Our place in the Divine Order is through its life and work. Through our participation in it we become part of processes stretching across eons of time, processes so vast that we must struggle even to see the possibilities.

Yet just as our development is restricted by our years, the same must be true of the Oversoul. It too cannot become more than it has time to become. Therefore we eventually want to inquire about its life expectancy. If, in the final analysis, we are alive as long as it is alive, just how much time does the Oversoul have?

I have spoken often of ten thousand years, but do we have any reason to stop there? Reincarnation tells us that as an Oversoul we are a being that can exist outside physical reality, a spiritual being that enters into but is not contained within physical reality. As a spiritual being not trapped within the life expectancies of the physical universe, we can perhaps begin to approximate our true age by drawing comparisons to galaxies millions and billions of years old. Yet even these expanded projections are metaphors, for time as we know it is a function of material existence and does not necessarily characterize the spiritual domain. Linear time is part of the space/time continuum. It is the fourth dimension of Einstein's four-dimensional universe. Outside the physical universe it ceases to function, or at least it behaves quite differently.

According to Robert Monroe, in the nonphysical domain there is movement and development, and therefore sequence, but not the confining restrictions of sequential time as we experience time here. I do not pretend fully to comprehend how there can be sequence without time, but I do not dismiss the possibility. Our language was created in and for the world of linear time and therefore hampers our efforts to think about, let alone describe, an atemporal universe. Clearly relativity theory has taught us to expect the unexpected from time.

My point here is that we cannot simply export time-concepts from the physical domain to the spiritual. Therefore, to ask how long the Oversoul lives is probably to commit what philosophers call a 'category mistake'; that is, to apply to something categories that do not properly belong to it. The category of life expectancy, conceived of in terms of linear time, probably does not properly apply to the Oversoul at all. To think of the Oversoul's life duration in terms of millions or even billions of years may perhaps serve at best as a suggestive approximation of an order of reality beyond our ken.

Rather than attempt to apply temporal concepts to the Oversoul at all, we ought to think of it as a being that lives outside time and that dips in and out of the time/space continuum. Even while part of it is immersed in time, its larger share hovers outside time. Within Western theology there is some precedent for these reflections. In Western theology spirit is seen as eternal. Properly understood, eternity means not an infinite extension of linear time but a different order of existence altogether. Eternity is not "forever and ever" but an all-encompassing simultaneity where the divisions of past, present, and future do not hold. Eternity is timelessness.

Perhaps I should stop here and be satisfied with the answer we have gotten thus far—that while we can safely project the longevity of the Oversoul to be vast, in the end we cannot mark its length in years because Earth-time does not properly apply to it. Yet I should mention another part to the answer, although it may introduce taxing subtleties.

The religious traditions that teach reincarnation agree with the Western religions that we are spirit, and as spirit we can never die. To this shared sense of immortality, however, these traditions add the observation that life in spirit is not static but dynamic. We can never die, but it is part of our nature to change and expand, even to transmute ourselves into higher life forms at critical stages of our development. This is the cycle of death and rebirth, the successive transmutation of form necessary to accommodate ever-expanding function. This is the cycle that carries us from life to life—even genus to genus—in our spiral of development.

Although the Oversoul exists outside time as we know it on Earth, perhaps it too participates in a similar cycle of death and rebirth as part of its own evolution. Perhaps it too must one day surrender its form in order to transcend limitations inherent in its structure, and become something new and larger. Here our speculations exhaust themselves. Yet, if we can extrapolate from the death/rebirth cycle of human experience to the Oversoul's experience, we have reason to assume that if the Oversoul does metamorphose into a higher life form, all would be preserved in the transformation. All would be conserved and carried forward. Just as the Oversoul collects and preserves the experiences of our many lives, so whatever comes next would preserve all the experiences gathered into the Oversoul. Change is perpetual throughout the physical and spiritual universes, yet life is eternal. Through the Oversoul, we are eternal.

THE OVERSOUL AND GOD

For those accustomed to thinking of there being nothing between us and God, the concept of the Oversoul may come as something of a shock. Our first reaction may be to think that the Oversoul distances us one step from God, but that is not in fact so. In the esoteric spiritual traditions that teach reincarnation *God* is the name given to the whole of existence, including both the physical universe and nonphysical universe(s). God is the intelligence that generates and incorporates all lesser intelligences. The trillions of stars we see in the night sky are but cells in God's body. Everything that exists is part of the reality of God manifesting Itself in different forms.

God is not only the mega-total of all that is but also the inner essence of every part as well. Within every particle of existence is the essence of Divine Life, the Divine Spark. Through this Divine Spark, the cosmos lives as a single being while at another level it simultaneously lives as many discrete beings.

Because everything that exists has this Divine Spark within it, we are always directly connected to the Whole. "You are closer to me than the jugular," says the Muslim of Allah, and it is true. In fact, we are more than intimately connected to the Divinity, we *are* the Divinity. Our substance is Its substance; our deepest identity is Its identity. Though we tend to lose awareness of this identity when we plunge into the physical world where matter emphasizes separateness, it is always there beneath the surface.

It is a paradoxical situation. We are at once the Whole and a single part. Our deepest identity is not our personality or the Oversoul but Divinity Itself. Yet we are also a small part in a drama larger than ourselves. As a center of consciousness entrusted with a hundred years of experience, we are also part of a larger consciousness, the Oversoul, entrusted with an indeterminate number of "years" of experience. That being is in turn part of an even larger consciousness—an Over-Oversoul, if you will. There is every reason to assume that this process of inclusion into larger wholes repeats itself again and again, moving higher and higher up the ladder of consciousness, eventually reaching the encompassing consciousness of God-as-All-That Is.

The traditions of enlightenment testify to the fact that each of us can experience within ourselves the God–Nature itself in its purest, predifferentiated form. Described alternatively as Undifferentiated Consciousness, The One, The Godhead, That Which Is Beyond Form, Emptiness, The Void, Non-Being, The Ground of Being, and so on, this reality presents itself as something indivisible and whole. Thus it is necessarily indescribable by words, which by their very nature divide the world into alternative categories.[8] Though impossible to describe, one can nevertheless experience this Reality. Those who do experience It, we are told, discover that It has always been their deepest identity. It has never been absent, only unknown to us.

Yet these same traditions of enlightenment teach us that when this Reality first chose to express Itself in diversity, It began a process of unfolding that generated many intermediate realms and many inter-

---

[8] Western philosophers have tended to take such disclaimers as evidence of the unreality of what the words refer to, but the enlightenment traditions are simply telling us that neither words nor our verbal intellect can penetrate or encompass this Reality. Those who love and trust words as the primary guide to truth will eventually have to choose between words and experience.

mediate intelligences responsible for these dimensions of Itself. These intelligences are acknowledged and honored in the many deities and Bodhisattvas of Eastern cosmologies. These are not Gods (as though there could be more than one God), but intermediate spiritual beings who direct and orchestrate the higher functions of the Whole. Though it looks at first like rampant polytheism, we are always reminded that "Only the One exists." As this One unfolded Itself into various spiritual realms, however, and eventually into our physical realm, Its body became a complex body. In manifestation, the spiritual domain is unified but not simple. It is filled with beings whose responsibilities and capacities exceed our imagination.[9]

The Oversoul is our bridge to these intelligences. Just as our life is nested in the Oversoul's life, its life, I would hazard, is nested in another even greater consciousness, and that in another, and so on. Information and energy would flow in both directions through the system, from top to bottom and from bottom to top—or if you prefer, from out to in and in to out.[10]

It might help us take in this idea of a hierarchical nesting of intelligences if we look for a moment at our bodies, for similar processes operate there. As a physical organism we are comprised of many organ systems, which in turn are made up of organs composed of various tissues. Tissue is but the organization of cells that are comprised of molecules made up of atoms. Atoms break down into nuclei and electrons, which then break down into subatomic particles and even subelectronic particles. At that point things get quite complicated, because particles as such tend to disappear and we are left trying to describe reality in terms of fields of energy (which more than one subatomic physicist has said behaves more like consciousness than matter). Thus our bodies are an incredibly complex hierarchy of

---

[9] It is not surprising that the Eastern religions, which have placed the greatest emphasis on systematically exploring the psyche, have generated more complex cosmologies describing these spiritual realms and the beings that inhabit them than have Western religions. It is not a matter of these religions being true and Western religions false, but simply of different religions tending to specialize in different areas. As a counterpoint, all of the major world movements of social reform have begun in Western countries, where the religions have tended to explore more deeply humankind's responsibility for bringing earthly existence into line with spiritual values.

[10] This idea that our intelligence is nested within a more encompassing intelligence which is in turn nested within an even more encompassing intelligence has a long history in Western philosophy. Plato saw the universe as a multilayered phenomenon, each stratum resulting from the outpouring of the one above it and all emanating from the mind of God. This ancient theory of emanation seems to be being revived in this century by the new discipline of systems theory.

interdependent systems nested within other systems. So many living organisms make up a single human body that Lewis Thomas in *The Lives of the Cell* has suggested that we think of our bodies as a huge city, with its many inhabitants coexisting in a mutually supportive balance.[11]

In a similar fashion the esoteric spiritual traditions invite us to see our consciousness as somewhat similarly nested within a complex web of consciousnesses which together make up God's consciousness. Ontologically—that is, with respect to our being—we are the Divinity; our essence is Its essence. Operationally, however, we relate to the Divine Totality through various intermediaries who, like us, are only different manifestations of the One.

INDIVIDUAL IDENTITY AND THE OVERSOUL

At the beginning of this chapter we asked "Do we continue to function as intact centers of experience even after the next incarnation has begun?" With the concept of the Oversoul now available to us, we can rephrase that question and ask "Does the Oversoul preserve my individual identity while integrating my experience into its more encompassing consciousness?" Is our life simply cut up into bits and pieces of data in the assimilation process or does it maintain its integrity? Beneath these questions, I think we want to know whether our individual life possesses a value beyond merely being an instrument for gathering new information, for we tend to think that only what endures intact has value. In addition, it is extremely difficult for us to imagine ourselves contentedly surrendering our present identity, even for a more encompassing one. We like to trade in our old cars, but trading in old identities is another kettle of fish entirely.

It is difficult to conceptualize the processes that must be involved here. In thinking about these matters I have repeatedly found myself

---

[11] Whereas scientific research has traditionally attempted to understand the greater of these systems in terms of the lesser systems (reductionism), many researchers today are convinced that the larger systems hold many of the secrets to the organization and function of the smaller systems. The flow of energy and information appears to run in both directions. The cells of our body cannot carry out their functions without input received from the larger systems. Simultaneously, we cannot perform any act out here in the world without continuous input from our body's cells. We are an extraordinary megasystem of mutually interdependent systems, each carrying out its individual tasks while simultaneously advancing projects beyond our immediate awareness.

With this shift in perspective, two hundred years of viewing the human body as a very complicated machine is coming to an end. The operation of a machine can be explained in terms of its parts, yet the body defies this kind of explanation. For a discussion of these developments in multiple disciplines, see Frijhof Capra, *The Turning Point*.

caught in language, having to disentangle myself from connotations of words that do not actually fit what I'm trying to understand. The question asked seems to require a yes/no type of answer. Yes, our individual identity appears to be preserved intact. It is less certain, however, that we remain as interested in staying invested in that identity as we now think we would. And if we no longer identify exclusively with a still-functionable identity, it would seem that we ought not call this thing an "identity" any longer. Part of the problem here is that our language was not designed to describe the workings of the Oversoul. The Oversoul blends what we are used to keeping distinct.

At this point I want to pursue the question of the fate of our individual identity by attending to the clinical evidence emerging from past-life psychotherapies. Looking to our past will show us our future, as we ourselves will one day be someone else's former life. What we are learning in these therapies about the fate of our former lives, therefore, is instructing us in our fate as well.

We must approach this evidence cautiously, of course. There are serious methodological complications inherent in collecting data from this deep in the psyche. These complications arise from the fact that there are many different ways of eliciting contact with our former lives in today's psychotherapeutic environment, and what approach we use will significantly influence how we experience them and thus what we take them to be. Before we discuss the evidence, therefore, we must take a brief detour into methodology.

To investigate that area of the psyche where the memories of former lives are stored—and we shall see that even to phrase matters this way is to prejudge the outcome—we must use consciousness to explore consciousness. We must use our present ego-consciousness to explore what we might call the deep psyche. When we do this, we find that *the deep psyche organizes itself differently depending on how ego-consciousness is focused as it approaches it.*

If you approach the deep psyche asking narrowly defined questions, you will probably get back narrowly defined answers. If, on the other hand, you bring to it a more fully textured problem you are living with, you will probably get back a more nuanced analysis of the problem. The psyche might point out aspects you have overlooked or show you ways in which you might reframe your thinking of the issues involved. To go still another step, if you approach the deep waters of the psyche as a whole person, as a complete life not focused on a particular problem or issue, you may very well encounter complete lives who will address your life as such. The posture we enter with will cause different experiences to crystalize around us. The exploring consciousness is like a seed that draws forth from the psyche only what the seed allows. It is not that we are experiencing a projection created out of our fertile imagination but that we are placing limits on the communication without even realizing that we are doing so. How wise we think the sage living on the mountaintop is will depend upon the quality of the questions we bring to him or her.[12]

The methodological problem we face here is the same problem that plagues research everywhere. As researchers, we are never able to study our subject from a completely unintrusive, neutral platform. Inevitably we must disturb our subject to study it. Because all knowledge of the phenomenon is experiment-dependent, there is no escaping the fact that to some degree we skew the data from the start simply by approaching it. This is particularly the case for studying deep areas of the psyche, for we can study them only by entering a highly interactive arena. The state of consciousness we enter with interacts with the consciousness we are exploring to produce our phenomena. There is no other way to collect data.

If we use hypnosis, therefore, to explore this domain, our previous lives will approach us in different operational modes depending on how we approach them. If we go looking solely for facts concerning the past, we tend to find just facts—who we were, when, where, and so on. If, on the other hand, we go looking for what we experienced in our former lives, that is what we will find. We will reexperience exactly what was experienced then, combined with a witnessing presence. This reexperiencing feels like watching a play while simultaneously being one of the actors on stage. As a spectator, we can choose to walk out at any time or see the play through to its conclusion, but we are not free to change the script. This strategy encourages us to think of these performances as a mere record of a once-vital being. Both of these first two approaches encourage us to assume that our former lives exist today only as static memories carried somewhere in "our mind."

But is this what our former lives truly are now, or is it simply a by-product of how we are approaching them? What if we approached the

---

[12] Some of the parallels here with quantum research are quite provocative. In quantum physics it sometimes appears that not only will the experiment we design determine what aspect of quantum reality will show itself to us, but that our experiment will in fact determine how quantum reality actually exists at a particular moment in time. That is, our experiment actually selects from among the several possible ways quantum reality has of configuring itself at that precise moment. The deep psyche also seems to behave in this mind-boggling fashion. Indeed, Fred Wolfe argues powerfully in *Star Wave* that consciousness is a quantum reality.

deep psyche without a defined agenda (as far as this is possible) and were willing to work with whatever came forward? If we gave the psyche permission to unfold itself in the focused awareness of the hypnotic arena according to its own choosing, how would our former lives be experienced then?

This more open-ended approach to hypnotherapy is quite rare in the literature on past-life therapy. Most therapeutic use of hypnosis to retrieve memories from previous lives is attempting to find solutions to specific problems and therefore tends to be rather directive. People are brought to therapy by their pain, not intellectual curiosity. They want relief, not research. In addition, financial considerations and the therapist's busy schedule often encourage a more targeted approach to the psyche. While this more directive approach may be appropriate and reasonable in these circumstances, however, we must appreciate the fact that it will restrict what comes forward from the psyche and how this material presents itself. If we want to understand not just what our former lives were but what they are *now*, if we want to understand the nature of their *present existence*, we must take a more permissive approach to the psyche.

For many years, Dr. David Cliness, professor in the counseling department at Youngstown State University, has been developing a therapeutic method that takes such an open-ended approach to the psyche through hypnotic states. My understanding of the psychological dynamics of rebirth has been deeply influenced by his research and through personally exploring these states with him over several years. While he has presented portions of his work at professional meetings, he is only just beginning to publish his voluminous research, carried out over fifteen years. Here I will restrict myself to sharing observations from his work that are immediately pertinent to the questions we are asking in this chapter. I include this material with his permission and kind support.

When the psyche is approached in an open-ended fashion, one's former lives tend to come forward not simply as static memories frozen in time but as living realities. They enter into dialogue with us, both to teach us things and to learn from us. They sometimes appear still terribly burdened by unresolved guilt, anger, pain, and the like. As we explore their pain, we come to recognize that the issues left unresolved during their lifetimes have come to form the nucleus of our own struggles in the present. Their conflicts have become our conflicts; their style of coping underpins our style, and so on. If in our encounters with them we relive various trauma they suffered during their lifetime, this often takes place as a reliving shared by *both* the former entity and our present self. In this encounter, two living presences appear to meet in common cause. Our reliving of this event with them seems to have the effect of freeing them as well as us from its influence. It also appears that this is not something they can accomplish by themselves, but for which they require our assistance.

They seem to be obligated to help us solve what is now our shared problem, perhaps because they were the original source of this problem. By helping us bring some aspect of their life into consciousness and resolving now what they did not resolve then, they seem to win for themselves the peace that has until now eluded them. Sometimes they appear to be reluctant, even unwilling participants in this process. The same limitations that made them unable to resolve a particular issue during their time on Earth may cause them to resist our efforts to resolve that issue now. For healing to take place they often must face extremely difficult truths about themselves. The pain they shunned during their lifetime is just as real now and sometimes just as hard to accept. Yet with persistence and compassion we can always bring into the open whatever burdens they are carrying and take them from their shoulders. They cannot resist our efforts indefinitely because we are the dynamic center of growth now, and our efforts to heal both our life and theirs is supported by nature itself.

These former lives do not appear to know what we know about changes that have taken place in society since their death. They may have developed some insight after their death into their own life and into their period of history, but for the most part their vision is limited to the world they knew when they were in a body. They appear to be suspended in time, as it were. We can sometimes provide them information about changes in customs or knowledge that have taken place since their day which may help them come to terms with their life.

During the phase of hypnotic work that involves the Collective, as Cliness calls them, one enters into a relationship with what appear to be dynamic, living presences. With some of them the issues connecting you are few and easily assimilated into consciousness. With others they are more numerous and more problematic. As work with the Collective continues, the difficulties they have passed on to you are eventually resolved and consciously assimilated. As this happens, these former lives tend to pass from the therapeutic scene. One by one, they are taken into a bright light, or into a being of light. Here they are received and made whole. One senses that they are finally home. If they return in later sessions, they tend to appear filled with light, clearly different from how they appeared before. (Similarly, when one meets former lives who have already fulfilled their individual mission—either through their own efforts during their lifetime or through the efforts of an intervening life—they tend to appear as luminous beings. One senses in them a richness that our still incomplete former lives lack.)

Once these lives have been restored to the light, they can be especially helpful to us. Occasionally they will return later in the work with information about our life and its mission or to help us with an issue that changing circumstances have only recently brought into focus. They may bring us wisdom and insights we can draw upon as we engage the challenges of our life.

Cliness's understanding of the dynamics of reincarnation is that our present life represents a composite of issues, abilities, foibles, and tasks drawn from not one but numerous former lives, assuming that we are dealing with someone who has had a few. He likens the process to playing cards. The deck includes fifty-two cards from which we are dealt a considerably smaller hand. The cards we are dealt are those lives that the Oversoul is now moving forward for work. Their issues are collected and organized into a new hand, and we are that hand. We are born into existence not free but deeply programmed from lives that, in one sense, we never knew. Cliness has found that typically anywhere from three to fifteen lives may be major influences in one life, sometimes more. While this hand is being played, one's other former lives appear to be effectively dormant, content to stand in the background until their turn comes, if they have not come already. Theoretically, we have access to everything that has gone before; practically, however, it is not so.

I have spent many hours pondering Cliness's data and my own experiences in our work together, trying to understand the implications these hold for how we are to understand the dynamics of the psyche and the nature of postmortem existence. Either this appearance of individual survival and continued interaction is a clever ruse orchestrated by the psyche for some unrecognized purpose or it reflects something real about the status of our former lives. After considerable thought, I tend to have more confidence in the second option, though I assume we are seeing only a small piece of what is actually going on and thus it is not at all clear what this "something real" is. It is not clear to me, for example, whether we should think of these as whole lives or as life fragments. That is, perhaps the dynamic presences we meet are not the integrated sum experience of the entire life but thematic fragments of experience that have become fixated or frozen by their attachment to a particular pain or circumstance.

Because our data are so incomplete, we must exercise great caution in attempting to extrapolate conclusions about the structure of spiritual reality from them. These encounters take place at the fringes of our awareness, where we are witnesses to processes over which we have little control and limited insight. While having a deep respect for the therapeutic efficacy of these meetings, I am also painfully aware of how incomplete our understanding of them is. New data are continuing to emerge and our understanding of the processes involved continues to grow. Furthermore, Cliness's results are themselves not entirely context-free. He works with his clients in a historical and cultural context that may be influencing how the psyche manifests itself in subtle ways we cannot yet identify.

If our former lives still live somewhere, what exactly is the nature of their existence? What is the character of their experience? For the reasons given above, my answers to these questions are tentative and subject to constant revision. For the present, I tend to think of these lives as still conscious somewhere in the universe. The conditions they live in appear to vary considerably from one to another. In a manner escaping precise formulation, many of them seem to live in an environment that often resembles the environment they knew on Earth. This is particularly true for those lives that are as yet unresolved. They appear to be animated but, until they are restored to the light, restricted. Those that emerge in therapeutically oriented hypnotic work often seem to remain burdened by issues they failed to resolve during their life on Earth. To the extent that these problems persist, the individuals (or large portions of the individual's life experience) appear to be frozen in time. They seem to be "on hold" and not to have yet gone into the light. Does this mean that they have not yet been consciously reunited with their Oversoul? I do not know. All I can report is that they *appear* to be unable to return to their source until a subsequent incarnation can rescue them by bringing to completion what they have left incomplete. I do not know whether this appearance of suspension is actual, a function of our psychological screening, or perhaps a creation of the Oversoul for the purpose of facilitating a productive therapeutic encounter. At this point I do not think we can rule out any of these possibilities.

If this suspension of their development is actual, it sometimes occurs, I suspect, not because they are being prevented from bringing their life to fruition in the postmortem state but because they simply do not know how to or are afraid to do so. They may be unwilling to let go of what is holding them back or afraid of the unknown. Their hurt, their rigidities, their expectations, their belief systems all can conspire to keep them where they are.

As they complete themselves through their work with us—either consciously in past-life therapy or unconsciously in real-life "therapy"— our former lives move on to planes of existence we cannot see into until it is our turn to enter the light. Their work finally finished, perhaps now they withdraw to enjoy more completely the wholeness they can now consciously participate in. If their individual contribution to the Oversoul is complete, ours is not as long as we still live on Earth. We are now the eyes and arms of the Oversoul exploring the undetermined possibilities in physical form. We are the new present where change is taking place, where the future is being written. For our few brief years we are the cutting edge of growth.

If all this is true, we should anticipate that we, too, will one day complete our mission and return to the whole. All life forms have their natural lifecycle. They begin, they develop through the middle years, and eventually they finish. Our personal identity does not die exactly when the body falls apart, and it may never die in the sense of disappearing entirely from existence, but it does conclude its work and then yield center stage to another. We yield not because we have failed but because we have succeeded. We drop this identity because it can no longer house what we have become through our labors. This transition does not take something from us but brings us into something greater. This is not loss but gain. This is not death but the rhythm of eternal life.

In the final analysis, all talk of death is misplaced. Our personality-based identity does not so much die as simply lose its hypnotic attraction over us. It may continue to be able to function on demand as a dynamic whole, but our awareness is no longer trapped there. Eventually, the Oversoul, through the sheer richness of its being, draws us away from our identification with this temporary form *it* adopted at our conception. Reunited with our larger life, we expand beyond this identity joyfully and without regret. We have come home and can finally drop the heavy bags we have been carrying all these years. Our aching muscles are instantly forgotten as we embrace the family we left behind so long ago. We are home again. The family is once again complete.

If there is work yet to do, tomorrow We may send someone else out, but tonight We celebrate the return of this one We love so dearly.

Our son has returned from his long, arduous journey. Our daughter has sacrificed for Us, struggled for Us, suffered for Us, all the while unaware of the selflessness of her undertaking. Now We can restore their truth to them and remind them of their true greatness. Tonight We can surround them with Our love and show them Our appreciation for all they have accomplished.

To discover that our life is connected to a series of lives does not reduce the value of this current life, as some at first fear. Similarly, to realize that our present life is only one cycle in the life of a being whose limits we cannot envision in no way diminishes the immediate self we now are. Like the chambered nautilus, one side cannot exist without the other. We are not rendered insignificant by this larger being but integral to it. If our past and future reach further than we once thought, this does not move us away from the present but paradoxically plunges us more deeply into it. We represent the current operational focus of all the lives that have preceded us. Everything that has passed before leads up to us, and we are creating the future. The more we appreciate the breadth of our larger life, the more we are led to focus our attention on our present life as it is unfolding here and now.

One final thought. Coming to reincarnation from a Western theological background, it seemed important to me in the beginning to emphasize the distinctness of the Oversoul from what Westerners are used to thinking of as the soul. In Western circles the soul is classically thought of as the surviving identity of the individual life, and the Oversoul is much more than this. Thus the term *Oversoul*, though somewhat awkward in itself, was useful to me as I struggled to expand my understanding of my identity beyond the conceptual habits ingrained through a lifetime of thinking of myself in terms of my body/mind identity.

Now that I have completed this transition, however, and have fully internalized the concept of this mega-identity, I am finding the term *Oversoul* increasingly cumbersome and somewhat artificial. It seems to erect unnecessary barriers between reincarnation theory and the Western theological heritage. In my present position, therefore, it feels more natural simply to call this encompassing identity the *Soul*—capitalized to distinguish it from the Western notion of soul—and to maintain contact with the Western discussion of the soul while expanding that concept as required by reincarnation theory. There are advantages to using either term, and the reader should use whichever most helps him or her understand and integrate the concepts presented here.

5
The Rhythms of Life

*L*ooking at our life through reincarnationist eyes tends to change our perception of its fundamental rhythms. Developmental psychologists have expended great effort mapping the intricate steps of our development from infancy through adolescence, from early adulthood to our advanced years. And yet if reincarnation is a fact of life, we must go further than this. We must place this one lifetime in the context of a larger life process and expand our concept of the developing human. We must come to understand that the stages we mark from the cradle to the grave constitute *only one half of the human lifecycle*. There is a second half of the cycle that is not being considered but must be addressed if we want to appreciate the larger rhythms of human existence.

We can back into this topic slowly by considering a question my students often raise: "What good is it to have former lives if we cannot remember them?" The question is a good one. If we could not remember our previous lives at all, then they would indeed be useless to us. How can we learn anything from experiences we cannot even remember? Another related set of questions that frequently comes up is "Why do we forget our previous lives in the first place? What purpose does this amnesia serve?" If there is strong evidence that at least some of us have lived before this life, why do we not naturally remember these experiences as we remember our experiences from this life? We tend to view amnesia as a sign of pathology, an indication that the normal, healthy process of remembering has broken down. What purpose is served by building amnesia into the normal scheme of things?

What these questions demonstrate is that reincarnation does not make much sense if we try to understand it only in terms of physical existence. They force us to look beyond our physical lives to form a more complete picture of the lifecycling process. We are accustomed to marking the stages of our development from birth to death, assuming that after death will come either eternal reward, damnation, or simply extinction. Yet if our present life is followed after some time by another life on Earth, then there must be a phase of our life that begins after the death of our body and continues to our next birth. If we fail to take into account this "hidden" phase of life, we are seeing only half of our full lifecycle. If we think of reincarnation only in terms of a succession of lives on Earth with some ultimate liberation waiting for us at the end, we are missing large pieces of the puzzle.

In this chapter, therefore, I would like to reflect on the balancing rhythms of the physical and spiritual phases of life as pieced together from a number of ancient and contemporary sources.[1] This discussion will build on some of the ideas developed in Chapter 3.

THE TWO PHASES OF LIFE

The full lifecycle of a human spirit/being runs not from birth to death but from birth to birth, with "death" but a transitional midpoint. Like the Taoist symbol of spinning yin and yang forces, our complete lifecycle encompasses two phases, one earthbound and the other spiritbound. The spiritual phase of our life is as important to our development as our earthly phase is. Our activities there balance and complement our activities here. It is therefore very important that we incorporate this hidden side of our lifecycle into our understanding of reincarnation if we want to have an adequate vision of how life works.

It would be foolish, of course, to think that we can know a great deal about the exact conditions of life beyond the grave, and yet it would not be foolish today to think that we can know at least something

---

[1] Foremost among these are *Beyond Death* by Stanislav and Christina Grof; *Far Journeys* by Robert Monroe; *Heading Toward Omega* by Kenneth Ring; *Life Before Life* by Helen Wambach; *Life Between Life* by Joel Whitton and Joe Fisher; and the Buddhist classic *The Tibetan Book of the Dead.*

about them. If we can lift the usual amnesia separating us from our previous incarnations by using various consciousness-focusing techniques, it should at least be theoretically possible to retrieve from our memory some information about our experience between death and the next incarnation. If consciousness records all experience, then consciousness might be persuaded to yield some information about the spiritual phase of experience.

I have said several times in previous chapters that you can never understand the inner logic of a person's life by examining it in isolation from its precedents. To try to do so is like reading one chapter from the middle of a detective novel and attempting to decipher what is going on. It is impossible. And yet we might ask: If novels do not make sense broken up into isolated chapters, why are we forced to live our lives this way? What purpose is served by constricting our awareness, trapping it in an isolated piece of body-ego, even if only temporarily? What purpose does this amnesia serve?

Simply put, the purpose seems to be to accelerate learning. Our amnesia gives us the *discontinuity required for exponential growth*, a growth so radically expansive that we struggle to envision what it might encompass. The system of reincarnating in relatively short, consciously separate cycles appears designed to accelerate learning by making it possible for us to immerse ourselves totally into many completely different human experiences for brief periods of time. After a stint in one body, one set of social relationships, one culture, one career, and one historical period, we are removed and inserted into a completely new set of conditions. Cut your imagination free from your present life and imagine the development a hundred such immersions would generate. We could know all sides of the human experience: wealth and poverty, fear and bravery, rebellion and tranquility. We could be the artist, the warrior, the priestess, the statesman, the pioneer, and the peasant. We could live both male and female lives, touching intimately all the mysteries reserved to each sex. We could know not just one continent and one culture but all of them, and not just one historical period but as many as we cared to sample.

In isolating us from our larger identity, our amnesia intensifies our learning experience by focusing us completely on the experience in which we are presently engaged. When we are distracted and give only half our attention to what we are working on, the results usually show it. When we do not focus ourselves completely on the lecture we are attending or the football game we are watching, we're going to miss things. Our amnesia causes us to believe for a time that we are only our

Birth

Integration
Planning
Remembering

Expansion
Actualization
Forgetting

Death

FIGURE 5.1

present body-personality. Through this ruse our energies are harnessed to the present moment. In the theater, people talk of the willing suspension of disbelief necessary to experience props on a wooden stage as the reality they represent. Somewhat similarly, we must believe fully in the conditions of our personal theater in order to engage the Earth-experience with maximum intensity. This our amnesia does for us. It keeps us from being distracted by memories of experiences that would disrupt the conditions of our present learning exercise.

For genuine learning to take place, of course, it is not sufficient merely to experience new things intensely. We must also remember these experiences, digest them, and integrate them into our previous knowledge. If we were constantly losing our experiences as quickly as we had them, there would be no accumulation of insight. Memory is essential to development. By this logic, if we do not eventually remember our previous lives, it is pointless to have had them. Thus the discontinuity of awareness necessary for acquiring new experiences must be balanced at some point by reestablishing the full continuity of our awareness if the cycle of learning is to be complete. The natural time for this to occur appears not to be during the Earth phase of the cycle but during the spiritual phase.

The basic rhythm of our lifecycle appears to be *expansion* and *integration* (see Figure 5.1). The acquisition of new experience takes place on Earth, the integration of that experience with our previous experience in the spiritual domain. The dynamics of each phase complement the other. Entering a new physical life is accompanied by a *constriction of awareness*; leaving our physical bodies is accompanied by a *reexpansion of awareness*. This observation is consistent with the experiences of those who come close to dying but are rescued through medical technology. They regularly report that while they were near death their awareness expanded to enormous proportions, allowing them to take in information and insights at an extraordinary rate.

FIGURE 5.2

Curiously enough, this expanded state feels familiar to them. Though it is unlike anything they have ever experienced on Earth, it nevertheless feels like "home."[2] The amnesia that accompanies birth is for a few brief moments lifted.

Another polarity is *planning* and *actualization*. We saw in the preceding chapter how a life plan is drafted in the *bardo* and brought to Earth for actualization. Work performed here is subsequently evaluated upon our return to spirit, thus completing the cycle. As we reincarnate again and again, we move through these phases in a lawful manner, dipping in and out of time in a spiral of open-ended development.

Although our forgetfulness on Earth is balanced with a remembering that takes place after separating from our bodies, we cannot assume that our full memory is restored to us after each and every incarnation. It may well be the case that there are cycles within the cycling process, that we might voluntarily enter—or be drawn into—phases of growth longer than a single lifecycle in which we would not be able to recall our full history after death. Thus while some expansion of identity would take place after each individual cycle, our whole identity might not again come into view until this larger cycle is completed. Eventually, however, if experience is not to be wasted and if we are to be whole, full memory of everything we have ever been and ever done must be restored to us.

THE HILLS AND THE VALLEYS

Pictures can help our imagination grasp concepts better than verbal theories alone. One picture I have found helpful in presenting the two phases of the human lifecycle to my students is that of the "hills and valleys" (Figure 5.2). I draw a sine-wavelike curve across the blackboard and invite my students to imagine our journey through life as traveling through a series of hills and valleys, each hill slightly higher than the preceding one. The valleys represent our life in the physical plane while the hilltops correspond to life in the nonphysical or spiritual plane.

---

[2] See, for example, Kenneth Ring, *Heading Toward Omega*, Chapter 3.

With the picture comes an exposition that goes something like this:

We can begin to describe our movement through the cycle at any point along the journey, but let us begin where we currently are, in the middle of a valley. We wake up in the valleys of time/space to a world we have no memory of choosing. We find ourselves surrounded by people, institutions, societal customs, and historical events that collectively shape and focus our lives. Responding to a sequence of opportunities and limitations that appear to be beyond our control, we tend to get caught up in the drama of our relationships, careers, families, mortgages, political causes, and the like, until eventually we are forced by the passage of time to begin the transition to higher ground. Thus in our old age we begin to leave the valley and enter the foothills outside town. As we begin our ascent, we find ourselves looking back over our life, searching for its patterns. The elevation gives us the overview we need to begin to see our childhood and adult years from a new perspective. With the wisdom of hindsight we begin to understand the impact of the choices we have made at key points in our life while also appreciating the constants of character that have been with us from the beginning.

As we move still higher into the foothills we eventually cross some dividing line where we must leave our bodies behind. Despite this change we continue much as we were, except that now we are liberated from many of the restrictions associated with a physical body. With this transition comes the encounter with the white light commonly reported by those who have experienced a near-death episode. Continuing our ascent, we go on to learn and confront what our lives were truly about. Now the lessons can be developed more deeply and broadly than before. The insights that survivors of near-death episodes have reported experiencing in their life reviews are just the first stages of a powerful process of self-discovery and self-confrontation that continues long after the loss of the body.[3]

As we continue to climb, we see more and more. We begin to understand more about the connections that tied our lives to the people we lived and worked with. We begin to see causal links that were not visible in the valley. Like turning over a piece of complicated needlepoint, two dots unconnected on the surface turn out to be linked by a common thread underneath. When viewed from the spiritual side of life, the tapestry of our lives begins to reveal its full logic and intent.

As the process of review and discovery continues, it begins to be

---

[3] Time appears not to behave on the hilltops the same way it does in the valleys, though it is useful to pretend here that it does in order to simplify the presentation.

combined with a process of remembering. As we draw nearer the top of the hill we begin to remember choices and decisions that we made before we took this human form many years ago. Slowly we begin to recall the mission we gave ourselves in entering this life, and with this recall we can now begin to assess how well we fulfilled our chosen tasks. We can also begin to appreciate in a different light the new experiences we have collected on Earth, experiences that have added to our richness and extended our capacities.

Like waking from a dream, we are reawakening to a larger identity, an identity that subsumes and integrates the many lives we have lived. As our vision broadens, so does our memory. Having climbed high enough to be able to see the valleys that preceded our most recent valley, we begin to understand how our life was a logical extension of the lives that preceded it. We begin to understand the key relationships in this life in the context of a deeper history of relatedness. We begin to appreciate the perfection of the flow of our larger life—how struggle in one life is tied to incompleteness in another, how ease here is related to victory there.

There is an exquisite balance to everything we are seeing, but it is much more than a static system of checks and balances. God is not a judge nor is karma merely an accountant. The orchestration of lives we are witnessing is designed to foster learning. It propels us on adventure after adventure, broadening our experience and teaching us as only experience can. There are rewards and punishments, but these are only the feedback that makes learning possible and accelerated learning inevitable. For this is an intensified learning curriculum quite rare in the universe. As we remember more of who we have been and what we have done, this becomes increasingly obvious to us.

Though I speak here of remembering, it is more a matter of resuming and reintegrating identities than simply remembering them. The metaphor of remembering suggests that the present personality continues as the organizing agent now augmented by memories of previous existences. However, the process is more like someone recovering from an extreme case of amnesia where remembering actually changes the identity of the individual. In terms of our original picture, this expansion of identity would take place at the top of the hill.[4]

If we are complete—as Oversouls—we can return to the source from whence we came. Otherwise we will eventually have to descend into yet another valley to seek the completion that can only be realized

---

[4] The reader may want to review Robert Monroe's description of reuniting with his former lives that appears in the preceding chapter.

there once the Earth curriculum has begun. After the equivalent of perhaps many years of Earth time spent in activities that reflect our interests and level of development, we eventually begin to prepare for our reentry into physical existence. The planning of our life is undertaken with the assistance of various spiritual beings whose responsibility it is to guide us in this task and in collaboration with the individuals who will be returning with us. While some may carelessly rush through this phase, we would be well advised to give careful thought to arranging our curriculum. Once a life is begun, options are significantly reduced and changes can be made only within a restricted set of alternatives.

With our planning complete, we can see both the lives which have gone before and the outlines of the one we are about to embark on. From this elevated perspective, we can appreciate the appropriateness of what we will be encountering in the valley below. Working collectively with other souls, we have orchestrated the people who will come together once again in this new valley, as well as those who will enter our lives for the first time there. We have chosen our parents, our socioeconomic status, and our sex. We have choreographed the major crises and influences that will introduce new experiences into our life, exercising capacities not previously developed or compensating for imbalances already accumulated. We have also chosen whether to live many years or few. The logic of these choices becomes inscrutable once the cloak of physical existence is shouldered, but it is a temporary inscrutability because we will remember the reasons for our choices when we climb out of the valley on the other side. (Or perhaps we will program in the option of consciously discovering some aspect of our destiny even while we are in the valley, introducing special consciousness-expanding disciplines into our lives for this purpose.)

Having designed the obstacle course that exists only to further perfect the being we now know ourselves to be, the time of return draws near. Giving our final assent to the exercise, we begin making our way down into the next valley. We keep descending until eventually we exchange the spaciousness of spiritual existence for the intimate embryonic meld with our next mother. Kicking and punching our way to differentiation, we soon are too developed to remain physically connected to her. Waves of building energy envelop us and violently push us through the birth canal back into the physical world, forgetful of any identity other than this one and oblivious to the mission that awaits us. Class has resumed and will not end until we climb out the other side of our valley, days or years from now.

In presenting this pictorial metaphor, I have obviously and undoubtedly oversimplified matters a great deal. The story I have told touches only the highlights of the lifecycling process and does so in an idealized manner. It makes the transitions into and out of physical existence look more systematized and standardized than they are. No doubt there are as many ways to move in and out of the valleys as there are travelers on the road. If some choose to plan their next life carefully, others probably plunge themselves recklessly back into the thick of life, inheriting a more haphazard array of conditions as a result. Different styles will produce different results. While some people might prefer to take few risks and will arrange their lives accordingly, others will be willing to wager more and set up more challenging circumstances for themselves. Different degrees of insight into the possibilities and purposes of reincarnation will produce different outcomes. Reincarnation seems designed to engender diversity, and we distort things if we diminish this diversity in the interest of theoretical economy.

HEAVEN AND HELL

We might at this point ask "If life cycles through phases of expansion and integration, if death leads eventually to rebirth, what does this do to the concepts of heaven and hell? What of final judgment, paradise, and damnation? Are they simply postponed until the end of a long series of lives or do they have no substance at all?"

The Tibetan Book of the Dead, or *Bardo Thodol*,[5] has some interesting things to say on this point. The *Bardo Thodol* is a Tibetan manual for dying and for navigating the various phases of life that occur between separation from one physical body and taking rebirth in another. Written down by the Tibetan guru Padma Sambhava in the eighth century A.D., the traditions it preserves are actually much older still.

According to *The Tibetan Book of the Dead*, most of us experience *both* heavenly and hellish phases on the hilltop between lives. These experiences are the direct result of our successes and failures on Earth and are therefore different in content and duration for each person. They are part of the process of facing the full ramifications of one's thoughts and actions on Earth, and thus part of the learning process itself. Much more than simply punishment, hell is part of the purification of our being, the burning away of impurities and the illumination of our spiritual essence.

---

[5] *Bardo Thodol* means literally "Liberation by Hearing on the After-Death Plane."

To take this a step deeper, the *Bardo Thodol* explains that after our body falls away and after the encounter with the white light, we enter a state or dimension it calls the *Chonyid Bardo*, the "Bardo of the Experiencing of Reality," in which our psyche is turned inside out, as it were. Here our unconscious emerges to dominate our experience while the less powerful ego moves into the background, compelled to participate in whatever emerges. One of the principles governing this *bardo* is "Thought creates reality," or "Thought creates experience." Our thoughts, whatever they are, become our complete and total experience. In this case, our thoughts are every thought, memory, or fantasy we ever stuck away in our unconscious. As these move forward, they interact with the energy field of this dimension and we find ourselves confronting beings, situations, and conditions that are actually external reflections of our internal state. In this way we, our total being, not just our ego, create our own heaven and hell. As most of us have stored away positive as well as negative thoughts in our consciousness, we will experience both to some degree, one following the other. The *Bardo Thodol* calls this "The Encounter with Wrathful Deities" and "The Encounter with Peaceful Deities."

Another principle governing this domain is "Like attracts like." Thus in both our suffering and our bliss, we will experience ourselves in the presence of other souls undergoing experiences similar to our own. The end result is strikingly reminiscent of Dante's *Inferno* and *Paradiso* with one exception—it is temporary. For all who have failed to reach enlightenment, the *Chonyid Bardo* is followed by the *Sidpa Bardo*, the "Bardo of Seeking Rebirth," and a new lifecycle is begun.

This ancient sketch of the interlife state is strikingly consistent with the account offered by Robert Monroe in *Far Journeys*. Drawing on his more than twenty-five years of experience traveling out of the body, Monroe claims that the dimension in which we exist between our Earth-lives is quite complex and highly stratified, with persons at different levels of development experiencing different realities. He describes thousands of "rings" surrounding the time/space dimension occupied by souls who are between incarnations. The conditions of existence in the different rings are said to vary widely. Those who are most deeply addicted to or absorbed in the Earth-experience, those whose conscious-ness is dominated even after death by the most earthy of the Earth emotions, inhabit the lower rings. Those whose awareness has expanded to include higher values and more encompassing identities occupy rings further out. As we make progress through repeated incarnations, we rise after each death to occupy that ring that reflects our new capacities.[6]

Whether blissful or painful, whether heavenly or hellish, our stays in this dimension are limited. From a reincarnationist perspective, eternal damnation makes no sense whatsoever. Nothing that we can do in a few years on Earth is so terrible that it could warrant eternal estrangement from God. Remember that no actions in the Earth school have genuinely permanent consequences, except perhaps learning how to love. Furthermore, according to the esoteric traditions, we are actually part of God. We are God-consciousness focused in differentiation rather than wholeness. For hell to be eternal, God would have to be willing to permit a permanent division within His own being, and this is beyond imagining. Estrangement from the source and very substance of Being cannot be permanent. It is simply part of the ebb and flow that advances the larger adventure we are all part of as part of God.

Reincarnation dispels the horrible specter of eternal damnation while preserving accountability. In some ways it actually intensifies our accountability, for according to reincarnationist theory, there is no savior who through his vicarious suffering can spare us from inheriting the consequences of our mistakes. This would interrupt the feedback essential for learning to occur and, from a reincarnationist perspective, learning is what Earth existence is all about. Metaphors of salvation are taken as describing graduation from the Earth curriculum into the bliss of enduring God-awareness—the true heaven—and saviors are thought to function primarily as teachers sent to guide us in the rediscovery of our divine nature, a nature in which all of us are one and the same reality. No one can learn this for us, but teachers can show us the direction we must travel and the most direct route to our ultimate destiny.

SOUL AGE

An adequate description of reincarnation, in addition to incorporating the spiritual phase of our lifecycle, must make room for the evolving awareness of an individual soul across its many cycles. We cannot, after all, expect a newcomer to Earth to show the same subtlety and skill at the game as a seasoned veteran, nor would we expect a veteran to make the same blunders as a novice. With experience should come some kind of maturity, some signs of development. But what does maturity consist

---

[6] Monroe does not see the existence of these rings as a necessary or inevitable feature of the spiritual landscape. Rather, he tends to see them as a tragic development in Earth's history, and one that can ultimately be reversed.

of in reincarnationist terms? If rebirth serves the purpose of perfecting our souls, what are the stages of this perfection? Can we determine these stages much as psychologists have tried to determine the stages of development within one lifecycle?

This seems like an appropriate request, and it has led many reincarnationists to develop the concept of *soul age*. Just as we often distinguish a person's emotional or intellectual age from their physical age, the attempt here is to measure the age of the soul. The concept of soul age suggests simply that some individuals have been in the Earth curriculum longer than others. Some are "younger" souls while others are "older." Some are taking advanced courses and are soon to graduate while others are still in elementary school. If we are justified in extrapolating from our experience in the local neighborhood school to the Earth school (and this is a big if) we would expect there to be some overall order to the curriculum. It seems natural to us that simpler lessons should precede complex ones. Would not the solution of certain problems require prior mastery of more basic skills that should therefore be learned first? If we are on safe ground taking these intuitions to reincarnation, we naturally would like to know which life issues constitute the elementary grades and which the advanced levels. What are the hallmarks of young souls compared to old souls, and what constitutes the themes of our middle years?

Though I believe there is merit in trying to answer these questions, I have less enthusiasm than I once had for the project—and more caution. I now recognize so many variables I did not see earlier that I wonder how many more I am still missing. So before I summarize a Hindu map of soul age, let me register a two-part disclaimer.

First, it would be a mistake to overemphasize the linearity of a soul's development across lives. Reincarnationists often speak as though each life picks up exactly where the previous one left off, but this is an oversimplification. It may be convenient for us to think of a soul staying with one set of issues until they are mastered, however long this takes, then moving on to the next set, but life doesn't seem to work that neatly. In any one life we are working on a small handful of issues, probably advancing some more successfully than others. In our next life we may divide these issues up, working at a more advanced level with some and reserving the others for a later life. We may work a particularly fascinating project for several lives, such as becoming a great composer, then drop it to experiment with a different project, returning only later to pick up where we left off with the music.

Some of the discontinuity of development from life to life is necessitated by the fact that we work many of our issues with specific people, all of whom have personal agendas other than the one they share with us. Imagine the extraordinary complexity of coordinating all the different facets of the various lives that must come together for people to work on their shared issues together. If we give some thought to it, we will quickly appreciate how unrealistic it is to think that all of us can neatly continue in our next life *all* the components of our previous life's work. There are simply too many variables for this to be possible for every person. Each lifecycle is a reshuffling of the deck, bringing to the surface issues (and relationships) from different centuries and different lifetimes. If there are signs of progress in our lives, we should look for them not in the specific themes of any one life but in the larger pattern of our development.

There is a second reason for taking any outline of soul age with a grain of salt. The metaphor of age suggests that everyone starts at the same beginning point and then progresses through a common developmental sequence from soul infancy to wizened maturity. Similarly, the metaphor of school suggests that everyone starts in kindergarten and must learn the same set of skills in order to graduate. But perhaps that is not the way it happens in life at all. Perhaps the Earth school offers an array of courses not all of which every soul needs. Perhaps a given soul's experience prior to its Earth cycles has left it requiring only certain of the lessons that can be obtained here. Thus its stay on earth might be brief compared to others of us who need more of the basics.

Of course, one's education may not always go as planned. A soul may enter the Earth curriculum with a very circumscribed objective only to fall under the hypnotic attraction of physical existence and become locked into a much longer educational experience. According to Robert Monroe, this is what happened to him and what happens to many of us. Most souls on Earth, he says, did not originate here but came from various nonphysical dimensions to take advantage of the unique learning opportunities Earth affords. Taking part in the Earth curriculum is tricky, however, because physical embodiment tends to be addictive. Repeated incarnations can come to obscure our original spiritual identity even between lives. Monroe describes an all-too-frequent lifecycling pattern of spiraling into increasingly dense levels of materiality over many lifetimes followed eventually by a spiraling outward again. Our spiritual identity is covered over and lost on the inward trip, while on the way out it is being uncovered and rediscovered. How many cycles are involved and how many lessons must be learned to complete the curriculum will depend upon how efficient a learner one is and how deeply into materiality one is drawn. At the very least, Monroe's account should lead us to approach any linear schematic of soul age cautiously and to examine carefully the assumptions hidden within that schematic.

To sum up my reservations, the concept of soul age can never be taken as referring literally to the length of time a soul has lived since its "first birth." It is simply a metaphor for describing the soul's progress through the Earth curriculum, nothing more, and even here there are traps. As helpful as this metaphor may be, it suggests far more standardization of the lifecycling process than is warranted. However plausible any description of developmental stages may be, life is undoubtedly more diversified and complex than we are recognizing. Staying mindful of these restrictions, let us look next at a map of soul age that comes from one of the oldest world cultures that has affirmed reincarnation. India.

THE CHAKRA MAP OF SOUL AGE

The *chakras* are a series of psychospiritual centers within a human being. The Sanskrit term is used by Hindus and Buddhists, but the same centers have been identified by other spiritual traditions as well. The chakras are classically described as seven psychic centers or "wheels" that link and integrate our physical and nonphysical bodies. They are located for the most part along the spinal cord and are associated with, but not equivalent to, major nerve ganglia and endocrine glands. The chakras are multidimensional phenomena, integrating physical, psychological, and spiritual aspects of existence. Each chakra has associated with it specific physical, emotional, mental, and spiritual processes, which accordingly are seen in Indian medicine as being interrelated.

According to Hindu teaching, our life force enters us through the highest chakra above our head and descends down through the other chakras until it reaches the lowest, located at the base of our spine. There this heavenly force mixes with our earth energy and begins its return, traveling back up the same way it came. All seven chakras are animated by this divine force and pass varying amounts of it into the systems they govern. A "closed" chakra passes less energy-awareness than an "open" one.

One's evolutionary status at any point along the journey is reflected in the status of all seven chakras taken together. A highly evolved being is said to have all chakras completely open and harmoniously integrated, while a less-developed being may have certain chakras relatively open while others are relatively closed. Numerous books on the chakras are available to the interested reader.[7]

Given their multidimensionality, the chakras can be approached in several different ways. Their functioning can be described in terms of subtle energy (*prana* or *chi*) or in terms of levels of awareness. A suggestive map of soul age can be derived from the chakra system if we approach them as symbol systems describing various levels of awareness or levels of being through which humans pass on their evolutionary journey, beginning with the first chakra at the base of the spine and continuing up through to the seventh above the top of the head. Approached in this way, we can view each chakra as describing a different existential posture taken in the world, a distinctive style reflecting a certain level of awareness. We can identify the components of each style by listing the various psychological characteristics associated with each chakra. Though the chakras can be thought of as describing recurring or archetypal levels of awareness, no individual can realistically be described in terms of a single chakra. Nevertheless, if approached with nuance, the psychological content of the various chakras do suggest the issues around which youth and age differentiate themselves. Because the chakras are always interactive and because their interactions are complex and subtle, the greatest danger here is oversimplification. What follows is a description of the seven notes of the scale from which the diversity of human life is composed.[8]

The first or *root chakra* lies at the base of the spine and relates to our most elemental survival instincts. It might be thought of as the bridgepoint between animal and human existence. It is associated with our instinct for self-preservation, with the fight-or-flight reflex, and more generally with feelings of fear and extreme existential uncertainty. When this level of awareness is fully developed, one feels safe and

---

[7] A particularly good introduction to the chakras with a strong psychological emphasis is found in Swami Rama, Rudolph Ballentine, and Swami Ajaya's *Yoga and Psychotherapy*, Chapter 7. The following account draws heavily from this source. See also Ajit Mookerjee, *Kundalini: The Arousal of the Inner Energy*.

[8] Ken Wilber, in his essay "Are the Chakras Real?" in John White's anthology *Kundalini, Evolution and Enlightenment*, cautions us against taking the chakras too literally even as the psychospiritual organs of the subtle body. He reminds us that from the position of enlightenment, the chakras are devoid of essence, as are all "things" that appear to exist. In this ultimate sense, the chakras are not real. Only Supreme Brahman, the Being-Consciousness-Bliss of one's True Self is Real; all else is transitory illusion masking the pervasive presence of this reality. Nevertheless, as Wilber himself points out, it is a central truth that in the world of appearances, "existence is graded, and with it, cognition [or awareness]" (p. 129). Within this world of appearances, the chakras can give us clues to the gradients of awareness that constitute human existence, even as we move step by step to penetrate the veil of this existence and rediscover its Ground.

grounded in the world, firmly rooted in existence and confident of one's ability to parry life-threatening attacks. Those who live in a "kill or be killed" world governed by the "law of the jungle" are dealing with unresolved first-chakra issues. In evolutionary terms, before one can do anything else, one must survive as an individual. This is the bottom line upon which everything else builds.

The second chakra, the *genital chakra*, secures the survival of the species. While still largely biological and instinctual, it also concerns our capacity for pleasure. One whose life is centered in this chakra will tend to be preoccupied with sensual pleasure, either getting it or avoiding it, and particularly with sexual pleasure. This level of being culminates in the capacity for rich and satisfying sensual experience. While capable of becoming an end itself, pleasure can also be put to the service of the higher chakras, as is always the case for any chakra lower than another. Freudian psychology can be thought of largely as a psychology of the second chakra.

The third chakra is the *solar plexus chakra*, whose theme is power. In time, sensual pleasure alone fails to satisfy us; it offers little challenge. Eventually we want to move beyond it to test our abilities in a larger arena, to challenge ourselves in competition with others. This is more than an extension of our survival instinct, for it sometimes leads us into projects that actually threaten our survival, such as dangerous careers or hobbies. Here the desire is to test the limits of one's personal power. Lives spent working on this level of awareness will explore both domination and submission, the two sides of power. Here we find both masters and victims, "authoritarian personalities" and the "inferiority complex." The themes of Adlerian psychology address primarily this chakra.

If the world consisted of beings comprised of only the first three chakras, it would culminate in a society of perpetual conflict, in which the exercise of power served no goal other than itself. Power alone seeks only the good of the individual. Untempered, it pits us against each other until someone wins and all others lose. Sooner or later, even the most aggressive of us will realize the ultimate futility of this game, and in so doing will begin to rise to our next evolutionary challenge.

The fourth chakra is the *heart chakra*, the chakra of empathy and compassion. This level of awareness reflects our capacity to establish alliances beyond the self. Here the individual discovers community and realizes the freedom of true equality. Here one discovers love in its highest form, what the Christians call *agape*, the Jews *hesed*, and the Taoists *t'zu*. This level of awareness culminates in the refined capacity to experience deeply what another feels and to choose as best for oneself what is best for everyone concerned. This is not self-sacrifice so much as the first stages of realizing an identity larger than the ego-self. Situated midway between the three lower and the three higher chakras, this chakra integrates what might be thought of as our earth functions with our spiritual functions. The first three chakras secure the position of the individual while the latter three teach transcendence of self. Some of the writings of Carl Rogers and Erich Fromm address the dynamics of this chakra.

As noble as equality is, humans are more than the founders of egalitarian communities on Earth. We are also creators, continually reaching beyond what already exists and discovering the new, the unprecedented. This capacity to create is related to the *throat chakra*, the chakra of creativity and nurturance. The two are related because to create requires that we commune with and receive from an order of reality higher than our finite selves. To genuinely create something new requires that we learn the secret of receiving. Whether we are creating new art, new music, new scientific formulas, or new solutions to long-standing social problems, creating puts us in touch with our higher nature, a subtle reality we can invite but not control. At the higher levels, creating becomes an inherently satisfying, even necessary activity in and of itself, apart from whatever artifacts are produced.

The sixth chakra is the *brow chakra*, the chakra of intuitive knowledge, the "third eye" located between and slighter higher than the eyebrows. The level of awareness associated with the sixth chakra reflects our ability to know things beyond what our senses tell us. As creativity develops, contact with the spiritual dimension of existence deepens, eventually awakening a capacity to accurately and reliably discern aspects of life that exist in that dimension. This paranormal intuitive capacity tends not to be taken seriously in the West but in the East is thought to be quite natural, though not necessarily common. Notoriously unreliable and unpredictable in the early stages, it can be refined and purified of distorting elements through years of meditation.

Our capacity for paranormal insight can be focused either on the world outside ourselves or on our inner world. The former will furnish us information on the outer world, such as clairvoyance or precognition. On a more modest scale, we might think of the major scientific breakthroughs where intuition jumped far beyond the data then available. When inwardly focused, this nonsensory mode of knowing can be used to gain insight into the truth of our innermost nature. Of the two, the inwardly focused intuition is considered a higher form of knowing and is said to characterize the greatest spiritual teachers of all cultures. This level of awareness culminates in our awakening to the Divinity-Within. Through the next chakra, we discover our true relation to that Divinity.

The seventh chakra is the *crown chakra*, traditionally located immediately above the head. This level of awareness reflects our capacity to enter into a state of consciousness totally unlike any that have preceded it. In this state our ordinary consciousness completely breaks down and we open to an awareness without limit or form. Recovering our capacity to experience the whole of Being, we experience what in the East is called enlightenment and what in the West is called Godhead consciousness. Here we discover what sages and saints have told us throughout the ages: "You are Children of God," "Atman is Brahman," "The kingdom of God is within," "That art Thou," "You are Divinity Itself." The crown chakra is often represented artistically by a halo of light surrounding the entire body or centered on the head. The last two chakras are explored in the psychologies of the world's major mystical traditions.

OUR EVOLUTIONARY POTENTIAL

The energy radiating through the seven chakras interacts to produce the balance of forces we experience as our personality. Taken together, they describe a range of development from near-animal existence to embodied Divinity. They should be thought of not as rungs on a ladder to be climbed one by one but as themes of a symphony lasting many lifetimes. As we grow, new themes are introduced and older themes are continually refined. Our development is not linear but interactive. As we develop one theme, others are simultaneously influenced.

It should be apparent by now that the concept of soul age tends to dissolve the conventional moral categories of good and bad. Once we understand that the soul's range of growth is too vast to be incorporated into a single lifetime, *good* and *bad* become relative terms. The same external action may represent an advance for one person and a regression for another. What is good for a young soul may be bad for an older soul who should be moving on to something more challenging.[9] Thus, judging others is a futile exercise that merely projects on them

---

[9] This is not to say that reincarnation leads to the philosophical position known as ethical relativism. Quite the contrary; reincarnationist traditions support the claim that certain values, such as compassion, are part of the fabric of existence and therefore are not arbitrary.

our individual life challenge. Inherent in the notion of soul age, therefore, is the permission to pursue our individual lives without worrisome glances left or right and without burdening others with our opinions of their progress.[10]

While it is probably inevitable that our first response to learning of the concept of soul age is to try to figure out where we are in our own evolutionary process, this exercise is not terribly productive; there are too many hidden variables for our calculations to be very accurate. Rather than use the map presented here to try to pinpoint our level of development, it would be more beneficial, I think, to use it to broaden our vision of ourselves and of our life tasks. By reminding us that we will have as much time as we need to perfect our souls, it encourages us to relax and stop worrying. As long as we think that we live on Earth only once, we cannot help but want to cram as many experiences (or as much growth) as possible into this one life. We feel that we must rush to bring everything to completion before we die. When we adjust our perspective to the larger horizon of rebirth, however, we can let go of these anxiety-producing expectations.

This map of soul age can also help us keep from identifying too narrowly with the themes of our immediate life. While our present life is where our work is, it is not in the final analysis what we are. By reminding us of the larger adventure we are on, this map can help us realize that we are *using* this life, we are not this life. I remember how strange this idea was to me when I first encountered it many years ago. And yet as one's insight into the deep structure of one's present life grows, as one begins to trace its underpinnings in previous centuries, it becomes more natural to think in these terms. I am not just this personality I had taken myself to be, but more. Before this life there was another and after it will come another still. In a poignant sense, I am just using this life. As we ponder these themes, our identification with our personality sometimes slackens. We begin to dilate and touch an identity larger than our body-mind identity. Through this crack in

---

[10] The esoteric spiritual traditions typically teach that while one cannot judge things either good or bad in any ultimate sense, one can always recognize one's duty in any situation. One can inwardly know the proper response to a situation without generating a system of judgments beyond ourselves-in-this-immediate-situation. This Eastern teaching strikes many Westerners as inconsistent. We have tended to place great trust in the construction of ethical systems and the formulation of universalizable rules of conduct that we see as necessary for making informed moral choices. Such systems, however, ignore the fact that souls of different ages may be learning different lessons from perhaps even "identical" situations. The point is precisely that two seemingly identical situations will not be identical if the participants are at different levels of development.

the door we can become absorbed, if only momentarily, into something larger, into some consciousness that cradles our existence in its own.

Even the mere intellectual realization that we are more than our present personality starts us on a journey of self-discovery. Once we see that we are not just this life, we must ask "What am I? If I am not just this life, am I my Oversoul?" Yet if the Oversoul is itself embedded in an encompassing Over-oversoul, and if this process repeats itself who knows how many times, we cannot simply take the Oversoul as our true identity but must look deeper still.

This search for our true identity leads eventually to the development of a level of awareness traditionally associated with the seventh chakra. If we are not just this life, neither are we just the lives that came before it combined with the lives that will come after it. If we are not just this personality, then neither are we just the Oversoul. The sages who have traveled this path before us say that in the final analysis, we are Being Itself. We are *Saccidananda*, Being-Consciousness-Bliss, manifesting in space/time. Once we experientially know this to be true, then we know that this body–mind identity and this Oversoul are but forms that Consciousness is taking in the adventure called Existence-as-Form. This is to abolish illusion and to awaken to one's True Nature. This is enlightenment.

It would be a mistake to conceptualize the chakras too linearly and think that enlightenment awareness can only develop after all the other levels of awareness have reached maturity. It sometimes happens that way and it can be orchestrated to happen that way, but it need not happen that way. This is because the identity that is discovered upon enlightenment is an identity that already exists before enlightenment. I already am Being-Consciousness-Bliss, even though I may not be aware of it this very moment.

If reincarnation can be said to have a goal in this phase of human existence, it is this: the experiential discovery of our Essential Nature. In this act we rediscover our true identity, we rediscover our wholeness, our oneness with everything that exists. In this experience all fear is ended, all desires satisfied, all scars collected on the journey healed. Those who have had this experience say that it is worth whatever it takes to realize it. They also say that it does not mark the end of our development but rather is simply a point of transition. From this point on our evolution no longer requires incarnating in space/time. We are free to come and go as we please.

Though it may be easier to know this truth about ourselves while existing in the domain of spirit, to experientially realize it while in physical form seems to carry a special significance. To wake to our Essential Nature while existing on the physical plane appears not only to advance our personal development but to contribute in some way to a collective evolutionary process of which we are a part.[11] It is here, perhaps, that our individual evolution fuses with the evolution of the species. If eventually the entire species were to become aware of its Essential Nature, surely the course of history would take a sharp turn into an exciting future.

---

[11] Again, we make this move via Rupert Sheldrake's concept of morphogenetic field (mentioned in Chapter 2, footnote 43).

6

A Reincarnationist Christianity?

*T*he conditions under which we live in the valleys of time lead us almost inevitably to see the physical world as the "real" world. They teach us to identify with our physical selves and therefore to doubt our continued existence beyond the grave. This doubt has been reinforced in the last two hundred years by a pervasive philosophy, supported by science but ultimately going far beyond science, that has held that the physical world is the only world that exists, or at least the world that really controls whatever else exists.

The only major social institutions in the West that have kept the vision of a nonphysical, spiritual universe alive in recent centuries have been its religions—Christianity, Judaism, and Islam. As metaphysical naturalism has reached ever deeper into the intellectual fabric of Western culture, they alone have continued to teach us to expect a surprise when our bodies fall away. Only they have preserved the vision that human life is more than physical existence and that its presence in the universe is more than a succession of fortunate accidents. Unfortunately, their vision has not extended so far as to include reincarnation.

Instead of rebirth, the Western religions have taught that though we are immortal beings, we live only a few years of that immortality on Earth. For better or for worse, the lives we are currently living are it, and how we will spend eternity hinges entirely on how we conduct ourselves here and now. Not all Western religious believers have accepted this restriction, however. There have been subcurrents that have found reincarnation to be a more compelling vision of life— Hasidism within Judaism, Sufism within Islam, and Gnostic circles within Christianity. Nevertheless, on balance, Western religious thought has endorsed a one-time-through philosophy.

It is not surprising, therefore, that many people who come from Western religious backgrounds approach reincarnation with consider- able resistance and anxiety. If they find themselves being persuaded by the secular research, they know that down the road they will have to make adjustments to their religious beliefs, and this is a frightening prospect for many. I have watched hundreds of my students go through this ordeal. The deeper their commitment to their religious lineage, the greater their discomfort. They often assume that reincarnation is an Eastern concept, and therefore necessarily at odds with Western theol- ogy. Sometimes they feel that by even considering the evidence for rebirth, they are betraying their faith, perhaps even risking their salvation. Yet, as college students, they also feel intellectually compelled to consider any hypothesis on the basis of the evidence. Ironically, those who suffer most are often those who combine considerable intellectual talent with a natural spiritual affinity that has flourished in the faith they were born into.

The questions that arise in the classroom repeat the same themes semester after semester: Does the evidence for reincarnation prove that the Eastern religions are true and Western religions false? Will this inquiry eventually force me to choose between Western and Eastern interpretations of life? Am I being untrue to my faith even to consider reincarnation? Is reincarnation compatible with Christianity? What would a Christian faith that incorporated reincarnation look like?

While all three Western traditions are represented in my classroom, most of my students come from Christian backgrounds. Therefore, it is Christianity that gets discussed most frequently. As many who read this book are likely to share these roots, this chapter addresses the challenges and opportunities reincarnation presents to the Christian faith. This focus is also in keeping with my competencies, for though I have studied Judaism and am acquainted with Islam, I am most familiar both by education and upbringing with Christian theology and sen- timent.

Let me state at the outset that I believe reincarnation is quite compatible with the Christian faith and that Christianity can incorporate reincarnation without losing its distinctive character should it choose to do so. Furthermore, I believe that Christian thought will be invigorated and strengthened by this expansion.

To my thinking, reincarnation represents an important missing link in Western theology. Despite centuries of theological discussion, the problem of suffering has remained essentially unsolved in the West. Theologians have never been able to satisfactorily explain the purpose suffering plays in a universe created by a benign God, nor why it is so inequitably distributed. Accordingly, the injustices of life have continued to gnaw at our insides and to erode our confidence in the Christian vision of life. Yet these problems, I suggest, derive primarily from adopting a one-time-through philosophy. When Christian theologians accepted the notion that there is no historical precedent to our present life, they cut the lines of causality that make life a meaningful tapestry. Unable then to recognize the logic or purpose of suffering within a single lifecycle, they had no recourse but to throw the burden of this inscrutability on God's shoulders, where it still sits to this day.

It's ironic, really. Christianity has taught us that God, the name given the Ultimate Reality in life, is loving, benevolent, and completely trustworthy. Yet it has also taken from us the key we need to recognize this love. Though we want to trust the Judeo-Christian God, we cannot help but experience a nagging doubt. How could an infinitely loving and powerful being inflict humankind with the tortured lives some of us are forced to live? It does not matter if I personally am spared tragedy, for if even one human life is wasted, this God cannot be completely trusted.

If we have but one life to live here, how could a God who plants us in such terribly disparate circumstances possibly be a just God? The argument that our different fates reflect God's foreknowledge of our choices and are therefore justified has never been persuasive because it is hopelessly circular. Our choices reflect the character that—in a one-life-only scheme—God designed for us "out of nothing," and for which He therefore must assume responsibility. Nor can we find much encouragement in the suggestion that we all deserve, because of some primal sin, the damning fate that only some of us are allowed to inherit. If God chooses to intervene in order to save only some of us from a fate we all deserve, where is the justice in this, to say nothing of the compassion? Our moral sensitivities are outraged at the injustice of it all, yet is God less morally sensitive than we?

As long as we restrict ourselves to thinking only in terms of a one-time-through option, the Judeo-Christian God will remain an enigma to us. The burden of God's inscrutability is so great that the entire theological edifice of Judeo-Christianity continuously threatens to crack under its weight. Perhaps it is for this reason that despite its lack of official sanction, 24 percent of the Protestants and 25 percent of the Catholics polled in America in 1981 have already accepted reincarnation.[1]

The Christian students in my classroom who grapple with reincarnation know that historically Christianity has rejected the idea of reincarnation, though few of them know when it did so or why. Most of them, however, do not feel prevented by past edicts from reopening the question. Faced with mounting secular evidence in support of reincarnation, the key issue to them is not historical precedent but whether reincarnation is compatible with the core insights of the Christian faith. Does it contradict anything important or weaken anything essential? Does it reinforce the Christian perception of what is ultimately true and valuable in life?

How one answers these questions, of course, will largely depend on what one construes the core insights of Christianity to include. Everyone knows that each religion contains an inner set of essential principles surrounded by a more marginal set of less important principles. History reshuffles the latter periodically without damaging the inner core. Will women ever be ordained as priests in the Catholic church? Will the Protestant denominations ever reunite? Our answers largely will depend upon what one takes the Christian core to consist of. Which principles in the tradition reflect eternal truths and which reflect transient cultural values? Every religion that lives long enough to outgrow the culture of its birthplace must ask itself this question. The longer it lives and the more culturally diversified its history becomes, the more frequently it must discriminate between what is essential and what can be changed without harm.

I believe that reincarnation is compatible with Christianity's core, yet I did not always do so. When I first became convinced that reincarnation was a fact of life, it seemed to me that to incorporate the concept, Christianity would have to undergo a drastic overhaul of its core doctrines. Today, the revisions seem much more modest. No doubt this shift reflects changes in my assessment of what constitutes the core of Christian faith, but it also reflects a growing sensitivity to the deeper themes that run through Christian symbolism. The concept of reincarnation expanded enormously my frame of reference for understanding

---

[1] George Gallup, Jr., *Adventures in Immortality*, pp. 192–193.

how life operated and what it was about. Yet within this expanded awareness I began to recognize even in Christian sources the archetypal themes of the soul's quest for God across many lifetimes. Underneath the details of theology, I heard echoes of a larger story—of souls losing their God-awareness and subsequently becoming lost in physical existence, of the causes leading to this condition, and of the cosmic and individual initiatives necessary to reverse this condition.

It is my belief that only a relatively small adjustment to Christian doctrine is required for Christianity to incorporate reincarnation today. The large majority of Christian teaching can remain essentially unchanged while making room for the concept of the Oversoul. Yet while only a modest redrafting of doctrine is required to incorporate reincarnation, I also think that considerably more rethinking of Christian theology is invited by its inclusion. The attention that reincarnation is receiving in the West is part of a larger encounter taking place between East and West, and this encounter holds profound social and theological significance for both hemispheres. In dramatically expanding our understanding of the life span of the individual, reincarnation radically expands our frame of reference for understanding what Christians have called salvation history. The logic of rebirth encourages us to view the world's religions as part of a collective enterprise, to see them as collaborators in history instead of as competitors. This represents a major turning point for those Christians who are not already used to thinking in these terms.

In this chapter, therefore, I look at both the minimum and the maximum options open to Christians today. I want to ask, first, how little do we need to change Christian doctrine to incorporate reincarnation and, second, what broader reassessments of Christianity's place among the world religions are we invited—but not compelled—to consider if we open to the concept of rebirth? Before describing these options, I want to mention two approaches to the topic of reincarnation and Christianity that strike me as unproductive.

AVOIDING TWO DEAD ENDS

Among the many claims one hears concerning the place of reincarnation in Christian theology, two strike me as dead ends. The first is the claim that Jesus actually taught reincarnation himself. The second is the contrasting claim that if reincarnation is not explicitly taught in the New Testament itself, it does not belong in Christian theology. Neither approach, I believe, is convincing.

Starting with the first claim, there are a number of passages in the New Testament which if read at face value seem to suggest that some of Jesus' disciples, and perhaps even Jesus himself, accepted reincarnation. I do not find these interpretations persuasive, but the technical issues they raise are too complicated to be dealt with here. (I examine these passages and the issues they raise in the Appendix.)

A second attempt to locate reincarnation in the teaching of the historical Jesus accepts the traditional view that reincarnation is not included in the New Testament. It then goes on to suggest that the New Testament did not record all that Jesus actually taught. The contention is that Jesus taught at different levels to different audiences and that the New Testament records only the teaching received by one audience, while reincarnation was part of a subtler teaching given to a second audience.

This old idea of a two-tiered teaching has been given new life by the discovery of fifty-two ancient manuscripts at Nag Hammadi in 1945, some of them dating as far back as the New Testament itself. These texts describe the beliefs of a very early group of Christians called Gnostic Christians who saw themselves preserving a teaching they believed derived from Jesus himself. This teaching included reincarnation as well as several other ideas that never made it into orthodoxy as orthodoxy was being defined by the major councils in the first six centuries of the Christian era. (Once again, the issues raised by the Nag Hammadi texts are rather technical and are addressed in the Appendix.)

On the whole, I am not yet convinced by attempts to place reincarnation into the teaching of the historical Jesus either through a few passages gleaned from the New Testament or through the Gnostic materials. Perhaps one day the historians will rewrite the history of this period, but for now I favor the view that reincarnation was not part of Jesus' original message. This does not mean, however, that Jesus taught against reincarnation, for he clearly did not. The Jesus portrayed in the New Testament never condemns reincarnation.

In John's gospel, for example, Jesus is presented with a man born blind and is asked, "Rabbi, who sinned, this man or his parents? Why was he born blind?" Were his questioners thinking that if the man himself had sinned, he must have sinned in a previous life, since he had been blind from birth? Perhaps, but their thinking is hard to reconstruct from this distance. In any case, John's Jesus bypasses the opportunity to criticize the possible reincarnationist assumption inherent in the question and answers instead that the man was born blind "so that God's power might be displayed in curing him" (John 9:1–2); that is, that Jesus might restore his sight now. Neither Jesus in the gospels nor Paul in his many epistles ever speaks against reincarnation. Both appear in the sources to assume the prevailing opinion that we live on Earth only once, but the safest conclusion is that they simply did not concern themselves with the question of whether humans live on earth once or many times. This was one of the many blanks that Christian theology had to fill in.[2]

The New Testament is not antireincarnation. This assessment stands despite one passage in the epistle to the Hebrews frequently quoted by antireincarnationists. The passage reads ". . . it is the lot of men to die once, and after death comes judgment . . ." (Heb. 9:27). (Once thought to be written by Paul, Hebrews is now widely held by scholars to have been written by a later, anonymous author.) When this verse is placed back into the context of the themes of the letter, however, it becomes clear that the author is not intending to adjudicate between alternative theories of the afterlife. He is concerned instead to champion Christianity's new covenant with God over the old Israelite covenant, which centered on the temple. Thus he compares Christ's sacrifice on the cross—which was a sacrifice of his own blood and which was made only once—to the sacrifices performed by the temple priests—which do not require them to shed their own blood and which must be repeated many times. In this context he says:

> But as it is, [Christ] has appeared once for all at the climax of history to abolish sin by the sacrifice of himself. And as it is the lot of men to die once, and after death comes judgment, so Christ was offered once to bear the burden of men's sins, and will appear a second time, sin done away, to bring salvation to those who are watching for him. [Heb. 9:26b–28]

The author of Hebrews is not arguing against reincarnation but against the Israelite temple-based religion. In this context, he mentions as an aside the common belief that men die once. Clearly, he does not espouse a reincarnationist world view, but neither can he be said to be arguing against reincarnation. Nor can he be taken as contending that reincarnation is incompatible with the Christian message. His attention is simply focused elsewhere.

---

[2] I agree with Professor Geddes MacGregor that the most plausible reason the early Christians in general did not concern themselves with metaphysical questions about the afterlife was their belief that Jesus would be returning to Earth in the immediate future, thus rendering such questions irrelevant. See his book, *Reincarnation in Christianity*, pp. 36–37.

This leads us to ask: Should Christians be bound to every belief mentioned in the New Testament, however unrelated it is to the central gospel message? To adopt an approach to scripture that does not even try to discriminate between the intended and the inadvertent locks us into a labyrinth of antiquity, unable to sort out the essential from the peripheral. Yet as our knowledge has grown enormously since biblical times, we have many times had to do just this. We have had to separate out those New Testament beliefs that are central to the gospel from those that simply formed part of the cultural backdrop to the gospel's entrance into history.

Even so, if one wants to play the literal-interpretation game, the reincarnationist still has a card to play. Even if this verse is taken alone and out of context, it does not technically rule out a reincarnationist reading. It is straightforwardly true that the person I now am will die but once, and then will follow the experience of judgment. This does not rule out the possibility that another human life will follow this one, and that its death will be followed by another judgment. The literal meaning of the verse is preserved within a reincarnationist framework.

The bottom line is that the New Testament is neither proreincarnation nor antireincarnation. It is simply silent on the subject.

Even if reincarnation is not part of the New Testament message, this fact alone does not mean that it could not or should not become part of Christian teaching. This brings us to the second claim—the contention that if reincarnation cannot be found in the New Testament, it does not belong in Christianity. Every religion that centers itself around the teaching of a historical personality must establish itself as a living reality that continues to grow intellectually after the historical founder has passed from the local scene. It must find ways of reaching beyond the original inspiration while simultaneously preserving that inspiration. Christianity has always recognized this necessity in its doctrine of the Holy Spirit. Though the historical Jesus is no longer present on Earth, the Church's link with God is preserved through the Spirit. It is this link that allows her to deepen and expand her teaching as she encounters circumstances that were not part of her original historical context. It is the Spirit she relies on when she turns to consider questions that were not asked or answered in the original gospel message.

The biblical record constitutes Christianity's starting point and the center to which she always returns to reestablish her balance, but it has never defined the limits of her thinking, nor should it. Over time, Christianity came to contain numerous ideas that were not part of Jesus' original teaching, such as the Trinity, the criteria of a just war, and the dual nature of Christ.[3] Catholic doctrines concerning Mary—both The Immaculate Conception and the Assumption—go beyond the biblical record. By these measures, at least, we could conclude that even if reincarnation was not part of the original New Testament message, it could still justifiably become part of Christian theology.

There is no doubt that if Christianity should decide today that reincarnation is an acceptable adjunct to traditional faith, it will have to pivot on its past to do so. Though this would require oiling some rusty joints, such a pivot is well within its means. Christianity has always felt free to reevaluate its past decisions and to reverse those it thinks no longer best serves truth. It has changed its mind before on matters it once felt deeply about and undoubtedly will do so again in the future. In the late nineteenth century, for example, there was no doubt that Roman Catholicism considered no form of the theory of evolution compatible with the doctrine of creation. Today, it has simply changed its mind, for it recognizes any number of ways in which one can simultaneously affirm both evolution and creation.

Many Christians are not willing to wait until Christianity's institutional offices make up their minds on reincarnation. If the Christian churches should decide to accept rebirth, the process may take centuries. My students cannot wait this long. They are taking the initiative themselves, weighing the evidence personally and considering the options largely without clerical guidance. In the end, all discussion of whether Jesus might have taught reincarnation or whether the early Church Fathers acted wisely in rejecting reincarnation in the sixth century is irrelevant to them, however fascinating it may be to the historian of antiquity. Such subtleties are a moot point, because the only Christianity *they* have known in their lives has preached a one-time-through philosophy. They want to know whether they can reverse this particular plank without dismantling the entire Christian platform. This brings us back to the question of what constitutes the core teachings of Christianity.

A REINCARNATIONIST CHRISTIAN FAITH

To make the core teachings of the Christian faith compatible with reincarnation, all that is required is that we change one tenet, that which restricts the soul to one cycle of years on Earth. Once we make room

---

[3] The proposition that Jesus was both fully God and fully man was not officially adopted until the Council of Nicea in A.D. 325. By themselves, the gospels allow several alternative interpretations of Jesus' status.

for souls to cycle back and forth to Earth many times on their long journey away from God and back to God, everything else in Christianity can remain practically as it was. Changes of nuance and context will not disturb the fundamental insights Christianity has deemed essential to its faith. Within orthodoxy there has historically existed a considerable range of acceptable interpretation of doctrine. A reincarnationist theology clearly favors one side of that range over the other, but it can stay within the larger boundaries.

Let us look at how much in Christianity would remain largely untouched by adopting reincarnation. I offer the following not as a definitive accounting but as a personal list that hopefully will promote discussion among others who are also thinking about this question.

God is the beginning and the end of all things. God is the source, the substance, and ultimate destination of all life. God is the whole that incorporates all parts. Ultimately, God is beyond concepts, beyond words, beyond thought, yet we confidently say that God's nature is love.

Ours is a created world. The physical universe is surrounded by, sustained by, and derives from a larger spiritual universe (or universes) that in turn derives from the Primal Reality, God. The details of this process are largely unreconstructible, though emanationist theories of creation are preferred over other options. Biblical pictures of creation can be seen as simplified, lyrical portraits of this basic metaphysical dependency.

God is our essence. (Optional) We are a manifestation of God in time–space. We are to God as sunlight is to the sun—the same, indistinguishable, one with, not separate from. Though ontologically we are always one with God, psychologically we tend to be ignorant of this connection. This is not pantheism, the belief that the physical universe is God, but pan*en*theism, the belief that the universe is part of God or is 'in God.' God is a reality that includes but is larger than the physical universe.[4]

---

[4] As Hinduism demonstrates, reincarnation is compatible with both monistic and monotheistic conceptions of God. Monotheism is the belief that God is One. In a monotheistic world view, God usually remains distinct and separate from what He has created. Monism is the belief that nothing but God exists. In a monistic world view, everything that exists is a manifestation of Divinity, and thus creation is not separate from God but a something that takes place "within" God. The formulation presented here leans strongly in the direction of monism, which will probably sound strange to Christian ears. This strangeness, however, derives not from reincarnation itself but from

Our life is eternal. Our bodies die, but our consciousness never dies. Because of our inherent divinity, it is simply not an option available to us.

Earth is not our home. Ultimately, we are spiritual beings whose natural home is the spiritual universe. We live at present as hybrid beings, part spirit, part matter. However intimately these may be intertwined, and however useful physical embodiment may be to our spiritual development, ultimately our essential substance is spirit and to spirit we will return.

Our present state is not our original state. As we exist now, we are only marginally and transitorily aware of our true nature. Yet we once possessed an abiding awareness of our essence. This change, or "fall," is connected to the taking up of physical existence itself. The conditions of material existence tend to cause us to forget our spiritual identity. Why this happens and how this happens is connected to our capacity to make choices and to the impact these choices have on our lives, including our choice to incarnate on Earth.

Our life on Earth is purposeful. This is true at both an individual and a cosmic level. The conditions of our individual lives are not accidental but intentional, thus "providential." Behind the seemingly inscrutable hardships we must endure is purpose, and behind that purpose is ultimately a benevolence that seeks only our perfection. On a larger scale, our lives are part of the purposeful movement of God in the universe. God is the God of history, and we are part of that history. We are part of an

---

monism, and one could quite easily generate a monotheistic version of reincarnation. Therefore, this particular postulate may be seen as optional. The monistic concept of God is closest to the Christian mystical concept of the Godhead. (On the differences between God and the Godhead, one might consult Huston Smith, *Forgotten Truth*, Chapters 3 and 4.)

Ultimately, monism and monotheism ought to be seen not as contradicting one another, but as being simultaneously true within different frames of reference. Monism is a more encompassing theory than monotheism. Monotheistic formulations can be regarded as valid, but eventually yielding to monism's more comprehensive frame of reference. A similar thing happens in physics where it is recognized that relativity theory gives us a more comprehensive and accurate model of the physical universe than does classical, Newtonian physics, but that Newtonian physics continues to be valid for understanding and working with a certain subset of this larger reality. For more on this, see Swami Ajaya's interesting discussion of dualistic versus monistic paradigms in *Psychotherapy East and West*, Chapter 1.

adventure God is on, the parameters of which lie for the most part beyond our vision.

The movement of religious life is essentially that of return. The going out from God is paired with a time of return. In the present phase of history, the story of humanity is one of return. Religions exist to facilitate this return to God, which can be construed as a recovery of our primal identity.

God's posture toward us is only that of grace and love. It is impossible for God to reject us in any way. God's love and support is universal, nondiscriminating, and irreversible.

We and we alone are responsible for the condition(s) we find ourselves in. God cannot reject us. If we are estranged from God, we ourselves must be the source of that estrangement. The story of Adam and Eve can be read as a archetypal story of our own past, describing choices each of us has made that have brought us to our present condition. Because God's grace is constant, we can always reverse the conditions of alienation and are always surrounded by invitations to do so. In the end, our return to God can be construed in terms of the Divinity healing Itself, for God is what we are.

Jesus was the Christ. His ministry was one of truth; his mission was redemption, the turning of humankind back to God. Nothing about reincarnation is incompatible with attributing a critical, even decisive role to Jesus in history. A reincarnationist Christology, however, would tend to view Jesus as distinct from us not *in kind* but *in degree*. He is an incarnation of divinity as are we all, but to a much more radical degree than we and therefore with a much greater impact on history. He is a prototype of human development, revealing to us fundamental truths about our own divine/human nature. Such a Christology lies at the fringe of but still within the repertoire of orthodox Christologies. While reincarnation does not rule out giving Jesus a unique status or role in history, the drift of reincarnationist sentiment clearly lies in the direction of recognizing Jesus as one of a small handful of highly developed beings, construable even as incarnations of the Divine Principle Itself, each uniquely tuned to their respective cultures and collectively changing the course of human history toward the rediscovery of the God Within.[5]

Love one another. Love is our way home. We all come from the same source, God. As our awareness of the oneness underlying and uniting all of us grows, love becomes the obvious and most natural path of conduct. Our love for each other reflects a spiritual vision of life and therefore should be independent of people's behavior toward us. If we are ever uncertain what love demands, we should do for the other persons what we would have them do for us in comparable circumstances. Because we all share the same divine nature, what we do to them, we are also doing to ourselves. If this is not immediately apparent, one day it will be.

Judge not and you shall not be judged. We are never in a position to judge another person's actions. Whenever we do so, we pass judgment on and limit ourselves. In this and in all matters, we should be guided by the law of reciprocity and extend to others the respect and compassion we naturally wish for ourselves.

Sin is conscious estrangement from God. Sins are any thoughts, words, or actions that *consciously* estrange us to varying degrees from the source of life, which is God. Thus our capacity to sin is relative to and restricted by our state of awareness, and changes with that awareness. To truly live in sin is to live more estranged from the essence of life and of our own being than our state of awareness allows. In essence, it is the choice to be less than we are. Sin is completely personal; we inherit no one else's sins. Yet there is a collective dimension to our acts that we cannot escape. Ultimately, sin is simply a function of our ignorance of who and what we are and a reflection of our preoccupation with mistaken identities.

We need each other. While reincarnation forces each of us to assume responsibility for our own fate, it also teaches us that life is an interconnected web of relationships. Ultimately, no one returns home alone.

---

[5] For a brief but interesting discussion of the Christological ramifications of making this shift in thinking about Jesus, see John White's essay "Enlightenment and the Christian Tradition" in his methodology *What is Enlightenment?*

Religious community. While reincarnation focuses our attention on the individual, it neither disparages nor discourages religious community. Indeed, the task of reawakening to our spiritual identity is so great that we are encouraged to gather with fellow seekers in mutual support and assistance. Similarly, religious rituals and liturgies are welcomed as instruments for reawakening our awareness of the transcendent. Ultimately, however, all ritual and all community is pragmatic, for the secret of return lies in the core of one's individual being.

We are accountable for everything and anything we do. This is true not because someone outside the system is keeping track of all our successes and failures, but because everything we do, say, and think impacts upon our inner being and thus is carried within us. It changes our energy in small ways that accumulate over time. In this way our behavior eventually defines the energy field in which we subsequently live and the circumstances through which we later experience the world. (More on this in Chapter 8.)

A hell of sorts exists and is often experienced between physical lives. The concept of eternal damnation, however, is simply a mistake.

Our destination after leaving Earth behind forever is beautiful beyond description. Glimpses that we are given in mystical experiences and near-death episodes are but brief foretastes of the transcendental peace and ecstacy that characterize "heaven." The joy we will feel there derives ultimately from our abiding awareness of God. Even so, reincarnation encourages us to see heaven not as a place of static rest but a field of ongoing activity and continued growth. The euphoria and God-saturation that we will experience there are the backdrop to a continuing evolution of our being, the end of which cannot be projected.

Reincarnation enlarges the size of the stage on which the spiritual drama of humankind is performed, but it does not change what Christianity has considered the essential elements of the script. Life still begins and ends in God. God remains the same, though with themes of immanence emphasized. The purpose of life remains the same, though our spiritual growth is viewed as unending. The diversity of life is honored while the underlying unity of all being is affirmed. Jesus' role remains largely the same, though we are encouraged to think of it in terms that complement rather than usurp the roles of other spiritual leaders in other cultures. The moral qualities of a spiritually oriented life-style remain the same. Overall, the script is the same. *The only thing that has changed is the age of the players.*

Instead of trying to fit the processes of salvation into one lifecycle, we can now view them as taking effect through many lifetimes. The soul that is struggling to make its way back to its Creator is not ten, fifty, or a hundred years old, but thousands of years old. The story of this soul's separation from and return to God is a tale that is enacted across the broad sweep of human history. The impact of initiatives taken in one lifecycle may not manifest until another, but there is a unifying coherence to the process. This coherence is provided by the larger being that we in fact are. The soul Christianity has traditionally talked about needs but to be understood as referring to the Oversoul, then everything else fits easily into place. The essential promises Christianity has made stand firm. Life is eternal. Purifying forgiveness is ours for the asking. We are ultimately safe in a benignly ordered universe. God has taken initiatives in history to draw us back to Himself.

If reincarnation is true, then it has been a fact of life at least since *Homo sapiens sapiens* emerged fifty thousand years ago and possibly longer. Each of our individual journeys away from God-consciousness and back toward it has been enacted against the backdrop of the history of intelligent life on this planet. Through reincarnation, all of human evolution is incorporated into what Christianity calls salvation history. All cultures, all peoples, all epochs are included in the plan. Salvation history is the story of the redemption of the entire human race—or, put slightly differently, it is the story of the retrieval of souls who have become lost for a while in the rebounding echoes of repeated human existence.

Christianity is part of this retrieval process, as are all the great religions of the world. Two thousand years ago it sounded eternal truths that were spiritually efficacious and thus unleashed new currents in history. To understand Christianity's true impact on history, we must remember the larger context in which it proclaimed these truths. This context was and still is the relentless polishing of souls through karma and rebirth. The human condition of estrangement from God that Jesus addressed did not develop overnight, nor was it inherited from some primal ancestor. It developed gradually for each of us through a long succession of individual choices that traded off one kind of awareness for another. Similarly, the purifying, restorative impact of Jesus' teaching did not and could not realize its full effect overnight or in a single lifetime. *Jesus came to save not human beings, as it were, but Oversouls who have become trapped in human disguises.* He came to remind us of truths long forgotten and to empower our reappropriation of these truths. The effect of his life and teaching was to bend the arch of our lives back toward the wholeness of God.

During his ministry, Jesus met people at all stages of their spiritual journey. Some were so close to spiritual reawakening that they fairly exploded into a higher spiritual consciousness simply from hearing him speak or from being in his presence. Confronted by Jesus, their lives were suddenly transformed; they were "filled with the Spirit"—able to heal, to discern men's inner hearts, and above all to love with overwhelming power. Others would take longer to come to an awakening this profound, perhaps thousands of years, but the promise of eternal life, of certain redemption, and of the continuous love and support of God holds true for them as well. The only difference operating here is soul age. It is a matter of timing, not substance.

The arch of our life away from and back to God carries us through many lifecycles. Each life takes us another leg of our long journey. Heaven waits for us both at the end of this present life and at the end of our odyssey. It is sampled to varying degrees between Earth cycles, but will be experienced in fullest measure only when our final homecoming takes place. If we are dismayed that the journey is longer than we once thought, we should take heart from the fact that the outcome is proportionate to the undertaking. We are on Earth to expand and refine our capacities to participate in Divinity. Though the curriculum of the Earth school is long and difficult, the outcome, we are told, is worth any cost.

While the basic thrust of my proposal for Christian theology is to redefine the soul in terms of the Oversoul, another approach should at least be mentioned here. I do so, however, at the risk of muddying the water.

As discussed in Chapter 4, the individual lives that make up a single Oversoul appear to exist somewhat independently of each other. There is a sense in which each individual life has its own autonomy while simultaneously participating in a larger configuration. I do not pretend to understand all the ins and outs of these matters. I observe, however, that in past-life therapy when a former life that has successfully fulfilled its karmic mission comes forward, he or she appears bathed in white light. It appears, therefore, that if an individual life does all that is karmically asked of it during its lifetime and advances the evolution of the whole its allotted distance, then that life comes to some form of spiritual fruition at its end. It does this even if other lives in the Oversoul remain unresolved and if subsequent incarnations must follow it to bring these lives to karmic completion.

In meeting the lives that preceded mine in my karmic lineage, it becomes clear that these lives are in a very important sense *not me*. They are mine by virtue of our collective inclusion in the Oversoul, and they constitute a heritage I am responsible to, but I am also distinct from what has gone before. They have made decisions I do not affirm. Some of them have committed atrocities I would never permit today. Others have accomplished great things that lie outside the scope of my present abilities. If we collectively form a greater whole, we nevertheless are distinct from one another.

From this perspective, we might view the religions of the West and the religions of the East as affirming two sides of a larger truth. One speaks of the individual life, the other of the lineage of lives that make up the Oversoul. The Western religions might be seen as emphasizing the truth that each individual life has the capacity to bring itself completion irrespective of what has preceded it or what will follow it. If we rise to the challenges embedded in our life, we can count on receiving our spiritual reward when our piece of work in the Earth school is finished. On the other side of the coin, the Eastern religions can be seen as reminding us that the definition of our life's work derives from a historical context larger than our present life. They remind us that while we are this present life, at another level we are much more than this life. In the end, these two perspectives are not contradictory but complementary.

The more we appreciate the relative autonomy of each life in the Oversoul, the more deeply we will appreciate the profound significance of the Christian doctrine of Christ's sacrificial death. Classically formulated, this doctrine says that Christ, who was himself innocent of wrong, died for the sins of the world, and through this act of generosity he redeemed the human race. Yet the archetype of sacrificial death, of the good person voluntarily suffering on behalf of others, has an even broader significance in a reincarnationist Christianity. Each one of us is completely innocent at birth. The individual I now experience myself to be did not exist before my birth. The karma I am working on in this life derives from human lives I do not even remember. Yet in incarnating on Earth and taking on their karma, I have volunteered to suffer on their behalf that they might be restored to their Source and be made whole. Seen from this perspective, each us is participating in the mystery of the sacrificial death. From the cross, Jesus instructs each one of us in the great mystery that to possess our life we must give up our life. We must surrender ourselves to working with the life script we find ourselves in, however unjust it is from our individual perspective, trusting in a beneficent outcome to our sacrifice. Each of us is here on a mission of redemption.

WHY DID CHRISTIANITY REJECT REINCARNATION?

Why did Christianity ever reject reincarnation in the first place? If rebirth did not challenge Jesus' teaching on God, eternal life, love, his mission on Earth, or any of the other components listed above, why was it deemed unacceptable to the Church? The Nag Hammadi texts demonstrate that reincarnation was a live option for many early Christians. If this is so, why was it excluded from orthodoxy at the Fifth Ecumenical Council in A.D. 553? Was it rejected on theological grounds or did other factors come into play?

In several books Geddes MacGregor has argued that the reason the Patristic Church rejected reincarnation lies not in the threat it posed to the theology of Jesus but in its threat to the institutional structure of the young church. In *Reincarnation in Christianity*, he writes:

> [Reincarnation] has a special tendency to cause those who believe in it to feel able to dispense with the *institutional* aspects of the Christian Way. . . . For reincarnationist systems of belief particularly call attention to the role of the individual will. They stress freedom of choice and the individual's capacity to make or mar his or her own destiny. My destiny is up to me. The Church may be immensely helpful to me. I may deeply reverence its teaching and thirst for its sacraments. . . . Yet if I accept a reincarnationist view I recognize that in the last resort I can do without the Church, as a boy can do without his mother, deeply though he may love her. [pp. 61–62]

It was characteristic of ecclesiastical thinking in the Patristic period to see the church as indispensable to a Christian's salvation. Its priests were mediators of God's grace channeled to believers through the sacraments they controlled. Reincarnation granted too much autonomy to individuals. It had too much potential to undermine the centralized authority the Roman church saw as critical to the survival of Christianity.

Yet what advanced the Christian cause in one century can hold it back in another. The development of a strong hierarchical system of leadership tightly controlled by a centralized authority may have insured Christianity's survival in its early years, but it is questionable whether it continues to serve her as well today. The old dream of one empire/one religion has yielded to a more pluralistic world vision. Accordingly, many observers feel that what was once an asset for the Christian Church has become a liability, and that her original self-concept should be exchanged for a new understanding of herself as a member of the sisterhood of world faiths. At the very least, we can say that if Christianity's rejection of reincarnation stems not from any basic incompatibility with the gospel but rather from an incompatibility with the Patristic theory of the Church, then no core tenet of faith prevents its being reconsidered today.

THE BROADER IMPLICATIONS OF REBIRTH

It should be clear that the logic of reincarnation invites Christians to go farther than the minimum distance in rethinking their religion's relation to other world faiths. The hunger for God and the thirst for transcendence is universal. Truth has been sought in every culture, and the awareness of Divinity has flowered around the globe. People have everywhere discovered or been shown the world of spirit and the laws of reciprocity governing our return to spirit. They are clearly stated in all the scriptures of the world.

Reincarnation so expands our frame of reference that we simply cannot take seriously any longer the contention that only one religion has the *real* answers to life while all other religions are false or incomplete. Our individual evolution has carried us around the world as we have traveled through time. We have incarnated on potentially all the continents, in all cultures, and in all religions. What one religion does for one culture, another religion does for another culture. Together they remind us that though our earthly existence is purposeful, it is transient. In every life they reteach us the rules of the game we are playing and redirect us toward our final destination.

Reincarnation is thoroughly compatible with Christianity's fundamental message, but not with the theological chauvinism that has until recently often distorted her sense of her historical mission. When Jesus was asked what was the greatest commandment, he answered: " 'Love the Lord your God with all your heart, with all your soul, with all your mind.' This is the greatest commandment. . . . The second is like it: "Love your neighbor as yourself" (Matt. 22:34–39).[6] When he listed the

---

[6] In Luke's version of this story, the question is "What must I do to inherit eternal life?" (Lk 10:25).

criteria that would be used in heaven to identify the saved, these criteria were feeding the hungry, clothing the naked, giving drink to the thirsty, visiting the sick, making strangers welcome, and attending to the needs of prisoners (Matt. 25:31–46). Not a word was said about belonging to a particular religion, let alone to a specific denomination. How did we come to lose this universal openness to goodness wherever we find it? How did we come to lose sight of the fact that wherever God is loved and humankind served, there Christ is active? How did we come to interpret the passage "No one shall come to the Father except through me" in the narrowest possible terms? Instead of recognizing that it was the universal Christ speaking, we took it to mean that one had to accept baptism in the historical Jesus' name in order to find God. Did the Jesus who taught that God is pure love intend to exclude from salvation all who were destined by birth never to hear the gospel? Is God's love so restrictive that it would exclude all who, having been nurtured for decades by their own religion, could see only dishonor in abandoning the faith of their ancestors for this new religion brought them by missionaries? How restrictive and foolish this concept looks today! If it made sense once, today it is nonsense. Fortunately, the intellectual and spiritual momentum of our times is away from such shortsightedness and toward a more collective embrace.

Once the Catholic church taught that "Outside the Church there is no salvation." Today that policy has been officially abandoned. Yet the theological formulations of Christian doctrine that are still widely used today in both Catholic and Protestant Christianity were drafted in the historical context of this older, exclusive world view. The traditional Christologies conceive of the historical Jesus as *the* unique mediator between God and humankind. They construe Jesus as generically unlike any other human who ever lived. His unique nature is said to reflect his unique role in world history. Recorded history is divided by his birth. All of the cosmos turns around his ministry and the events that followed. The logic of the traditional Christologies implies that whatever the universal Divinity is doing in other cultures, whatever contact humans on other continents are making with Spirit, these do not compare with what happened in Galilee two thousand years ago. Thus there is a contradiction that has not been fully resolved between such exclusive doctrinal formulations and the genuine ecumenical respect Christianity is beginning to show other world religions. The present theological challenge is to find ways of distinguishing between a *decisive* manifestation of Divine Truth and an *exclusive* manifestation.

The historical momentum of our times might be described as a shift from a singular to a collective perspective. Within the singular perspective, religions were approached in an either/or fashion. For one religion to be true, all others had to be false. In this perspective, we asked "Which religion is true?," for we assumed that they could not all be true. Our first response was usually to assume that our religion was the true one and that all other religions were false, but our growing sociological sophistication gradually undermined that option. Because everyone tends to believe that his or her culture's religion is the true one, this preference for the familiar simply reflects our cultural indoctrination. In an effort to escape religious enculturation, many took up the comparative study of religion, attempting to weigh the good and bad points of all the religions, again on the assumption that only one could be the "most true."

The collective perspective rejects this either/or approach to religion in favor of a both/and approach. It holds that other religions need not be false for one to be true, and that no one tradition has the exclusive purchase on truth. It applies not to transient cults but to religions that have proved themselves in history, that have demonstrated sufficient staying power to be classified as a true world religion. The collective perspective affirms what the single perspective denies, that all the religions of the world can be simultaneously true. If it is not immediately clear to us how this can be, we are encouraged to continue deepening our understanding of their teaching, constantly reassessing the intellectual assumptions that may be preventing us from seeing how they fit together into a larger whole.

Early formulations of the collective perspective tended to minimize the differences among the world religions. They typically stated that all the religions were saying essentially the same thing and that the differences between them could be accounted for by differences in cultural contexts. "There is only one truth appearing in many translations, one message with many cultural variations." This formula was conceptually neat, easy to grasp, and therefore became popular with those who were looking for some way of expressing their growing awareness of the global village. But, according to many scholars of comparative religion, this formula oversimplified matters, naively emptying the different religions of their philosophical distinctness. It simply wouldn't wash.

A more sophisticated formulation of the collective perspective goes something like this: The fundamental truths of the world religions are either (1) identical or (2) complementary. When we sift through all the peripheral beliefs and customs and identify the core of each tradition, the insights contained in that core will either be intertranslatable or complementary to each other. The first half of this formula simply restates the notion that there is considerable common ground beneath the theological subtleties of the world's many religions. Where there is common ground, we should be able to translate one set of concepts into the corresponding concepts of another faith. The second idea introduces a new theme that is appearing in works on comparative religion and therefore deserves more attention here.

If two religious traditions contain philosophical insights that are complementary, this means, first, that they are compatible with each other and, second, that each contains something that the other lacks. What is a well-developed insight in one religion may be underdeveloped in another, and vice versa. A major theme in one culture may have been relegated to a minor position in another and therefore may have received less critical attention. By combining the two perspectives, we realize greater insight into the whole.[7]

For example, it is widely recognized that the art of meditation has been refined to a higher degree in the East than in the West, and therefore that the Eastern religions have generally produced more detailed maps of the transcendental dimensions of the psyche than have the Western religions. Christianity, for example, has had its contemplatives ever since the Desert Fathers of the third century, but they have always constituted a minor current within the Western mainstream. Consequently, the introspective techniques developed in Western monasteries, while effective in themselves, are typically not as sophisticated as those found in Eastern monasteries. This was the conclusion, for example, of Thomas Merton, the Trappist monk who traveled to India in the last months of his life after a lifetime spent in one of the great Christian contemplative monasteries of America, Gesthemani.

If the Eastern religions have the edge on meditative techniques, what complementary strengths have the Western religions developed? Perhaps one is their eye for social injustice. Is it an accident that every major world movement of social reform, for example, the rejection of racism, sexism, and caste, has originated in a Judeo-Christian-Muslim culture? This seems to reflect the fact that one of the major themes of Western theology is humankind's responsibility for remaking society

---

[7] For simplicity's sake and because it fits the themes of this chapter, I shall draw the contrasts between East and West, but the same principle can be applied as well to two religions from within the same hemisphere.

according to God's standards.[8] By contrast, the religions of India, for example, have tended to stress the theme of liberation (*moksha*) from the pains of earthly existence into transcendental bliss, and therefore have paid less attention to reforming the conditions of earthly life.

The introspective techniques of meditation and the extroverted drive toward social justice are not contradictory tendencies but complementary strengths. Together they produce a whole that is larger than either of the two taken alone.[9]

Rather than present a lengthy philosophical or historical argument in support of this shift to a collective perspective, I will offer several pictures that can help us think about religion in collective terms. Many of us are so accustomed to thinking in terms of the singular perspective that we need the calisthenics these images provide to begin seeing religions in a new way.

I often ask my students, for example, to imagine that they are outside a large, square building about the size of a high school gym. In the center of this dark and otherwise empty building is a modern abstract sculpture. On each of the four walls is a large window; the only light that enters the building comes through these windows. We are outside the building, looking through the windows, trying to see and understand the sculpture inside.

In this analogy, the modern sculpture represents God, Ultimate Reality, or perhaps the "meaning of existence." Each window represents a religion embedded in a different world culture. Each culture gives us a "window of discovery" for looking at God, for trying to fathom what life is about. Each culture contains unique experiences and conditions that allow it to see some truths of life better than others. Each culture's unique history, social structure, historic personalities, and even geography have sensitized it to certain aspects of life and thus to certain aspects of the Beyond.

Through each window flows the light that illumines one side of the sculpture. What we see from any one window is real, but it is also incomplete. If we want to develop the most comprehensive and accurate

---

[8] We can note this pattern while simultaneously acknowledging that these same religions have also participated in and helped perpetuate the very social evils they later sought to eliminate, and still do to a degree.

[9] See also the discussion in Chapter 9 of the functional complementarity of Buddhist meditation practice and the Christian ethical directive of *agape* (pp. 210–213). Examples of an identical principle occurring across different religious traditions might be the Golden Rule (see pp. 65–66) and the importance of forgiveness (see pp. 213–214).

picture of the sculpture, we would naturally want to look at it from all sides, to walk around the building spending time at each window. The windows nearest our own would show us a view that overlaps with our original view, while the window on the wall opposite ours would show us aspects of the sculpture we could not see at all from our side.

Now imagine that each group of window-watchers does not even know of the existence of the other windows and therefore that each develops theories of the sculpture on the basis of individual perspective alone. When contact with the other window-watchers is first made, arguments about the sculpture would naturally ensue. How could the other window-watchers not see what we see? How could they describe the same sculpture so inaccurately? Only slowly would everyone discover that the other window-watchers were seeing a different facet of what we were seeing. Only once we get past the stage of arguing over who is right and who is wrong can we begin the exciting task of reconstructing the whole from the different perspectives—or at least the whole as the religions of Earth have discovered it up to this point in time. According to this analogy, Christianity has nothing to fear from the Eastern religions and much to gain. The more windows we have to view the sculpture from, the more complete will be our understanding of it.

One of my students did not like the inaccessibility of God in this analogy and proposed an interesting revision. In her model, we are inside the building and God surrounds the outside. The windows are transformed into doors, for the purpose of religion, she felt, was not simply to allow us to understand God conceptually but to actually experience God. In her revision, the different religions are culturally attuned doorways to transcendence. They are ways out of our limited condition. They exist to mediate contact with a larger reality that surrounds all life. Because each doorway is tuned to the particulars of its culture, it is somewhat different from the others. Yet the function each performs for its people is the same.

The experiential component in this student's revision is carried over into a third analogy often given for the collective perspective. In this analogy the different religions of the world are likened to different climbing parties scaling different faces of a single mountain. On the eve of the ascent, each team gathers in the village located at the foot of their side of the mountain and celebrates the climb according to the local customs of the province they are in. As they depart and enter the lower foothills, the parties can see the contours of the valleys which cradle the villages they have just left. As they continue to climb, they can see more and more of the broad landscapes that spread out below them. Eventually the vistas begin to overlap. The higher the parties climb, the greater the overlap becomes. Only when they have all reached the top of the mountain, however, do they all see the full, unobstructed sweep of the horizon. Only from the crest do they finally see how all the various folds of the lower hills are connected to one another.

This analogy suggests that the deeper (higher) one's experience of the essential truths of one's religion, the more obvious becomes the common ground with other faiths. To me, the climbers who reach the top of the mountain represent the mystics of the various faiths, those whose advanced spiritual experiences lift them above the ordinary believers' view of things. This concept of experiential convergence is supported by the psychological assessment of mystical experiences as they occur in different cultures. When mystics first venture beyond the physical world into the spiritual domain, their experiences are still colored by their culturally ingrained expectations. With repetition, however, their experiences are slowly cleansed of personal and cultural programming. The mystical traditions around the globe tell us that if we want to experience the reality called God as it is in itself, we must give up every preconception we have about this reality. This means surrendering every religious concept of God and every culturally programmed expectation of what the encounter will be like. We must enter the "veil of unknowing" through which no concept, not even a conceptualizing mind, is allowed to pass. At this highly refined level, the differences that marked earlier mystical experiences disappear. Not all mystics reach this advanced level, but those who do offer the same report upon their return. Beyond the veil, they tell us, lies a reality beyond words, beyond concepts, beyond dogmas. Here there is only a bountiful transparency that underlies even the Oneness of life.

A final analogy for the collective perspective. Imagine a huge table on which have been dumped the pieces of a massive jigsaw puzzle. You are one of ten people sitting around the table, each trying to piece together one section of the larger puzzle. As you find and assemble the pieces that belong to your section, you discover a beautiful, complex design, filled with archetypal themes and aesthetically complete by itself. Meanwhile, each person around the table is discovering a similar phenomenon—a unique design, different from the others but with overlapping symbolism. Each design is so beautiful that it is inherently satisfying to view, so much so that for a while it looks as though the pieces come from not one but ten puzzles jumbled together. With continued work, however, the puzzle-menders begin to find that the ten designs can be interconnected. As they bring the individual parts together, something startling emerges. Each design, while complete in itself, fits together with the other designs to form a massive picture of incredible complexity and scope. As beautiful as each individual design is, the beauty of the assembled whole is many times greater.

It is my belief that we are at a point in history that is comparable to the position of the ten puzzle-menders joining their puzzles into a larger whole. We have long appreciated the richness of our individual religions and now are moving into a new phase of the game. The challenge of the twenty-first century is to understand the larger whole that each culture, each race, each religion contributes to. We must find ways of affirming the truth contained in every part while simultaneously opening ourselves to the larger truth expressed in the whole. Is the timing of this convergence accidental, coming as it does at precisely that point in history when we are collectively trying to come to terms with our unprecedented ability to exterminate all life on this planet? It seems that on both religious and political fronts, to continue in adversarial confrontation hastens our destruction, while opening to a larger vision of what our collective life is about moves us into the next phase of history. I deeply believe that our future lies in expanding our concept of nation, of history, and of Spirit to global proportions.

The popularity of reincarnation in the West is a symptom of this blending of world views into a larger synthesis. The invitation reincarnation extends to Christians is to open to a larger understanding of God's activity in human history. It invites Christians to enter an arena of exchange where the outcome is yet to be determined. Reincarnation encourages them to learn freely from other religions while remembering that they have something unique to contribute as well. It reinforces those forces in Christianity that are already moving past the religious exclusivity of the past, helping to build a common future while there is still time.

The fact that approximately one quarter of the adult Christians in America have already adopted reincarnation is not a sign that their faith is decaying but that it is growing. Their faith is not weak but adventuresome. It is being revitalized by serious contact with the other side of God's globe. If reincarnation is, as it is assumed in this book, simply a fact of nature—a fact that requires not faith but only careful research to discover—then it is a fact that Christianity will eventually accommodate itself to. It will do this because its God is the God of creation, and therefore anything that is part of the natural order of creation cannot be rejected. Nor can anything in the natural order threaten Christianity's message of eternal life and the abiding love of God.

7

Reincarnation and the Family

For most of us, the family was the nucleus within which we first experienced life. Here we first learned what human beings were, what we meant to each other, and what sharing life entailed. Through it we first met ourselves, discovering who we were by interacting with those who were here before us. Years before we even realized what was happening, the family was holding our soul in its hands, profoundly shaping how we would thereafter touch life.

If the people with whom we spend these critical years are connected to us only through chance, then surely chance rules the Universe and every semblance of meaning is just accident. As there is no meaning in accidents, we are without meaning, however much we desperately try to assign some to ourselves. We are an anomaly of life, an experiment created out of a trillion chance events randomly thrown out over billions of years. Yet anyone who has ever experienced deeply the presence of meaning in life knows that it cannot be this way. Reincarnation tells us that it is not so and helps us understand the presence of meaning in the beginnings of life.

From a reincarnationist perspective, infancy and childhood is a long, protracted process of awakening. As most of us have been on this planet many times before, reached maturity and known death many times, we are not seeing this for the first time. Yet each time it has a quality of freshness, as though it truly were for the first time. We have cycled again. It takes many years before we discover who we are and what our life is about, many years before we begin to see the project of our life in any outline, before the challenges we have chosen to incorporate into this lifecycle emerge and confront us. But long before any of this, we rest within our family, being prepared for the journey. Here our innermost self is shaped by those beings into whose care the Universe, God, or karma has entrusted us when we were at our most fragile and impressionable stage of development.

If we live thousands of years, cycling time and again to earth, taking form in different bodies, different centuries, and different cultures, what could be more natural than to collect traveling companions along the way? Once we see ourselves as beings of infinite duration, it becomes obvious that relationships that would last through many lifecycles would tend to develop. How utterly artificial if it were otherwise, if every relationship we started in life had to be completed by the time both bodies had perished. How much more natural the vision that in every life we are beginning some relationships, developing others in the complex middle years, and finishing still others, separating in peace and eternal friendship.

Once we open to these possibilities, don't they seem true to our experience? There are persons we meet with whom we immediately feel a depth of connectedness that is completely inappropriate to the circumstances. After we scrape away the projections, much remains that is not projection. We feel somehow at peace with them, as though we have weathered much together, and our spirits naturally open to them. They may be persons we meet only once or persons introduced into our lives at any stage. They may be our age or not, but we experience how easy it is to know them and to be known by them. With them there is often an uncanny sense of picking up where we left off. This kind of rapport bespeaks years of work together, with much explored and much overcome.

With others there is a contrasting kind of familiarity. With these people we experience an immediate threat the minute we enter their presence. We cannot be around them without being on guard, no matter how innocent they appear to others and even to ourselves when we attend only to outward appearances.

The variations on unfinished relationships are endless. Occasionally we meet someone toward whom we experience an immediate and powerful attraction, something very deep but more a raw intensity than something deeply explored. Possibly a love relationship has been started somewhere but has not yet run the full cycle of development and closure. Perhaps the next stage of development will take place in this life, perhaps it is marked for another, but we feel the connection as we pass each other in time.

From a reincarnationist perspective, there are two types of families in which we are imbedded, soul families and biological families. The concept of soul family carries different meanings for different authors, but in general it speaks of a family of beings whose relatedness extends beyond one lifecycle. In some contexts, the concept of soul family reflects the belief that people travel together in groups from the beginning to the end of their human experience. We might think of them as classes going through school together. These family members might not ever cross paths during one physical lifecycle, but they are always connected to one another psychically. If one of them succeeds in resolving a particular life challenge, all of them are nourished, while another's failure also touches them all.

In a broad sense, as I shall use the term here, one's soul family consists of those with whom one shares joint adventures extending over many lifetimes. They may be persons we have come to know, trust, and love through our previous lives together, or conversely ones we have wronged. Through our many lives we've obviously made mistakes, and mistakes injure people, creating bonds of ill will. Thus we may be in conflict with members of our soul family because of misunderstandings that have not healed, injuries sustained without compensation, and wounds still unforgiven. These persons too become our traveling companions, badgering us until we treat them with the respect they deserve or until we compensate them for the loss we have caused them.

In shared dreams and joint projects, in struggle and conflict, in love and hate, our soul family is comprised of those persons we are working with in this lifecycle. They are the cast in our karmic script. They know us better than most, influence us and receive from us more deeply than most, and are usually the pivotal people around whom we make our most important life choices. These are the people who, if we do not "do right by" now, will resurface later in our life, if not in this cycle then in another. They are bonded to us because they present us with those basic predicaments in life where we must choose either to grow into a larger being than we are or to resist development. If we resist, sooner or later we must be brought back to the same choice point, for the nature of all life is toward growth. When we are brought back to this point, it will often (though not always) be in the company of this same person who, for reasons of his or her own development, is involved in the flip side of our predicament.

Of the two families, obviously the soul family is more seminal to our journey. It is with them that we take the next step in our development, that we polish ourselves, that we become more than we are. Is it any surprise, therefore, that we should often find some members of our soul family in our biological family? How natural to discover in these enclaves that shape us so profoundly individuals with whom the life-bonds are especially strong. Karma is marked by intensity of relationship, and some of our most intense relationships are often found here.

How would adopting a reincarnationist perspective influence how we think about and experience our biological families? What options would open if we came to see our family members as time travelers gathered together in this particular configuration for mutual growth? In exploring the possibilities, we must keep our eye on both our family of origin and the family we give birth to ourselves. Let us begin by looking at birth and the early parenting experience.

Few experiences in life can match the experience of giving birth. For those couples who give themselves over to it deeply, who prepare for it physically, emotionally, and spiritually, it can open life to its core. It is simply an awesome event, one to which words seldom do justice. We may go on and on about the energy, the power, the insights, and the love, but unless the person we are talking to has had the experience, he or she just nods politely and thinks we have simply become caught up in the euphoria of birth. And of course we have. It is one of the places where the currents of life run close to the surface, and it's completely intoxicating.

For one-timers, the experience of birth is often surrounded by an awesome feeling of creating life, perhaps of co-creating life in partnership with God. Such a couple tend to experience their infant as coming "from them." It represents a blending of their two natures and thus is an expression of their love and their choice of each other as life companions. They watch carefully to catch a glimpse of a physical feature, a mannerism, or a personality trait that echoes some aspect of their partner or themselves, sometimes reaching far back into the family tree for the resemblance. Before she is two weeks old, little Stephanie will be divided up a hundred different ways by her grandparents, aunts and uncles, friends and neighbors, but all this is their way of welcoming her and loving her. She is a new creation, a unique mixing of two lineages that reach back further than our records can trace.

Reincarnation does not negate these sentiments so much as place them in a larger context, shifting the emphasis to the preexisting (Over)soul that is returning to earth in this child. Because Stephanie existed before this birth, as her Oversoul, the body and personality she takes from us are not what she *is* but more the *medium* she has chosen to live and work in. From among all the thousands of parents available, she has chosen to draw her form from us and to complete with us the next phase of her development. Reincarnation does not cheapen the experience of becoming a parent, as one-timers often fear. The fact that Stephanie has in some other life been someone else's child does not make our relationship with her less special or less sacred. To live many lifecycles does not water down the significance or experience of this lifecycle. Reincarnation simply reframes the parenting experience. It invites us to see ourselves *cooperating* with creative processes of enormous complexity. We open our lives to the Universe and a being comes to us who needs us to complete itself; in the process we receive exactly whom we need to complete ourselves. The extraordinary intricacy of the pairing of parents and children is breathtaking and unerring. It is a coupling of destinies every bit as precise as the genetic coupling biologists attend to. The fit is always precise; a delicate interweaving of necessities and opportunities, of what must be and what might be.

Understanding the logic of reincarnation helps us understand something every mother has always known, that each of our children is unique from the start, with its own distinctive likes, dislikes, fears, and aptitudes. Each comes into life with its own agenda, behaving differently even in the womb. We do not condition their personalities into them but from the very beginning work with a personality that is already in place.

From a reincarnationist perspective, our responsibility as parents is to help our children discover and develop the persons they already are. We are entrusted with the responsibility to watch over this unfolding, to help our children through the rough spots, perhaps to help them learn the limitations of certain ways of being in the world, but always to begin by deeply accepting the person before us. Reincarnation encourages us to watch carefully and assume little about what our child should and shouldn't be. As guardians of this soul, we must be attentive to signs of its agenda in life. We did not create it nor do we own it in any way, even for a time.

We are gardeners assisting but never mastering the processes of creation. We prepare the ground but we do not actually create the being who comes, even though it draws its shape from our genetic codes. We do not ultimately control the forces of nature we direct. Each tree has its own shape. We water it, pour the energy of our life into it, and wait attentively to see what it is, how it will grow, and what it will need. We make decisions for it—pruning it, guiding it in a new direction, removing obstacles—always based on our best sense of what is good for the tree itself. We are stewards of life, guardians of the next generation of incarnating souls.

There is so much that we don't know about our child. What adventures has she already collected from life? What lessons has she learned and what gifts does she bring to share with us? We seldom even know how old she is. We know the minute her body was born, but how old is her soul? Is she a young one, with only a few cycles under her belt, or is she one of the old souls we've heard about, well seasoned through thousands of years of cycling? Such a basic thing and we usually don't have a clue. We don't even know what her age is in relation to our own. The soul of the little bundle we cuddle on our chest in the dark hours of the night may be thousands of years older than ourselves. It gives one pause.

Reincarnation's great gift to the parent–child relationship, it seems to me, is that it leads us to approach our children with great openness. Because we cannot simply use ourselves as reference points for understanding them, we can only wait to see who and what they are in their own right. Reincarnation invites us to see our children truly as guests in our home, entrusted to our care for purposes of mutual development. It restores true equality of spirit without telling us to abandon our roles as parents.

This last point is important. I have sometimes heard foolish parents invoke reincarnation as an excuse for poor parenting. "Mary is an old soul, that's why we let her make her own decisions." (Too much of the time.) Tommy is a sandbox tyrant; "he must have former lives as a warrior." (If so he was probably belligerent then too.) These speculative fantasies are capricious and dangerous to our children. To be aware that our children have a history that predates their present life does not mean that they are not now children or that we are not now their parents. In the larger scheme of things my child may be centuries older than I, but in this life I am still her parent and as such must assume the often unpleasant responsibilities of discipline and training. As I do so, however, I can never lose sight of the larger picture, of the soul living for a few years in a child's body. The body is deceptive. If we pay attention only to it, it will always lead us to underestimate the deeper truth of the person.

Our destinies are inseparably linked to those of our children. From a reincarnationist perspective, there are no accidents in life. Fate is karma, and our children's karma is not outside our own but part of it, and vice versa. The web of energy that brings events into our lives includes our children's destinies as well. Thus we can meet their tragedies and good fortunes with the same openness with which we meet our own. How do we rise to its challenges and escape the traps hidden within it? What are we to learn from it?

This is true both for external events, such as car accidents and premature deaths, and for the karma of their personalities as well. At times our children's personalities seem exquisitely crafted to rub ours the wrong way. Beyond their uncanny ability to find and inflame every flaw in our psychological makeup, these children seem to possess a nature in diametric conflict with our own. They want from us things we do not know how to provide, or they hit all our sensitive spots simply by being themselves. From a reincarnationist perspective, these conflicts must be accepted as karmic and therefore not made the fault of the child, who in this case simply happens to be the agent of forces larger than herself. All of these difficulties have cause and purpose in our life. However difficult these karmically embedded conflicts initially are, they always hold great opportunity for us if we accept their challenges and manage them well.

Turning to our families of origin, to our own parents and siblings, what possibilities for reenvisioning these relationships emerge from adopting a reincarnationist perspective? Can it help us come to terms with what has already happened, and if so, how?

Schooled in popular Western psychology from our birth, most of us are accustomed to understanding the traits of our personalities as deriving from our treatment in the home, primarily from our parents but sometimes from siblings or other caretakers. If only they had done a better job, then I would not be the way I am today. "If they had paid more attention to me when I spoke to them, perhaps I would not be such a compulsive show-off now." Or "If they had been more generous to me then, perhaps I would not feel like a bottomless pit of needing now." From a reincarnationist perspective, however, this gets everything backward. It puts the cart before the horse.

The rule of thumb for reincarnation is "I do not have the problems I have in life because I have these parents, but rather I have these particular parents because I have chosen to work on these particular issues." Our existence predates our birth. Our larger history has positioned us to work on certain specific issues in this lifecycle. These issues will be the ones around which our entire life will focus. They will recur in one form or another in different areas of our life—in childhood relationships, in courtship, in marriage, in our career, in our health, with our children, with ourselves. They will keep confronting us until we solve them, until we break their code, until we free ourselves from the inner programming that binds us to them.

Viewed from this perspective, our parents are not the cause of our problems but the first occasion of their manifesting in our lives. Our life has drawn these particular people to us, not the other way around. Their assets and liabilities as parents are exquisitely used to force a particular issue to the front of our awareness. In the deepest sense, what is in our lives can only come to us from within ourselves. Our early caretakers only create the conditions that bring certain patterns latent within us to the surface, where we can face them. These patterns become fixed in our personality structure in the early formative years where they will remain to assist or torment us until we do something about them. The Hindu term for these constitutive life-patterns is *samskara*. The samskara form the riverbed through which our awareness of life flows. The dynamics of karma operating through our parents is the same as for karma in other contexts. Karma orchestrates circumstances and events in our lives to bring to the surface attitudes, emotions, or beliefs that are already within us. Karma is not something that happens to us but is always an expression of a preexisting conditioning that derives from another time and place. By reactivating that conditioning we create the opportunity to resolve and transcend it.

Our parents are karmic for us and so are their foibles. Their imperfections are put to the service of our perfection by awakening our own imperfections within us, forcing us to see them and hopefully to deal with them. As for our parents and us, so too for us and our children. Try as we may to be the perfect parents for our children, we fail. If we don't repeat our own parents' mistakes with us, we make new ones. Our children must struggle with the imperfections we awaken in them as we do with those our parents awakened in us. As enigmatic as it may sound at first, our imperfections are perfect for the beings entrusted to our care.

Let's not get ourselves trapped into thinking of these imperfections solely in terms of clinical psychopathology, for that would be to see only a small part of the whole. From one's parents, for example, one may learn that material wealth is important in life, even crucial to one's sense of self-value. Some individuals leave home with this belief deeply ingrained in their world view only to find that their life seems fiendishly contrived to demonstrate its invalidity. Perhaps they will amass enormous material wealth and still feel a persistent hollowness gnawing at them from within, or perhaps they will lose everything repeatedly until eventually they discover a contentment that has nothing to do with material goods. Or to take another example, perhaps individuals learn from their parents a particular formula for what it means to be "a man" or a "real woman," and yet when they use that formula later in relationships, their world comes crashing down around their ears. Life is giving them feedback on certain pieces of programming they have picked up along the way, programming moved to the front but not genuinely initiated by their parents.

The perfecting of life is a lengthy adventure with many truths to be discovered and refined along the way. One may acquire, for example, an unquestioning respect for and allegiance to the Church or State in one life that needs to be balanced out in another by learning the consequences of entrusting too much responsibility for one's life to institutions. Or one may learn the early lessons of self-sacrifice in one life only to balance this out in a later life by learning what ought not be sacrificed even for the apparent good of another. There is no way to catalogue everything Life has to teach us; only a fool would attempt to define grades and lesson plans. We look around us and see millions of people struggling with their unique trials and can trust that all of them are part of the curriculum.

Which slice of this curriculum we have singled out for ourselves is often foreshadowed in our nuclear families. Our families focus us in life, not unalterably but profoundly. Their service for us ultimately is to distill something in our lives, to launch us on our adventure by crystallizing something within us. How liberating it is for all parties when we finally learn enough about how life works to absolve our parents and siblings from all the supposed injuries we suffered at their hands. From a reincarnationist perspective, even if they were at fault, they are not to blame. We alone are completely responsible for everything that occurs in our lives, and in this responsibility lies a tremendous freedom. Once we assume full responsibility for our destinies, our destinies suddenly become easier to change. When we assume responsibility for writing the script, we naturally forgive the actors for their parts in the play, and in that forgiveness we demonstrate that we have learned what the play is about, at least up to this act. Forgiveness is a tricky thing. There are levels and levels to it before we reach rock bottom, before we truly forgive without holding something back. At the deepest levels, we must forgive the Reality which is behind all intermittent realities. We must forgive the Universe itself, or the Tao, or God, or whatever name we give to the source of everything that exists. When we begin to forgive this we truly begin to make giant strides.

8
The Web of Life

Reincarnation speaks to us of a connectedness to life. It tells us that this moment in time is connected to other moments in the distant past and future. It reminds us of the existence of deep currents moving through history, trajectories arching across hundreds and thousands of years. It embeds our present in a history that is larger than our physical bodies can partake of. It reminds us that we are essentially spiritual beings whose contours only emerge when we look beyond the physical body and peer deep into history and beyond time itself.

Yet the connectedness reincarnation speaks of is more than a connectedness reaching across lifetimes; it is also a connectedness that saturates our present life. If we imagine our connectedness across lives as vertical, this connectedness is horizontal. It is our connection to specific people, places, and conditions. It encompasses the givens of birth and the "accidents" of history that together interact to create our personal destiny. I call this horizontal connectedness the *web of life*.

The web of life is a web of energy that underlies and underpins the other causalities of our life. It is the spiritual-causal matrix within which our physical lives are suspended, the energy constellation of our interlocking karmic scripts. The web of life includes all those people who belong in our lives and in whose lives we belong. It includes our parents, our brothers and sisters, our husbands and wives, our children, our lifelong friends and enemies, and a wide assortment of people who insert themselves at strategic points in our lives. It includes everyone who influences us deeply and whom we influence. It even includes the driver of the car that may run the red light twenty years from now and end this cycle for me.

Though we can think of ourselves as living at the center of this web, in actuality there is no center. Or better, we might say that there are many centers and *no absolute center*. Each of us is the center of our own web while simultaneously standing on the perimeter of other webs. In our many capacities, we are drawn into each other's lives. With some we are lifelong companions while our tenure with others is brief. The karma of these interactions is always balanced. I would not be in your life nor would you be in mine if the karmic draw were not reciprocal. To bring us together, the karmic filament must be fastened at both ends. Because of this reciprocity, it is in the end pointless to think in terms of "my web" or "your web." It may be helpful for us to do so to make a particular point, but the metaphor of the web discourages such distinctions. It emphasizes instead the larger patterns of life we are embedded in. These larger patterns are not vague, amorphous fields but patterns of precise and defined relationships. There is nothing fuzzy about karma and therefore nothing fuzzy about an individual's particular web.

The web of life is a metaphor that can help us reconceptualize not only our social embeddedness but also our relationship to time. If we think of ourselves as centered within a constellation of energy that is drawing certain people, certain places, and certain events into our lives, we can begin to develop a feeling for ourselves as a being existing outside of this particular moment—as spread across time, so to speak. If people and events that will prove to be decisive to my unfolding are already being slowly drawn to me through some reciprocal attraction, then I might think of myself as existing in some sense outside today. If part of my karmic script is to find, fall in love with, and marry a particular person, then part of me is even now reaching out across time to bring this person into my life and vice versa. Therefore, at least part of my energy—part of *me*, if you will—is not confined to the energy of this twenty-four-hour period, but instead reaches outward toward a future that is, in some respects at least, inevitable. If my energy reaches beyond the present, in some sense I reach beyond the present. I exist then in addition to now.

Similarly, we can use the concept of the web of life to reconceptualize our spatial identity, to begin thinking of ourselves as existing outside the particular physical place our body occupies. If my life is connected to lives separated from me not only by time but by great distances, then somehow my very being must be such as to allow these connections. In the end, it seems artificial to distinguish between the energy that constitutes me and the energy that creates the relationships that hold the key to my future unfoldment. I am not some solid "thing" connected to other things through filaments of energy. Rather, I exist as living energy who together with other nuclei of living energy form the tapestry of energy I call here the web of life.

As we begin to appreciate our connectedness to other humans, we eventually are led to expand our conception of the beings that generate this connectedness. If our interconnected webs reach out across time and space, then we reach out across time and space. It is only our bodies and that part of our minds most closely associated with our bodies that are caught in the space/time intersection of here and now. The spiritual side of our being ranges free of such limitations. We might therefore think of our bodies and our body-minds as crystallizations in time-space of a larger life form that also exists even now beyond time-space.

THE WEB IS ALIVE

As we saw in the preceding chapter, karmic scripts are not predestined necessities that squeeze all choice out of life. They are rather the careful bringing together of people and circumstances to create opportunities for learning. How we choose within these opportunities influences not just our distant karmic future but our present as well. This brings us to the single most important characteristic of the web: It is alive. The web of life is conscious and reactive. It responds to us in subtle ways that exceed our understanding of causal processes. It expresses a creative intelligence by responding to our choices as we go through life. The flow of events in which we live is itself alive to our choosing.

How strange this idea sounds to our ears! It is practically impossible to go through twelve years of schooling followed by college and professional training without becoming deeply conditioned to think of nature as a massive, lifeless machine. Quantum physicists may have begun to demonstrate that particles behave at times as though they were conscious, but most of our scientific and social-scientific disciplines still conceptualize the universe in mechanistic, Newtonian terms. Thus the only causations our educational institutions train us to recognize are those we can quantify and summarize in mathematical equations. The world we quantify is intelligent in its own way, but its intelligence is of a lower order than human intelligence. It does not think or make choices as we do.

What is true of nature is also true of history. Though the calculus of history's ins and outs is more subtle in some ways than the calculus of nature's causes and effects, historical events are also seen as lacking intentionality. If we learn something from history, that is an option we exercise as conscious beings, but it is not something history sought for us.

Trained to think in this intellectual environment, it is practically inevitable that we come to view the flow of events that carry us through life as devoid of personal meaning for us. In this world view, we exist as inflated molecular chains, bumping into each another in an atomistic world of meaningless association. Randomness tears blindly through the fabric of life, throwing us back upon the virtues of accommodation and heroic gestures. In today's intellectual environment, to suggest anything else smacks of superstition, yet that is precisely what is being suggested here.

It is an ancient idea—that the rhythms of our life express an intentionality beyond molecular, electromagnetic, or genetic intentionality. That within the pulsations of our life is an intentionality that responds not just to the choices we have made in previous lives but to the choices we are making now. Though we cannot quantify these responses or explain them to our complete satisfaction, we can often observe them if we watch life carefully and know where to look.[1]

WORKING WITH THE WEB

The key to working with the web of life is to understand the rhythms of our life as an ongoing dialogue that exists to facilitate our personal growth. The web is alive and reactive. We make choices and it responds to our choices. It reconfigures itself around us, surrounding us with new conditions, giving us feedback on the choices we've made. When the Chinese consult the *I Ching* to better understand what life is trying

---

[1] By invoking the metaphor of the web of life I am attempting to point to patterns that manifest in life. I am not suggesting that we understand very much about the intelligence or mechanisms that are generating these patterns. When I speak of the web "sensing and responding" to our choices, I am using personification to describe intelligible relationships, not a ghostly "thing." Though we would like to know more than we do about the underlying mechanisms (or agents) responsible for these interactions, our incomplete knowledge should not stop us from recognizing the patterns themselves.

to teach them in a given situation, they say they are "consulting the Sage." Some sages live on mountain passes or in remote ashrams. This Sage, however, is always near at hand. It is the field within which we live and breathe; it is the ever-changing context of our existence here and now.

Carl Jung, a famous Swiss psychiatrist, often observed in therapy that when his patients engaged what he called the archetypal level of the psyche, synchronicities frequently began to occur in their lives. He defined synchronicity as an "acausal connecting principle," by which he meant that two events were meaningfully related even though they were not physically related. (Rather than call these acausal events, I would rather say that their causality is mediated nonphysically, rather than physically.) When Jung's patients reached this very deep level of exploration and self-healing, the world surrounding them would often begin to behave magically, as it were. Meaningful "coincidences" would begin to multiply in their lives. It was as though the universe itself were conspiring to support their search for wholeness. Jung speculated that reaching the archetypal level of the psyche released or engaged powerful energies that had the capacity to orchestrate even physical events in some unexplained way.[2]

Synchronicities occur in many contexts and take many forms. Examples are more common than one might at first think. Many people have had the experience of being wakened in the middle of the night by a striking dream in which a close relative comes to them and tells them good-bye. He or she reassures them that all is well, that they are content, and then they leave. The next morning word is received that this person unexpectedly died overnight. One of my students described a variation on this pattern in her journal. She wrote: "Recently, I was playing golf and I got the overwhelming sense that something was terribly wrong. I couldn't put my finger on it, but something was awful. When I got home, my husband told me that he had gotten a phone call telling of the death of a very dear friend in North Carolina." No presently known physical causal connection links this woman's sudden shift in mood and her friend's death, but there does appear to be a meaningful connection nonetheless.

Perhaps we are working on an important project and getting nowhere. Events seem to conspire to prevent us from accomplishing what we want. Then we pull back and reassess the situation. We may

---

[2] See Carl Jung *Synchronicity: An Acausal Connecting Principle*. A good secondary on synchronicity is Ira Progoff's *Jung, Synchronicity and Human Destiny*.

change only our attitude toward the project and suddenly doors begin to open and phones begin to ring. In these situations it is not just wishful thinking to suspect that there might be a relation between changing something inside ourselves and the outer world's availability to us.

When synchronicities come up in our lives, it is as though the universe is speaking to us. It is getting our attention or pointing us in a particular direction. They tend to occur at times of great import. Sometimes they help us see where we should go, warning us of a hidden dead end behind a particular choice or of unexpected turns in the road ahead. At other times they come to us only after we have made a difficult decision, as if to comment on our choice.

One of my students not long ago shared with me an experience in the latter category. She was a woman in her early thirties, divorced and raising two children. In her journal she wrote:

> I had an experience this week which proved to me something I've known but at times doubted. When a person follows a true path you can't go wrong. I've said this but must not have believed it, because when it happened it was like, "Wow! It does work!" I'll try to relate this in as few words as possible.
>
> I broke up a long-term relationship three weeks ago after I realized the other person was not willing to work on the relationship anymore. I felt that to stay in it would be compromising my integrity since I knew how unhealthy it would be to stay. Financially, this break was disastrous. I'm at school on a 4-year scholarship and grant but needing to run my household and support two kids on next to little is scary. So I said to myself if I do what I know is right and put myself back on my true path, I know my physical needs will be taken care of. I've believed this over the years, but it's easy to believe something one has never had to test.
>
> So, I made the break and the next couple of weeks were havoc with my significant other moving out. Several times I kept telling myself the above (perhaps out of desperation). Anyway, yesterday, my professor told me I will be getting paid for the research I'm assisting on and long-overdue child support started coming in unexpectedly.
>
> Now, what does any of this have to do with reincarnation? A lot. We are spiritual beings living on this physical plane and apt to fall into human traps and forget who we are and the bigger picture of our existence, and this week I was reminded of the big picture and validated through positive reinforcements for following it.

As I was preparing the final draft of this book I came across a passage from Joseph Campbell that struck me as being almost a commentary on this woman's experience. It reads:

> But if a person has had the sense of the Call—the feeling that there's an adventure for him—and if he doesn't follow that, but remains in the society because it's safe and secure, then life dries up. And then he comes to that condition in late middle age: he's gotten to the top of the ladder, and found that it's against the wrong wall.
>
> If you have the guts to follow the risk, however, life opens, opens, opens up all along the line. I'm not superstitious, but I do believe in spiritual magic, you might say. I feel that if one follows what I call one's "bliss"—the thing that really gets you deep in the gut and that you feel is your life—doors will open up. They do! They have in my life and they have in many lives that I know of.[3]

The Taoist sages say that we can be sure a given path is our proper path when it lies "downhill where the water runs." When we are aligned with our karmic scripts, our lives have a sense of flowing like water running downhill. Things will tend to fall into place without strenuous exertion. It may have the feeling of "what we'd rather be doing anyway." Thus Taoism encourages us to pursue our destinies by following the path of least resistance. This does not mean that finding and following this path will not require work or sacrifice, but rather that when we find our true path, it will feel like the most natural course for us to take and therefore—all things considered—it will offer us the least resistance.

As we incarnate in order to learn through being challenged, we do not find "downhill where the water runs" without accepting the challenges embedded in our lives. The most dramatic instances of synchronicity I have witnessed have occurred when someone is struggling with one of those fundamental questions that will determine the course of his or her life for a considerable period of time. These contests are what give our lives their distinctive shape. They are the big choices: Which career will I pursue? Will I forgive a long-standing grievance or

---

[3] The passage continues: "There's a wonderful paper by Schopenhauer, called 'An Apparent Intention of the Fate of the Individual,' in which he points out that when you are at a certain age—the age I am now—and look back over your life, it seems to be almost as orderly as a composed novel. And just as in Dickens' novels, little accidental meetings and so forth turn out to be main features in the plot, so in your life. And what seem to have been mistakes at the time turn out to be directive crises. And then he asks: 'Who wrote this novel?'" (From *An Open Life*, Joseph Campbell in conversation with Michael Toms, pp. 24–25.)

retaliate? Will I take the risk and change careers? To list the choices is to recite the litany of the human drama. Will I end the marriage or try again? Will I accept the fact that I am addicted? Will I be a coward when the shooting starts? Sometimes these crises jump out at us suddenly—as in Steve Logan's case, when he had only seconds to choose whether to forgive his father or let him die. More typically, however, they confront us slowly and repetitively. Usually the most important karmic choices we make are those we struggle with through many years.

My sense is that when all is said and done, we spend our entire lives usually learning only a small handful of lessons. Underneath all the details of our lives, beneath all the ins and outs of career, family, health, and so forth, we are actually struggling with only a few basic recurring issues. These are the really big problems or blocks that keep limiting us: "If I could just ease up and not be so driven all the time"; "If I could just stop trying to control the lives of those around me"; "If I could just trust the creativity I feel rising within me"; "If I could just accept myself for who I am"; "If I could just tame this temper of mine"; "If I could just finish what I begin." However we fill in the blanks, we know that if we could just resolve this one particular thing, a new life waits for us. This one thing is the keylog, as the loggers call it, that's jamming up all the others. If we could just free that one log, everything else in our life would begin to flow again.

These basic confrontations take us into an intensely personal arena and present us rare opportunities to change our destinies. The changes may not be immediately apparent to even a careful observer, as in Steve's case with the bicycle accident, but at times they may be. We make a difficult choice, but one we know in our gut is right, and our circumstances slowly take an unexpected turn for the better. We choose to accept a responsibility or to take a gamble, and suddenly things begin to fall into place. I have also seen it appear to happen the other way around. I once watched someone presented with an important opportunity to grow decline it. Shortly thereafter he was passed over for an important job that he seemed ideally qualified for. One never knows how to read such matters, but I have often wondered what might have happened had he accepted the earlier challenge.

Sometimes the blocks in our life exist outside ourselves and reflect conditions over which we appear to have no control. The national economy is driving our business into bankruptcy. A drought has destroyed our crop for two years running. A car accident has shattered our family. A disease is stealing my life from me bit by bit. Yet if karma, reincarnation, and karmic scripts are trustworthy concepts, these events too are part of our curriculum. We have placed ourselves into these experiences for reasons only we can discover. However inscrutable they are at present, in some way we need these experiences. They hold something that we can use, otherwise they would not be in our lives. What is required is not necessarily to understand their meaning for us at a cognitive level but to respond to them as deeply as we can. Our challenge is to use these experiences, to draw from them whatever they hold for us, and to follow them wherever they lead us.

Something inside us has brought these experiences to us. They contain some hidden key for us. If we can find that key and use it, one of two things will happen. Sometimes when we turn the key, the outer circumstances of our life begin to change. Slowly the dark clouds gathering on the horizon begin to break up. The circumstances of our life begin to turn around, now that they have accomplished their end and are no longer needed. At other times, the outer conditions continue unchanged, and we change. Sometimes life simply refuses to let us continue to live as we were. It brings together conditions that mercilessly grind our old self into dust. Perhaps we will not live to see our children grow up. Perhaps we will never get our big break. Perhaps we will never have that one thing we wanted most from life. Sometimes when we turn the key, we find it releasing whatever it is in us that originally convinced us that we needed this particular thing to feel complete. Sometimes it is only by taking from us what we wanted most from life that life can teach us that we are more than we thought we were. We are more than our longings, even our most cherished longings.

There is a distinct feeling that comes with finding and using this key. Whatever happens after that, we know that we have done what was asked of us; we have fulfilled a part of our destiny. This feeling of being on our path, of having just come through a major test and having made the right choice, is unmistakable. It brings a peace that is completely independent of outer circumstances. It is what the *I Ching* means when it says that the greatest good in life is "to live without blame." To live without blame is to be fulfilling our karmic script. Only this sense of fulfilling our destiny brings lasting peace in life. In the end, it matters little how much suffering comes into our life, for suffering alone cannot take away this peace nor can the absence of suffering confer it. What matters is how well we use the suffering that comes to us—or, for that matter, how well we use whatever comes to us.

As I said in Chapter 4, I do not think we should assume that *every* detail of our lives is karmically intentioned. It may well be that even some of the major difficulties we must face in life were not central to our karmic script. Perhaps they were seen as inconveniences we were willing to put up with or risks we were willing to run in order to take advantage of other possibilities that this particular life offered us. Perhaps they were not foreseen at all. In the end, it makes little difference, because unanticipated events can be used for personal growth just as well as anticipated events. What is important is not what happens to us, but how effectively we use what happens to us. Asking "Why is this happening to me?" is much less productive than asking "How can I maximally respond to what is happening to me?" None of our effort is wasted. We will find out the whys after class is over, and no doubt there will be some surprises. What appears significant to us in the valley may not look the same from the hilltop, and we may discover significances there we are totally unaware of here.

CHANGES IN THE WEB

Karmic causalities are variations on the theme of growth. We make choices within a field of possibilities and the web responds. These changes may surface suddenly or gradually. The sudden ones are easier to spot, but I suspect the more common pattern is for these changes to enter our life gradually—so gradually that we may not even notice their arrival or associate them with our previous choices.

To see the causal rhythmns of our lives, we must look at large blocks of time. To recognize the connections between choices made and changes in circumstance, we must develop a feeling for our lives as an organic whole. A life is an organic process of great complexity. It therefore tends to move slowly. There is a trajectory to each of our lives, an arch that gives it its distinctive character and familiarity. This arch expresses our karmic momentum in time space. This momentum is defined by our relationships, our careers, where we live, and so on. *This momentum cannot be changed suddenly.* However change manifests in our lives, its roots reach deep into the fabric of our choices. When major turning points come upon us suddenly, they are the cumulative expression of many smaller choices we have made over many years.

When we decline an opportunity to grow, our life loses a little of its momentum toward change. If we decline another, it loses a little more. If we keep this up, eventually opportunities for growth begin to disappear completely. Our lives may take on a flat appearance. There is little going on except the day-to-day routine. Nothing new enters the horizon, nothing exciting, nothing challenging. Our life has slowed down to its lowest evolutionary track. We begin to experience our life as something we are passively inheriting instead of something we are creating. Worst of all, there does not appear to be anything we can do to change this condition.

But if we begin to seek growth earnestly, even if we just want it deeply, an opportunity for growthful change will be drawn to us, often unrecognized at first for what it is. An opportunity may come up to exchange something we have for an unknown. Usually we must give up something to make room for the new, and we typically can see what we are giving up much more clearly than what we are getting. Whatever it is, it is different and it asks something from us. If we give it, growth gains a little momentum in our life. If we could step back and watch the process from a distance, we would soon see another opportunity come along. The Universe is interested in promoting our growth. It cannot help but respond to our efforts to grow by giving us more openings. As the saying goes, "God helps those who help themselves."

Each time we accept an opportunity to grow, change gathers a bit more momentum in our lives. If we are open to genuine personal growth, we will find that the opportunities coming to us will begin to point us in that direction. What we are asked to give up will become more difficult, the confrontations more challenging, and the rewards greater. This happens simply because growth is the natural order of things. When we choose to grow, we align ourselves with Nature and therefore begin to receive her full attention and support.

When we begin to accept the challenge of changing how we live our lives, a certain flowering starts to take place. This may take either an external or internal form, or both. A person may begin to experience a certain material prosperity in his or her life or a more subtle, but unmistakable, interior sense of well-being. For those deeply committed to personal growth, this prosperity may take the form of being given still further opportunities to grow. Externally their lives may appear to be filled with one hardship after another, yet through these trials they are being given opportunities to engage and release karma.

Because these are lawful processes, they occur with a certain predictability, though not the predictability we associate with controlled laboratory experiments. In the laboratory we simplify nature by eliminating as many variables as possible in order to track the one variable we are interested in. When we study nature outside the lab, however, we seldom have this luxury. Karmic predictability is more like making geological predictions about earthquakes or volcanic eruptions. We can say with reasonable certainty that the quake is going to occur "soon," but we cannot predict the exact day. There are theoretical variables we have not yet identified and factors we cannot quantify. And yet we can monitor the pressure building on the fault, and we can reasonably predict that the plates will begin to slide explosively past each other in the "near future."

The web can bring us people, information, or opportunities exactly when we need them if we are committed to making use of them. I have seen this happen so often that I have almost stopped being surprised by it. How common this experience is was demonstrated to me once again just before I began writing this chapter. After finishing Chapter 7, I needed to clear my head before continuing, so I took a day away from writing to explore the Oregon coast close to where I was then living. In a tourist-information office in a small coastal town, I got into a conversation with a charming lady who worked behind the counter. Her bright eyes sparkled from within a face seasoned with many years. After giving me the information I had asked for, she asked what I did for a living. One thing led to another, and when she found out that I taught, among other things, psychology of religion, she brightened and said that she was doing a lot of study in that area herself. She told me that she was finding her senior years the best years of her life. They were giving her the time and composure to undertake the study and personal development she had come to value so highly. Then she asked if I was familiar with a particular author, which I wasn't, and went on to explain how this person's books had suddenly fallen into her lap recently, bringing her exactly the information she had needed to take the next step in her personal growth. As I smiled and nodded, she went on to say that that's the way it was always happening to her these days. She paused and then said, "Because of this I've finally come to trust Life. I never did before, you see. Now after all these years, I trust Life. This has been the greatest gift of all." I could see in her face and feel in the quiet pause that followed how much this change had meant to her.

This chance meeting, if that's what it was, reminded me that these basic truths are part of all of our lives and will be discovered by anyone who opens to them. There is nothing hidden or esoteric about them. This is simply how life behaves if we allow ourselves to see it. From a reincarnationist perspective, these events make perfect sense. As human existence itself is about learning, we should not be surprised to observe the processes of life supporting our efforts to learn.

Unless we reject the plan proposed to us by our spiritual guides, we enter life with a karmic script. From the start we are embedded in a web of relationships. As we become conscious, we begin making choices and from that point on our life becomes a dialogue between our choices and this web. This dialogue takes place whether or not we are consciously aware of it. Once we become aware of what is happening, we can begin to take greater advantage of the feedback the web gives us. We can listen to it more attentively and learn from it more efficiently. Once we begin to realize the rules of the game, we can become more conscious players. The point of this game is to learn, and we all have the option of becoming more conscious learners.

THE INNER COMPASS

Our curriculum is completely individualized. Our contract is with our Higher Self alone. No one else can tell us what our script is about—not our parents, teachers, drinking buddies, priests, or therapists. One person's script may bring him to religion while across town another person's challenge may be to leave religion for something more personally demanding. My task may be to break free of traditional values while another's may be to learn from them. There are no external rules we can follow to guide us through the most difficult ordeals we face in life. At such points we have only a subtle inner voice to guide us, a gut sense of where our true course lies.

I sometimes ask my students to consider carefully what they would choose if they could have either a map of their entire karmic script or an inner compass with which to orient themselves on their journey through life. With a map they would know the general features of the trail they are on, while with a compass they would know only if they are on or off their path. As tempting as it would be to have a map of our lives, the compass is always the better choice. Even with a map, we can get lost, but never with the compass. Our inner compass is a living awareness of our alignment with our karmic script. If we learn how to use it, it will always tell us whether we are off our course or on, whether we are falling behind or moving ahead of schedule. It is an inner knowing that can be refined into a highly sensitive moment-to-moment guidance system. It is standard issue in the Earth school.[4]

Freud did us a great disservice when he persuaded us that our conscience was just our superego, and our superego just the internalization of parental injunctions. These parental scripts are only the surface layer of a much deeper living voice. The concept of conscience is itself too shallow to do justice to what this inner knowing offers us. It

---

[4] The refinement of this inner compass of intuition is much discussed in New Age literature. See, for example, *Living in the Light*, by Shakti Gawain.

is our lifeline to our Oversoul. As such it has access to information our rational mind lacks. It is not restricted by either time or space as the rational mind is, and this gives it an interesting perspective on matters, to say the least. Most importantly, it knows our karmic script. It is the quiet voice guiding us to and through the confrontations we arranged for ourselves before we were born. It has access to all the information we need to bring our lives to a fruition beyond our wildest dreams.

LIVING IN THE PRESENT

Reincarnation teaches us about a connectedness that stretches across the centuries and runs throughout the fabric of our present life. Yet the more deeply we understand this connectedness, the more we are led to focus our attention on the here and now. Everything of importance crosses our present again and again until it is resolved. If we want to grow spiritually, we need only focus our energies on our present as it exists today, not as we imagine it ought to exist when we get involved in spiritual things. Handling the present well is the key to improving our quality of life. This is what is so grounding about understanding reincarnation and the web of life. It recommends that we do what we were doing anyway—live our lives as they exist right now—but that we do so as consciously as we possibly can. It teaches us to appreciate the full significance of the choices we are making and then to choose boldly. All movement comes from our conscious attention to the ever-changing present.

There is a Zen story that illustrates this point. A Zen master was once asked by an emperor to paint a scroll for the court. On it he was asked to write the essence of the Buddha's wisdom, the secret of his teaching. The master sat down, quickly drew the sign for "Attention," and handed the scroll to the king. The king was surprised and said "Surely there must be more than this." The master obligingly took back the scroll and under the first sign again wrote "Attention." At this point the king, thinking he was being made a fool, became angry and insisted that the master do what he was instructed or forfeit his life. The master again took up his brush and wrote "Attention" a final time. There was simply nothing else to add.

The spiritual masters have always told us that the key to our lives is right under our noses. The spiritual journey begins where we are presently standing. The essence of spirituality is to live fully in the present. This means, first, fulfilling our karmic script, a script that was crafted for our spiritual awakening. Many of the exotic-looking practices we associate with spirituality are simply techniques to deepen our capacity to experience the present moment fully and without distortion. Buddhist *vipassana* meditation, Japanese *kin-hin* (walking meditation), and the Christian practice of the presence of God all focus our attention on the immediate moment of experience. The present is the gateway to our ultimate spiritual destination. We have been on our spiritual path, in dialogue with the Sage, since the day we were born. Once we understand how the web functions, we can make this dialogue more conscious. We can live our lives knowing how the game is played and what is at stake.

Reincarnation teaches us that life is about learning and that all the trappings of our life are merely props to facilitate this learning. Just props. Our careers, our responsibilities, our tragedies, our personalities, our deepest social commitments, our causes. Nothing but props. Nothing is actually as we feel it to be while we are in the valley. We feel so deeply that this or that aspect of life is vitally important. This is real or that is real. My children are real or my disease is real. But none of them would be in our life if they did not play a part in a larger developmental process. Remember that we could have inserted ourselves back into life anywhere on the planet. We could have come into any family, any body, any culture, any nation, perhaps even any historical period we wanted. We are in *this* time and place, with *these* particular people, and living *this* particular script to advance our evolution and that of others. Everything in our life is real in its own right, each person is here pursuing his or her own education along with us, but they are not real in any ultimate sense. We are characters in each other's scripts, props on each other's stage. We are not ultimately real as we exist here in this particular valley. When the time of this valley is over, we shall all climb the hill and resume truer identities. Everything that surrounds us here below is a prop. Even death is a prop, perhaps the greatest prop of all.

This is what the Hindus mean by calling the world *maya*, "illusion." Things are not as they appear. In saying that the world is in the highest sense an illusion, they did not intend to disparage life but to remind us of the larger context in which the physical universe exists. Our amnesia is so complete in the valley and we become so preoccupied with our individual life lessons that this call to remember another world strikes us at first as ridiculous. It is hard for us to pull ourselves away from our personal scripts long enough to remember that they are means and not ends in themselves. They are just courses in school. There is another world, a world of spirit, a world outside linear time. This is where we came from and where we will ultimately return. Large as our physical universe is, we are told by those who have remembered more than we that this spiritual universe is even more vast. Beautiful as our physical world is, the beauty of the spiritual world is greater. Satisfying as life here can be, it does not compare with what awaits us upon the completion of our work. Everything here is part of a larger drama.

The sages tell us that to participate in this drama, we have only to "pay attention." Simply pay attention to what is going on right in front of us and choose wisely. We are exactly where we belong. There is no reason to go elsewhere, just pay attention. At a time when we understood more than we understand now, at a time when we had the advantage of wise counsel, we chose this life. We chose the events that have brought us to this present moment in time, and we can trust that decision. We can trust everything that went into it and the entire system that made it possible. We can trust the benevolence of the Universe and be confident of our ultimate safety in it. We will never know death, and life need only get better from here.

However we choose, the web of our life cannot fail to respond. Its response is not magical but completely natural. We are anchored in the web of life by the collective energy of our past choices. As our present choices change the balance of this energy, the web cannot help but adjust. In the next chapter we examine these processes in greater detail.

The Field Effect

*T*he first verse of the *Dhammapada*, an important Buddhist scripture, reads "You are everything that you have ever thought."
This means that what we now *are* derives from what we have
thought in previous existences and in this existence. In the relentless
chain of causes and effects, all experience follows mind. Where we have
repeatedly focused our attention has created the life form we now exist
as. Our body, our situation in life, our tragedies and good fortune, all
follow mind. What is large in our life does not simply pop into existence
out of nowhere but was cultivated from small beginnings. Our present
aptitudes and "natural talents" reflect skills that have been practiced
elsewhere. The questions and themes that dominate our lives today
have history somewhere. And always it is mind that determines which
themes are growing and which are diminishing in our experience. We
are thus *self-selecting fields of experience*, and these fields have two sides
to them.

THE TWO-SIDED FIELD

In every moment of our life we are living within a field of experience
that we have generated through countless individual choices while

simultaneously making new choices that will either reinforce this field or change it. This field is two-sided. On one side, it is the field of our inner, subjective experience—our interests, aptitudes, wishes, dreams, fears, and so on. On the other side, it is the outer, objective circumstances of our life. These two sides are deeply intertwined and constitute a single karmic configuration. In this chapter we explore various ways in which these two sides interact. In particular, we explore how changes made in one's inner field can sometimes produce startling changes in one's outer field.

Every choice we make creates an experience that possesses a certain emotional energy. As we move through life, the energy of each new experience is added to the energy already collected through our previous experiences to form what we might think of as an aggregate energy mass. This energy mass will obviously reflect the themes of our experience. If we cultivate humor, we collect humor; if we cultivate anxiety, we collect anxiety, and so on. We carry within us the residual feeling-tone of every experience we have ever had. We are the walking repository of all our experiences.[1]

Once an experience enters our system, its emotional energy stays within the system until it is released. Nature has provided us, of course, with many ingenious ways of releasing this energy. Troublesome experiences keep haunting our thoughts, forcing us to attend to what we wish had never happened. Our muscles tense up, inviting us to massage the accumulated stress out of our bodies. Each night in our dreams we dissipate undigested energy collected during our waking hours. And let's not forget how often we yell at our families because we've had a hard day at the office. The point here is that while we have many ways of cleansing this emotional energy from our psychophysical system, the energy we do not remove stays trapped within the system. What we do not remove day by day—either spontaneously or through deliberate exercises—accumulates within our psyches and our bodies. The longer experiences are allowed to stay in our system, the further removed they get from our present awareness and the more difficult they are to retrieve and release.

The energy we collect within ourselves over time cannot avoid eventually precipitating a response in the energy field of our web. It is a natural and inevitable reaction. As a net of energy, the web of life

---

[1] For more on how experiences are internalized and organized according to their emotional content, see Stanislav Grof's description of COEX systems ("systems of condensed experience") in *Realms of the Human Unconscious*, Chapter 3.

InnerOuter
world world

FIGURE 9.1

responds to the energy we gather within ourselves as we go through life. Sooner or later the outer circumstances of our life will shift in response to changes in our inner energy.

The two sides of our field of energy are in constant interaction. To help convey this concept to my students, I sometimes draw the following picture on the board (Figure 9.1). I trace the figure many times to emphasize the repetitive, cyclic quality of the processes involved. The dot at the center of the figure represents the present moment. The right loop represents the outer, physical world and the left our inner, mental world. The purpose of the diagram is to portray the interaction between our inner and outer worlds as mediated by the choices we make in the present. It also depicts the continuous recycling of our past in our future.

The right side of the image pictures the flow of events as they approach us in the physical world. The dot in the center of the figure is our moment to moment consciousness. When an event reaches this point, it has entered our immediate awareness, and we must choose how to respond to it. Our choice will either reinforce or weaken this particular theme in our life. In choosing our response, we create an experience. At that point the physical event becomes a mental event that will now exist as a dynamic force in our inner life.

If we choose to engage a particular event when the moment of contact comes, we reinforce this particular theme in our life and thus increase its energy within the system. For example, if something irritates us and we respond in quick anger, our bad temper is reinforced. Conversely, if we choose not to respond to this trigger with anger but simply let the situation pass, anger's hold on us is reduced. By choosing how we meet the events that confront us in the flow of experience we are constantly altering the energy mass that holds us suspended in our web.[2]

The millions of choices we make as we go through life collect within

---

[2] If we choose to avoid an event altogether or to repress the emotion it triggers, the energy of the event is *increased*, not decreased. Only by admitting something into our awareness but choosing not to engage it is its energy genuinely reduced. Avoidance always signals a continuing entanglement of some kind and thus is a form of engagement.

us and pool their energies. Eventually this energy "curves around" and moves out again into the physical world, drawing to us new events that reflect our changing inner state. Yet even at this advanced stage it is still possible to influence the process, as we shall see below. Thus this movement back out is also drawn through the present, a later present than before. Round and round the energy cycles—the web of life responding to our choosing, our choosing redirecting our lives through time. Self-selecting fields of energy.[3]

INTERVENING IN THE KARMIC CYCLES

As Figure 9.1 indicates, karma cycles through our awareness twice, and we can intervene in the cycle at either point. We intervene in karma first when we choose how we meet events coming at us in the physical world. How we respond to everything life throws at us will either reinforce or weaken these karmic themes in our life. After we have made this choice and an event has entered the mental side of the cycle, we can still influence it. We can reinforce it through mental repetition or fantasy, or we can move to neutralize it. This is an important point. We are not committed to experiencing all of our karmic feedback in the physical world, either later in this life or in a future life. We always have the option of interrupting the cycle before mental karma becomes more physical karma.

The great advantage of intervening on the mental side of the cycle is efficiency. Like the wheels of justice, the wheels of karma move slowly in the physical world. If we choose to engage our karma through repeated rebirths, we can only deal with so much karma each time

---

[3] As the picture is drawn, the loop that gives us feedback on our choices is closed, suggesting that there are no factors influencing our present awareness other than the choices we have already made. If this were truly the case, we would be locked into a closed, deterministic system, condemned to repeat the same choices we have always made in the past. Obviously, I do not want to imply this. No picture can represent every aspect of a situation, and this picture does not depict all the variables operating here. It seeks only to model the feedback loop operating between choice and circumstance. If we wanted to include some representation of the variables that introduce creativity into this feedback loop, we might add an hourglass-shaped funnel extending vertically through the center point (see Figure 9.2). This open-ended funnel would represent our connection to the Oversoul and other spiritual resources.

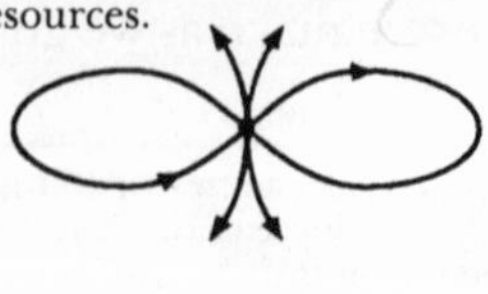

FIGURE 9.2

around. The circumstances and conditions required to produce the confrontations needed to expand our awareness take time to orchestrate on the physical plane. Fortunately, if we are interested in accelerating the process, we can choose to engage our past mentally rather than physically. We can "pay attention" to the deep currents of our inner life through some form of past-life therapy, for example. We can enter into dialogue with our former lives and consciously appropriate their lessons without waiting for these to manifest in the physical domain. Karma only requires that we learn the consequences of our choices; it gives us wide latitude to choose how this learning takes place.

THE FIELD EFFECT

By bringing former-life experiences into our awareness and by appropriating their lessons, we can neutralize the karmic carryover of these past lives in our present life. When we do this, we should expect to be able to observe changes taking place in our physical world, because the external conditions of our present life are rooted in this karma. This is precisely what sometimes happens. I call this the *field effect*. When an individual follows the psychotherapeutic journey to the level of former lives, he or she engages those events which form the matrix of their present life experience and in the process changes this matrix. Changing one's inner field precipitates changes in one's outer field, sometimes rather dramatically.

As discussed in the preceding chapter, we are surrounded by people we have pending karma with. We may be married to them, parenting them, working for them, teaching them, buying a house from them, going into business with them, and so on. They may be intimately close to us or simply in the vicinity, "waiting" for the proper time to come forward in our lives. If we begin to engage and clear the karma that connects us to these people through some type of former-life therapy, we can often observe dramatic changes in our relationships with them as the web of life adjusts to our initiatives. Relationships that were on the brink of self-destructing may be renewed. Other relationships that were just beginning may dissolve precipitously once the karma underpinning them has been made conscious and released. People may move into and out of our lives with amazing speed and intensity. Persons who were on the fringes of our life may suddenly be moved to center stage and demand immediate attention.

Experiencing the field effect can be dizzying and disruptive, especially if you do not understand what is happening. As you engage your former lives, people may come at you from out of the blue and approach you with an intensity that surprises even them. They may be angry at you for little apparent reason, or guilty, or helpful, or romantically interested. Often they feel somewhat at a loss to understand their own emotions and behavior. Meanwhile, you may feel welling up within yourself the emotions that belong to your side of this karmic dyad. You may suddenly feel romantically drawn to people, repulsed by them, responsible for their problems, and so on. If you can resist becoming involved in the scenarios they offer you and simply continue the inner cleansing, you will eventually uncover the former-life connection that ties the two of you to this particular dance. When this connection is made conscious and resolved, the tie is severed. Slowly or suddenly, this person stops coming forward and begins to recede from your life. If you remain friends or acquaintances, at least this particular phase of your relationship has ended.

Even if only you consciously appropriate and integrate the former life memories, both parties are affected. It's like two people holding the ends of a rubber band: Only one has to let go for both to spring apart. As I understand the process, your letting go produces one of two effects on the other persons involved. Either they too will be completely cleared of this particular karmic scenario or they will retain the need to repeat the scenario—but not with you. Either way, you are out of the picture. If they need to repeat the scenario for their own learning process, they will eventually draw to themselves someone to play your role. This may be either someone with whom they have a similar karmic bond or a karmic stand-in; that is, someone who is karmically suited to fulfill this particular role but who comes from a different karmic lineage.

While hypnotherapy is probably the most common method in use today for exploring former lives, the field effect can be triggered by any therapeutic method or spiritual practice powerful enough to access this deep level of consciousness. These methods include Jungian therapy, meditation, and various forms of highly experiential psychotherapy.

Stanislav Grof, for example, has for more than thirty years been a pioneer in developing very intense forms of experiential psychotherapy that combine a number of techniques to precipitate extremely deep therapeutic encounters. While not specifically oriented toward past-life recall, his therapeutic approach sometimes triggers vivid experiences from earlier historical periods that his clients themselves interpret as coming from previous lifetimes. While they are experiencing these sequences, they often are able to identify specific persons in their present life who are the karmic descendants of the protagonists in these former lives.[4] Dr. Grof writes that when this occurs,

> present interpersonal tensions, problems, and conflicts with these persons are frequently recognized or interpreted as being direct derivatives of the destructive karmic patterns. The reliving and resolution of such karmic memories is typically associated [for the subject] with a sense of profound relief, liberation from oppressive "karmic bonds," and feelings of overwhelming bliss and accomplishment.[5]

Even more striking for our purposes is the effect such intrapsychic encounters have on the other parties involved. Grof reports that many subjects who relived and cleared a karmic pattern during a session felt that their respective partner in the present life had in some way been involved in the process and had undergone a similar release. Because the person in question was sometimes hundreds of miles away and completely ignorant of his client's activities at the time, Grof did not see how this was possible, and thus he tended to dismiss the observation. Later, however, he was forced to change his mind. He writes:

> When I became sufficiently open-minded to make attempts at verification of the relevance of these statements, I discovered to my great surprise that they were often accurate. I found out that in many instances the persons the subject denoted as protagonists in the karmic sequence experienced at exactly the same time a dramatic shift of attitude in the direction that was predicated by the resolution of the past incarnation pattern. This transformation happened in a way that could not be interpreted by linear causality. The individuals involved were often hundreds or thousands of miles away, they did not know anything about the subject's experience, and the changes in them were produced by an entirely independent sequence of events. They had a deep transformative experience of their own, received some information that entirely changed their perception of the subject, or were influenced by some other independent development in their environment. The time of these synchronistic happenings was often remarkable; in some instances they were minutes apart.[6]

---

[4] See, for example, the case of Tanya cited in Chapter 2.

[5] *Beyond the Brain*, p. 47. See also *The Adventure of Self-Discovery*, pp. 84–93.

[6] *The Adventure of Self-Discovery*, p. 90. Grof goes on to note: "This aspect of past life experiences suggesting nonlocal connections in the universe seems to bear some similarity to phenomena described by Bell's theorem in modern physics."

When the therapeutic cleansing is particularly deep and intense, therefore, our web responds nearly instantaneously, making the field effect easy to spot.

The field effect can also be triggered by a number of psychotherapeutic encounters other than those dealing specifically with former lives. In the extremely deep states of consciousness that Grof's innovative techniques facilitate, his clients regularly experience a wide range of transpersonal phenomena that have nothing to do with former lives and yet also trigger the field effect.[7] These may include encounters with Jungian archetypes and experiences of mythological sequences and other collective elements from specific cultures around the world. For example, if during therapeutic work a subject engages a particular archetype such as the *Anima* or *Animus*, Grof reports that ideal representatives of that archetype tend to appear synchronistically in the client's everyday life. Similarly, if a subject engages themes from the collective unconscious pertaining to a specific culture, this is sometimes accompanied in everyday life by "a striking influx of elements related to this particular geographic or cultural area." These might include the sudden appearance of members of that particular ethnic group in the subject's life, unexpected letters from, or invitations to visit, the country involved, or gifts of books from that country. When the subject completes this particular phase of work and the culture-specific themes disappear from his or her sessions, these synchronicities cease.[8]

When we engage former-life memories, whatever method we use, we often cannot tell whether the people who come forward in our life are the present incarnation of our former karmic partner or a karmic stand-in. In the final analysis, it matters very little. If our original karmic partner is not in our vicinity when we are doing this work, or is not available to us for whatever reason, someone else may step forward, drawn to us because of the energy we have released into the web through engaging our past. If a stand-in comes forward, our relationship with that person will mirror the primary karmic relationship in its essential characteristics. If this happens, the stand-in's karma warrants his or her coming into our life in this particular capacity. The draw is

---

[7] Transpersonal states of consciousness are states of consciousness in which personal identity is transcended. The term *transpersonal phenomena* refers to phenomena one can experience while in transpersonal states of consciousness. Though one accesses these phenomena through one's individual consciousness, the phenomena themselves are transindividual and have little to do with one's individual identity or history.

[8] See Stanislav Grof, *Beyond the Brain*, pp. 44–48.

always reciprocal. Whoever we find in our web at any point in time belongs there, however they come to be there.

The field effect will cause whatever issues we are engaging in our inner psyche to be mirrored in the circumstances of our outer life. If the issue is a romantic attachment from a previous life, the web may respond by inviting us back into romantic involvement. Or perhaps I once helped someone in a way that left him dependent on me, and this dependency now returns to haunt us both. Perhaps someone injured me long ago and now her descendant, or stand-in, feels terribly guilty around me without knowing why. Whatever the particular karmic connection is, when the tie cycles through our life again, we always have the option of jumping on for another ride around the loop or clearing the relationship.

Obviously, not all the karma that cycles through our lives is unpleasant karma. Many of the karmic scenarios the field effect may present us with can be quite appealing. But whether we deem it positive or negative, karma is still karma. There are not two types of karma, of course. Karma is simply karma, causes and their effects. If we experience some karma as more burdensome and other karma as less so, these are Earthbound, valley distinctions. From a spiritual perspective, all karma commits us to future valleys, and the valleys are not our true home. They are not where we experience our greatest joy. Thus, even when a karmic invitation appears sweet, we would be well advised to weigh our choices carefully before we act.

The Eastern spiritual traditions are unfortunately often represented as teaching that we should abandon all our desires, thereby shedding all karmic entanglements in order to return to our spiritual home as quickly as possible. Because few of us can envision our lives completely devoid of all desires, we tend to dismiss these philosophies as either unrealistic or simply not relevant to us. Though some Eastern teachers take this hard-line approach, a more nuanced description of Eastern teaching would be gentler and more patient. These philosophies recommend only that we fully understand the consequences of reinforcing our desires and then make conscious choices within our means. We are always choosing to let go of some desires in life while holding on to others, and we will always be free to do so. Once we understand that holding on to these karmic loops commits us to future valleys of rebirth, it seems to me that we will naturally begin to choose our loops very selectively.

By the time we learn how karma and rebirth work, we undoubtedly have collected many desires and formed bonds with many people. The more entanglements, pleasant or unpleasant, we can bring to completion now, the quicker we will actualize our full spiritual potential. Knowing this, we may want to forgo the cycles of reattachment that present themselves in our lives as quickly as possible or we may want to move more slowly. It's entirely up to us. There is no imperative outside our own desire for spiritual ecstacy.

If we choose to forgo a pleasing karmic scenario, we do so not out of coldness but from compassion. This is a terribly important distinction. We never step back from the person, but only from the karmic loop they present to us. If we decline their invitation, we reject not them but the cycle of emotions that tie us to a particular dance with them. In the end, we can share no greater gift with someone than freedom, and we can only bring this gift to them if we choose it for ourselves. This is the greatest compassion.

KARMA, MEDITATION, AND AGAPIC LOVE

Though there are two points at which we can intervene in our karmic loops, the field effect demonstrates that in actual practice these two are often intertwined. Inner initiatives often precipitate changes in our outer world, while changes in our outer world invite us to engage our inner process. Having said this, we can nevertheless use these two points of intervention to observe how different spiritual practices intervene at different points in the karmic loop. In developing this contrast, I would like to tie this discussion to the discussion of religious complementarity at the end of Chapter 6 on Christianity. There it was suggested that the most productive way to view the different religious traditions was to see them as (1) asserting some essential insights in different formulas and (2) asserting some unique insights that are complementary to one another. The discussion of karmic loops gives us an opportunity to demonstrate one example of this complementarity.

Though it involves an oversimplification to draw the comparison this way, we can say that certain meditation practices usually associated with Eastern religions intervene on the mental side of the karmic cycle while the Christian ethical imperative of agapic love intervenes on the physical side. This contrast oversimplifies matters because both Eastern and Western religions teach practices that intervene on both sides of the cycle. Nevertheless, if we recognize its limitations, the comparison can be instructive. By demonstrating that meditation and agapic love are complementary ways of intervening in the cycles of karma, we can better recognize the larger whole that both religions are part of.

There are many meditation techniques, of course, each designed to have a different effect on consciousness. One entire family of meditation techniques is designed to cleanse karma from our system by focusing our awareness on the ever-changing present moment. In Buddhism this form of meditation is called *vipassana* meditation, "insight" meditation.[9] The key to vipassana practice is the cultivation of a focused yet open, nonjudgmental awareness. After learning how to calm the mind and quiet its background chatter, the meditator is instructed simply to watch his or her consciousness as it exists moment to moment. Anything is permitted to enter our awareness, though it is not allowed to stay long. Techniques are taught that facilitate being open to whatever surfaces from the deep psyche while not getting caught up in it. The key is to be open to but not to react to what emerges. This is called *bare attention*, or nonreactive awareness. Once something enters the empty field of our awareness, we accept it but then gently usher it along. This is not repression, for repression seeks to prevent something from emerging. Here everything is accepted but not indulged in.[10]

When we withdraw from the world for a period of time each day and focus our attention nonreactively in the present, we find that the mind begins to cleanse itself of its accumulated mental toxins. Every moment we are interacting with the world the mind is taking in experience and storing it away. Not all that it takes in is healthy for it, and in our meditations we can watch the mind removing the unhealthy elements and restoring a harmonious balance to the system. If we keep this practice up for a number of years, supplementing our daily meditations with periodic intensive meditation retreats, the toxins that surface come from deeper and deeper within the psyche. At first stresses from the present come forward, followed later by stresses left over from last year and the year before that. Eventually traumas or subtler poisons left over from childhood surface, sometimes with sufficient cognitive content to allow us to locate them accurately in our past, sometimes not.

---

[9] Many sacred traditions teach forms of meditation that are functionally equivalent to vipassana practice. The comparison being drawn here, therefore, is actually much broader than between Buddhism and Christianity alone.

[10] For more on these meditational practices see *The Heart of Buddhist Meditation* by Nyanaponika Thera; *The Experience of Insight* by Joseph Goldstein; and *Gradual Awakening* by Steven Levine. For a useful introductory comparison between many different meditation techniques, see *The Meditative Mind* by Daniel Goleman.

We may simply experience intense emotions without understanding exactly what period of our life they come from. Yet, as all we have done is turned our awareness inward and taught it to register nonjudgmentally whatever it sees, we know that whatever comes forward comes only from us.

With continued practice the cleansing deepens until the fragments that emerge eventually begin to come from our former lives. Once again, sometimes these surface sufficiently intact to allow us to recognize the original historical circumstances, while at other times they do not. At times we are simply confronted with experiences or raw emotions that do not belong to our present life. During such periods of intense cleansing the field effect may be triggered. This is especially likely when the elements surfacing in meditation are major themes in our present karmic script.

The purification process activated in vipassana meditation parallels in certain respects the cleansing that takes place in past-life therapy. Though the methods for accessing the archives of our consciousness differ, they both share this uncovering of karma from previous lifecycles. The karmic cycle is being interrupted on the mental side of the feedback loop, and karma is being "burned up." Slowly our energy field becomes clearer. Our transcendental nature is uncovered bit by bit, occasionally absorbing us into its spaciousness, giving us glimpses of what awaits us when the purification process is complete.[11]

While Christianity has always had its own meditational traditions, they have for the most part been a minor current running beside the Christian mainstream. Mainstream Christianity has emphasized a different form of spiritual practice—agapic love. Agapic love is an ethic of radical equal-regard that embraces all persons as equally valuable members of the human family. For this reason, we are to treat others not on the basis of how they might treat us but according to a higher

---

[11] As the cleansing continues it becomes more difficult. Toward the end, the fragments that surface can be particularly dark and primitive, mercilessly attacking the remnants of our attachment to our ego-identity. If we are to fully recover our transcendental nature, we must break through the illusions surrounding the personality identity we have assumed in this and other births. In the *Vissudhimaga*, an important Buddhist text on meditation, this particularly difficult stage of practice is called the Stage of Higher Realizations. As a matter of comparative interest, the Christian mystical tradition also knows of these dark experiences. St. John of the Cross, a Catholic Spanish mystic who lived in the seventeenth century, described them in *Dark Night of the Soul*, as did his colleague St. Teresa of Avila in her *Autobiography*. Their descriptions closely parallel that found in the *Vissudhimaga*. For more on these comparisons, see Meadows and Culligan (1987) and Bache (1981, 1985, 1991). Daniel Goleman discusses the *Vissudhimaga* in light of modern psychology and meditation research in *The Meditative Mind*.

ethic. Not only must we treat all people as equals, we must also reflect God's love to them. We must love even our enemies and forgive those who injure us. Our concern should be for the "widows and orphans"; that is, for those in society who have no one else to look after them. In this way we demonstrate our acceptance of God as the source of all our lives and of Jesus, who demonstrated God's true nature in his self-sacrificing love.

Following this ethic has the effect of intervening powerfully in the physical side of our karmic cycle. By practicing it we neutralize the karmic loops that confront us in our day-to-day lives. If we refuse to respond in kind to people who treat us harshly, unjustly, manipulatively, exploitively, and so on, we are refusing to reinforce these negative karmic cycles in our life. If we respond to these injustices with a compassion and forgiveness that is grounded in the conviction that love is, despite appearances, the ultimate force in the universe, we daily exchange good karma for bad. If we reinforce the mental states of forgiveness and love in our daily prayers, we dissolve even more negative karma.

Forgiveness is an extremely powerful means of clearing karma from our lives. To genuinely forgive is to assert great power and control over our destiny. Perhaps for this reason it is such a universal theme in the world's religions: "Forgive us our sins as we forgive those who sin against us." "Judge not and you shall not be judged." On all continents, the refrain appears: as you forgive, so shall you be forgiven. Often what we are asked to forgive in others are the same failings we have come to recognize in ourselves, for here too we find the field effect operating.

A number of religious practices can trigger the field effect without our being aware of it. Certain types of prayer can do this, as can the practice of positive affirmations. When we pray to be forgiven for or freed from a particular flaw in our character, or when we attempt to plant a countering trait through positive affirmations, we may soon find ourselves beside someone who burdens us with exactly the same failing we are trying to get rid of in ourselves. If we do not put together what is happening, we may fail to spot the opportunity we are being given. We are being offered the chance to actualize our request by forgiving our flaw in other people. By forgiving someone for injuring us in ways that parallel our treatment of someone else at another time, we resolve a piece of karma and cleanse it from our system. However, if we do not extend to others the forgiveness we seek for ourselves, we will remain stuck at this impasse.

The spiritual mechanisms operating here are subtle but quite simple.

Our request has been taken at face value. To receive forgiveness, we must be willing to forgive. The demands of reciprocity are exacting and precise. The parity the Universe insists on is merciless. Its mercy lies in the fact that the Universe never gives up on us. It will continue to teach us these lessons until we surrender to the cosmic processes that we are part of. When we do this, we will experience the extraordinary kindness and benevolence behind all the pain we may have suffered at the hands of others.

CONCLUDING THOUGHTS

For those who undertake deep therapeutic work, the field effect is an important phenomenon to understand and track. With powerful psychotherapeutic interventions on the rise in our culture, we can expect more and more people to experience this complex interaction of inner and outer worlds as time goes on. The field effect tends to dissolve the illusion that boundaries can be neatly drawn between what happens in the therapist's office and what happens in the outer world. The individual who pursues his or her spiritual journey to this deep level of the psyche often comes to live in a supercharged world filled with opportunities and significances. Only by understanding the natural processes driving these events can we maintain the centered balance needed to deal with them.

For those who do not carry their personal growth into such deep waters, the field effect is important too, because it demonstrates the dynamics of the web of life, the interaction between our inner choices and outer circumstances. It highlights a relationship that is usually subtle and difficult to spot. It reminds us that we always exist in a living field of energy that is responsive to our choosing. If we meet the flow of events that surround us as a living web, life becomes an interactive game and each of us becomes a powerful player directing the action on our board. When life becomes a conscious game of personal evolution it becomes the sport of kings and queens.

Finally, once we understand that our inner and outer worlds interact to ensure our spiritual development, we can recognize that Christian agapic love and Buddhist vipassana meditation represent complementary spiritual practices. They both interrupt the cycle of karma, but at different places. If reincarnation is true, anyone who followed the code of ethics taught by Jesus would move in the same spiritual direction as someone who practiced the meditational practices taught by the Buddha. These are simply two paths up the same mountain.

*I*f reincarnation is true, it is a fact of life that predates the birth of all the religions in existence today. This suggests that long before Jesus, Lao-Tzu, or the Buddha lived, most of us had been spiritually evolving through thousands of years of successive rebirths. Reincarnation is part of an evolutionary process more ancient and, in a sense, more fundamental than any of the world's religions. This raises a provocative question. If rebirth and the spiritual evolution it secures have been facts of life from prehistoric times, what exactly have the great spiritual teachers added?

The answer, I think, is that they have added awareness, and through awareness empowerment. Without commenting on how the current world religions came into being or on how we should understand the special status of their founders, I think these systems of belief have functioned to guide us through the larger evolutionary process being realized through karma and rebirth. Whether or not they have specifically taught reincarnation is less significant than the fact that the teachings that have echoed through the temples, churches, and synagogues around the globe have been placing in our hands the tools of our individual evolution and thus have been slowly changing the collective trajectory of human evolution.

Popular wisdom holds that "Experience is the best teacher," and most would agree that no lessons are more deeply learned than those gathered from personal experience. If life is our greatest teacher, we might view the teachings given us by the great spiritual masters as instructions in how to learn from life. They have universally assured us that we continue to live when we leave here and that our earthly existence is in some respects a trial or test. They have insisted that we are safe and, despite the considerable evidence to the contrary, that we are loved and nourished by the source of existence itself. They have then proceeded to teach us how best to meet whatever challenges we are asked to face in life. There are no shortcuts to getting an education in the Earth school, but there are attitudes and values that can accelerate and ease the learning process.

The ethical teachings of the world's religions are remarkably consistent. The fundamental values of compassion, fair play, and forgiveness seem universally distributed. We are told that we should meet whatever happens to us with equanimity and forbearance. In all our dealings with each other, we should follow the Golden Rule. By adopting this principle of equal-regard, we break the cycles of karma that are rippling through our lives from a past we can no longer see. By treating others as we wish to be treated, by not responding to evil with evil, we right the wrongs of the past and deepen our awareness of the underlying unity of life. Above all, we should know that we are safe, that nothing could possibly separate us permanently from the source of our life, and that the rigors of life are ultimately for our own benefit.

Human existence itself is about spiritual growth. We have taken birth in the Earth school to learn and to grow, but there are different tracks through this school. The slowest track is to follow passively the course of our karma as it winds through one valley after another. The less aware we are of the rules of the game, the slower will be our progress, but progress will nonetheless be made. As we become more aware of the causal laws governing the process, we are able to make more informed choices and thus can progress more rapidly and smoothly. The world's spiritual traditions have been teaching us these basic rules for more than two thousand years and thus have been giving us the tools needed to escape from the labyrinth of conditioning that has imprisoned our true nature inside this succession of body/mind identities.

But the contribution of the world's religions to the spiritual evolution of the species has not stopped there. The esoteric branches of these traditions have developed numerous practices that can accelerate our deconditioning even further, thus hastening our liberation from the illusions created by physical existence. These practices include a simplified life-style, fasting, extended silence, group chanting, meditation, various breathing and bodily exercises, and so on. Without minimizing the complex ways these diverse practices impact on our bodies and psyches, their cumulative effect is to accelerate the evolution that would advance at a slower rate through living the moral life alone. The more advanced the practices we adopt and the more consistently we integrate them into our lives, the faster we will evolve. It all boils down to how aware we wish to be and how aggressively we wish to pursue our evolution. In the final analysis, the most intense form of spiritual practice is to live completely in the present, to be fully conscious to the flow of life as it unfolds around us and through us moment to moment. The present is both the means to and the end of our awakening.

Two final points. First, if the religions of the world have made possible a more conscious participation in our own evolution, it is clear that they have no monopoly on spiritual growth. We exist on Earth in order to grow, and we will grow whether or not we affiliate with any religion, let alone with any specific religion. Religions are not the only institutions that have supported this evolutionary process, and we must admit that they have at times seemed to work hard against it. The history of the failings of religion is well known. They too have been subject to the cycles of decline and rejuvenation that govern all historical institutions. Nevertheless, they have encompassed the bulk of humanity and have preserved important truths that might otherwise have been lost.

Second, though we often tend to describe the spiritual journey in terms of its end stages, in fact every stage of human growth is part of one's spiritual evolution. When people talk of taking up a "spiritual path," they are only describing a point at which the spiritual path they have always been on has become a self-conscious choice. This is a significant point on the journey, but certainly not its starting point. In our personal lives as for the planet as a whole, we are waking up to something that has been going on for billions of years. If the themes of the end stage of the journey concern the reappropriation of our essential divinity and learning how to combine particularity with wholeness, there were many other lessons that came before these, and none of them was trivial.[1]

This encourages us to recognize that, contrary to conventional parlance, all of us have taken up a spiritual vocation, not just those who have taken formal vows. By virtue of our presence on Earth, we have all demonstrated our commitment to a rigorous course of spiritual training. There is no one we see around us, therefore, who does not deserve our sincerest respect.

---

[1] In fact, we have no reason for thinking that this particular stage is the "end stage" at all. In all probability, it is but the current chapter in a story that has been unfolding for at least fifteen billion years and that will continue to unfold for at least that long still. If reappropriating our divinity and learning to combine wholeness with particularity is but a transition point midway in the plot of physical existence, the possibilities for the future are staggering.

Reincarnation in Early Christianity

1. REINCARNATION IN THE NEW TESTAMENT

A number of passages in the New Testament appear to reflect a prior acceptance of reincarnation among some of the Jews to whom Jesus spoke and even among his disciples. If this is so, some have argued, and if Jesus did not take the trouble to refute this belief, might it not be possible that Jesus himself accepted reincarnation? If he did not teach it directly, might this simply be because it was an assumed belief among his audience?[1] For example, when Jesus asked his disciples "Who do men say that the Son of Man is?" they answered "Some say John the Baptist, others say Elijah, and others Jeremiah or one of the prophets" (Matt. 16:13). (See parallel passages in Mark 8:27–28 and Luke 9:18–19.) The argument is made that if the people expected that one of the prophets might return as the Son of Man, this must assume a belief in reincarnation, for how else could a dead prophet return to earth?

This argument works, however, only if it is assumed that the people are necessarily thinking that the "Son of Man" would be a human being

---

[1] The arguments critiqued here are taken from Cranston's summary in *Reincarnation*, pp. 206–213.

and thus required to take physical birth. Though this is the interpretation eventually given the title in Christian theology, it would be anachronistic to assume that the Jews of Jesus' day necessarily thought in these terms. In Jesus' time, the Son of Man was often thought of as an angelic figure expected to accompany God's final intervention in history, not a human being at all. The figure is taken from Daniel 7 and has a complex history in the intertestamental literature (works written between the Old and New Testaments). Given this complex background, we cannot assume that the people cited in Matthew 16 are necessarily conceiving of the Son of Man as a human figure, and therefore we cannot infer that they were thinking in reincarnationist terms.

A second set of passages concerns John the Baptist and reflects the widely held belief among the Jews that Elijah the prophet would return as forerunner to the Messiah. In these passages, Jesus states either directly or indirectly that John the Baptist is Elijah, thus ful- filling the prophecy (Matt. 11:2–15; Matt. 17:10–13; Mark 9:9–13). If Jesus accepted the idea that John the Baptist was Elijah returned, and if John was "born of woman" as Luke 1:13–17 indicates he was, would this not imply that Jesus himself was accepting some theory of reincarnation?

The problem here, however, is that the historical validity of these passages is questionable. Many biblical scholars doubt that these passages reflect statements actually made by the historical Jesus. They seem instead to derive from a later period, when Jesus' and John's disciples were competing for the same audience. By relegating John to the status of forerunner, the early Christians were asserting the supremacy of Jesus while simultaneously claiming fulfillment of an ancient prophecy. Though actually arising after Jesus died, these passages were placed in Jesus' mouth when the gospels were eventually written many years after his death.

The same historical skepticism applies to other passages sometimes quoted as possibly reflecting Jesus' belief in reincarnation. In John 10:15b–18a, for example, Jesus says:

> I lay down my life for the sheep. And I have other sheep, that are not of this fold; I must bring them also, and they will heed my voice. So there shall be one flock, one shepherd. For this reason the Father loves me, because I lay down my life, that I may take it again. No one takes it from me, but I lay it down of my own accord. I have the power to lay it down, and I have the power to take it again.

Was Jesus saying that he had incarnated more than once in history in order to bring salvation to more than the Israelites? It's a possibility, but not a strong one, I think. Even if Jesus actually said these words, having the power to "take his life again" is most likely a reference to the resurrection, and the "other sheep" are probably the Gentiles who would have the gospel preached to them only after Pentecost.

Similarly, we are not compelled to assume that Jesus is thinking in reincarnationist terms to make sense of John 8:56–58, where Jesus says in response to taunts for setting himself up as greater than Abraham:

> "Your father Abraham rejoiced that he was to see my day; he saw it and was glad." The Jews then said to him, "You are not yet fifty years old, and have you seen Abraham?" Jesus said to them, "Truly, truly, I say to you, before Abraham was, I am."

If the passage is historically reliable, which is suspect, it should be read as claiming a preexistent divine status, not a former life.

As I see it, there are essentially two problems with these attempts to place reincarnation in the lifetime and teaching of Jesus. The first is that they approach the New Testament without adequately taking into account developments in biblical scholarship over the last century. During this time we have learned that the gospels came to be written considerably after Jesus died (from forty to eighty years after) and were not written by eyewitnesses to Jesus' ministry. Despite the venerable tradition that Jesus' own disciples wrote the gospels, the textual evidence has not supported this interpretation. Neither Jesus' own disciples nor other first-generation Christians appear to have taken the trouble to write down Jesus' teaching, probably because they believed that Jesus would be returning to Earth in the very near future, certainly during their lifetime. (This expectation seems to have been widespread among early Christians, and is clearly visible in Paul's early epistles—notably I Thessalonians 4:13–18 and I Corinthians 7, probably written in A.D. 51 and 54/55 respectively.) There was obviously little point in creating a permanent record of Jesus' teaching if Jesus himself was shortly going to be back among them in person. It was only the death of the first generation of believers combined with the shock of losing the Jerusalem community to the military campaign waged against the city by the Romans in A.D. 69–70 that forced the Christians to drop these expectations and to begin gathering its oral traditions into written summaries for future generations.[2]

The information contained in the gospels was thus passed along orally for many years before being organized and preserved by second-generation Christians. During this oral phase and even in the writing itself, the material was added to and reshaped many times. From a historian's perspective, therefore, we cannot naively assume that every statement that issues from Jesus' mouth in the gospels is something the historical Jesus actually said. Yet this is precisely what is assumed by those who would argue from isolated passages to reincarnationist conclusions. Very frequently, the statements cited are statements that historians have good cause to doubt were actually said by Jesus himself and that appear to have been incorporated into the growing body of Jesus stories at a later date.

The second problem with attributing belief in reincarnation to Jesus is this: If Jesus did believe in reincarnation, why is there no explicit discussion of it in the gospel record? Why are there only these indirect, veiled references to such a fundamental and important idea? If Jesus taught reincarnation, we would certainly expect to find some explicit discussion of it in the gospels. It is always possible, of course, that references to rebirth have been systematically edited out of the gospel record, but a convincing historical argument for this hypothesis has not yet been forthcoming. Alternatively, some have suggested that Jesus taught at different levels to different audiences and that the New Testament only records the teaching received by one audience, while reincarnation was part of the esoteric teaching given to a more selective second group. Have we finally discovered this second audience in the texts recovered at Nag Hammadi?

2. REINCARNATION IN EARLY CHRISTIANITY

The fifty-two texts discovered at Nag Hammadi in 1945 describe a form of Christianity different from the one recorded in the New Testament. Called Gnostic Christianity by the scholars, the beliefs of these Christians have finally been brought to the attention of the general public by Elaine Pagels's widely read *The Gnostic Gospels*.

According to Professor Pagels's reading of the sources, Gnostic Christianity was a mystically oriented version of Christianity that em-

---

[2] The tradition that the Jerusalem community escaped the brunt of this military onslaught by escaping to Pella is a legend not substantiated by historical sources.

phasized the importance of actually experiencing the God that dwells within each of us. It was not so much a formal doctrine as a way of thinking that permeated the early centuries of the Christian era, influencing even the gospels themselves, especially John. Gnosticism emphasized the transformative effect of this inner knowing, or *gnosis*, instead of a sacramentally mediated salvation.

It differed from what eventually became orthodoxy on a number of other points as well. It taught that God was both male and female and spoke freely of "God the Mother." Accordingly, it treated women as equals and did not deny them access to positions of authority in the community. It also drew no distinctions between clergy and laity, preferring democratic political structures to hierarchical ones. Finally, it appears that the Gnostic Christians believed in reincarnation. They taught not only the preexistence of the soul, but its rebirth in successive incarnations following the karmic laws of cause and effect. In the Gnostic text called the *Pistis Sophia* or Faith Wisdom, for example, Jesus teaches his disciples how failings in one life are carried over into another. Someone who curses others in one life will in his new life be "continually troubled in his heart." An arrogant, overweening personality could find himself reborn into a deformed body, and thus come to be looked down upon by others, and so on. "Ideas that we associate with Eastern religions," observes Professor Pagels, "emerged in the first century through the Gnostic movement, in the West, but they were suppressed and condemned by polemicists like Irenaeus."[3]

Gnostic Christianity was condemned as a heresy by the ecclesiastical Church in the second century and persecuted with Emperor Constantine's assistance in the fourth. So successful were these efforts to stamp out the Gnostics that the only information we had on their beliefs before the discovery of the Nag Hammadi texts derived from hostile Orthodox sources. Orthodoxy saw the Gnostics as tainting the true gospel with alien ideas derived from outside sources, yet the Nag Hammadi texts clearly demonstrate that the Gnostics saw themselves as true Christians keeping alive a tradition that derived from Jesus himself.

Did the Gnostic Christians preserve aspects of Jesus' teaching that other forms of Christianity let slip away? Do the documents of Nag Hammadi represent a long-lost source that will eventually place reincarnation back into the historical Jesus' teaching? Or is the more accurate

---

[3] *The Gostic Gospels*, p. xii. This reading of the Gnostic texts is also supported by the French Egyptologist Jean Doresse in *The Secret Books of the Egyptians*, pp. 112–113, and Geddes MacGregor, *Reincarnation in Christianity*, pp. 43–44 (both quoted in Cranston, 1984, p. 219.)

portrait of Jesus the New Testament one devoid of reincarnation? The historical questions are complex and as yet unresolved. The possibilities are provocative, but the jury is still out. All I can say is that I am not aware of a convincing historical argument that has proved that the beliefs that distinguished Gnostic Christianity can be reliably traced back to the historical Jesus.

One thing is clear, however. Gnosticism can no longer be regarded as merely an heretical second-century aberration, but must be seen as a pervasive world view in which Jesus' teaching flourished, at least for a time. As non-Gnostic forms of Christianity gained the upper hand politically, other forms that might have originally been equally viable expressions of Christian faith were systematically repressed. Pagels writes:

> The process of establishing orthodoxy ruled out every other option. To the impoverishment of Christian tradition, gnosticism, which offered alternatives to what became the main thrust of Christian orthodoxy, was forced outside. The concerns of gnostic Christians survived only as a suppressed current, like a river driven underground.[4]

Whatever Jesus himself may have taught, the Nag Hammadi literature demonstrates that reincarnation was a live option within early Christianity. This in itself is a significant discovery.

---

[4] *The Gnostic Gospels*, pp. 149–150.

BIBLIOGRAPHY

Ajaya, Swami (1983). *Psychotherapy East and West.* Honesdale, Pa.: Himalayan Institute.

Atwater, P. M. H. (1988). *Coming Back to Life: The After-Effects of the Near-Death Experience.* New York: Dodd, Mead.

Bache, Christopher (1981). "On the Emergence of Perinatal Symptoms in Buddhist Meditation." *Journal for Scientific Study of Religion,* 20 (4): 339–350.

———— (1985). "A Reappraisal of Teresa of Avila's Hysteria." *The Journal of Religion and Health,* 24 (4): 300–315.

———— (1991). "Mysticism and Psychedelics: The Case of the Dark Night." *The Journal of Religion and Health,* forthcoming, spring, 1991.

Bateson, Gregory (1972). *Steps to an Ecology of Mind.* New York: Ballantine.

———— (1979). *Mind and Nature: A Necessary Unity.* New York: Dutton.

Bernstein, Morey (1989). *The Search for Bridey Murphey.* New York: Doubleday.

Campbell, Joseph (1988). *An Open Life: Joseph Campbell in Conversation with Michael Toms.* Burdett, New York: Larson Publications.

Cannon, Alexander (1950). *The Power Within*. London: Rider.

Capra, Fritjof (1975). *The Tao of Physics*. Berkeley: Shambhala.

——— (1982). *The Turning Point: Science, Society and the Rising Culture*. New York: Simon & Schuster.

Combs, Allan, and Mark Holland (1990). *Synchronicity: Science, Myth and the Trickster*. New York: Paragon House.

Cranston, Sylvia (1967). *Reincarnation in World Thought*. New York: Julian.

——— (1970). *Reincarnation: An East-West Anthology*. Wheaton, Ill.: Theosophical Publication House.

Cranston, Sylvia, and Carey Williams (1984). *Reincarnation: A New Horizon in Science, Religion, and Society*. New York: Julian.

Cranston, Sylvia, and Joseph Head (1977). *Reincarnation: The Phoenix Fire Mystery*. New York: Crown.

Doresse, Jean (1960). *The Secret Books of the Egyptians*. New York: Viking.

Edwards, Paul (1986–1987). "The Case Against Reincarnation, I-IV." *Free Inquiry* 6 (4): 24–35; 7 (1): 38–48; 7 (2): 38–49; 7 (3): 46–53.

Evans-Wentz, W. Y. (1973). *The Tibetan Book of the Dead*. New York: Causeway Books.

Feher, Elizabeth (1980). *The Psychotherapy of Birth*. London: Souvenir Press.

Feldenkraise, Moshe (1972). *Awareness Through Movement*. New York: Harper.

Fiore, Edith (1978). *You Have Been Here Before*. New York: Ballantine.

——— (1987). *The Unquiet Dead*. New York: Doubleday.

Fisher, Joe (1985). *The Case for Reincarnation*. New York: Bantam.

Flynn, Charles P. (1986). *After the Beyond: Human Transformation and the Near-Death Experience*. Englewood Cliffs, N.J.: Prentice-Hall.

Francuch, Peter D. (1981). *Principles of Spiritual Hypnosis*. Santa Barbara, Calif.: Spiritual Advisory Press.

Gallup, George, Jr. (1982). *Adventures in Immortality*. New York: McGraw-Hill.

Gawain, Shakti (1986). *Living in the Light*. San Rafael, Calif.: Whatever.

Gyatso, Tensin, His Holiness the Dalai Lama of Tibet. Translated and edited by Jeffrey Hopkins (1988). *The Dalai Lama at Harvard*. Ithaca, N.Y.: Snow Lion.

Goldstein, Joseph (1976). *The Experience of Insight*. Santa Cruz, Calif.: Unity Press.

Goleman, Daniel (1988). *The Meditative Mind*. Los Angeles: Tarcher.

Grof, Stanislav (1976). *Realms of the Human Unconscious: Observations from LSD Research*. New York: Dutton.

———— (1980). *LSD Psychotherapy*. Pomona, Calif.: Hunter House.

———— (1984). *Ancient Wisdom and Modern Science*. Albany: State University of New York Press.

———— (1985). *Beyond the Brain*. Albany: State University of New York Press.

———— (1988). *The Adventure of Self-Discovery*. Albany: State University of New York Press.

Grof, Stanislav, and Christina Grof (1980). *Beyond Death*. London: Thames and Hudson.

Grof, Stanislav, and Joan Halifax (1977). *The Human Encounter with Death*. New York: Dutton.

Humphreys, Christmas (1983). *Karma and Rebirth*. Wheaton, Ill.: The Theosophical Publishing House.

Iverson, Jeffrey (1976). *More Lives Than One? The Evidence of the Remarkable Bloxham Tapes*. London: Souvenir Press.

Jung, Carl G. (1965). *Synchronicity: An Acausal Connecting Principle*. In *Collected Works*, Vol. 8, Bollingen Series XX. Princeton, N.J.: Princeton University Press.

Kelsey, Denys, and Joan Grant (1967). *Many Lifetimes*. New York: Doubleday.

Klimo, Jon (1987). *Channeling: Investigations on Receiving Information from Paranormal Sources*. Los Angeles: Tarcher.

Leonard, John, and Philip Laut (1983). *Rebirthing: The Science of Enjoying Your Life*. San Rafael, Calif.: Trinity Publications.

Levine, Stephen (1979). *Gradual Awakening*. Garden City, N.Y.: Anchor.

Lilly, John C. (1972). *The Center of the Cyclone*. New York: Julian.

———— (1974). *Programming and Metaprogramming in the Human Biocomputer*. New York: Bantam.

———— (1977). *The Deep Self: Profound Relaxation and the Tank Isolation Technique*. New York: Warner.

MacGregor, Geddes (1978). *Reincarnation in Christianity*. Wheaton, Ill.: Quest Books.

———— (1982). *Reincarnation as a Christian Hope*. Totowa, N.J.: Barnes & Noble.

Monroe, Robert (1977). *Journeys out of the Body*. Garden City, N.Y.: Anchor.

———— (1985). *Far Journeys*. Garden City, N.Y.: Doubleday.

Mookerjee, Ajit (1983). *Kundalini: The Arousal of the Inner Energy*, 2nd ed. New York: Destiny Books.

Netherton, Morris (1978). *Past Lives Therapy*. New York: Morrow.

Orr, Leonard, and Sondra Ray (1977). *Rebirthing in the New Age*. Berkeley, Calif.: Celestial Arts.

Pagels, Elaine (1979). *The Gnostic Gospels*. New York: Random House.

Progoff, Ira (1973). *Jung, Synchronicity, and Human Destiny: Non-Causal Dimensions of Human Experience*. New York: Julian.

Rama, Swami, et al. (1976). *Yoga and Psychotherapy: The Evolution of Consciousness*. Honesdale, Pa.: Himalayan Institute.

Rinbochay, Lati, and Jeffrey Hopkins (1979). *Death, Intermediate State and Rebirth in Tibetan Buddhism*. Valois, N.Y.: Snow Lion Press.

Ring, Kenneth (1980). *Life at Death: A Scientific Investigation of the Near-Death Experience*. New York: Coward, McCann.

———— (1984). *Heading Toward Omega: In Search of the Meaning of the Near-Death Experience*. New York: Morrow.

———— (1986). "Near-Death Experiences: Implications for Human Evolution and Planetary Transformation." *Revision*, 8: 75–88.

Rinpoche, Kalu (1986). *The Dharma*. Albany: State University of New York Press.

Rofa, Ida (1977). *Rolfing: The Integration of Human Structures*. New York Harper.

Rogo, D. Scott (1985). *Search for Yesterday*. Englewood Cliffs, NJ: Prentice-Hall.

St. John of the Cross (1959/1584). *Dark Night of the Soul*. Trans. and ed. by A. Peers. Garden City, N.Y.: Image.

St. Teresa of Avila (1960/1565). *The Life of Teresa of Jesus*. Trans. and ed. by A. Peers. Garden City, N.Y.: Image.

Scholem, Gershom (1941). *Major Trends in Jewish Mysticism*. New York: Schocken.

Schuon, Frithjof (1984). *Transcendent Unity of Religions*. New York: Harper.

——— (1986). *Survey of Metaphysics and Esoterism.* Bloomington, Ind.: World Wisdom Books.

Selfe, Lorna (1977). *Nadia: A Case of Extraordinary Drawing in an Autistic Child.* New York: Academic Press.

Sheldake, Rupert (1983). *A New Science of Life: The Hypothesis of Formative Causation.* Los Angeles: Tarcher.

Smith, Huston (1958). *The Religions of Man.* New York: Harper.

——— (1976). *Forgotten Truth: The Primordial Tradition.* New York: Harper.

——— (1982). *Beyond the Post Modern Mind.* New York: Crossroad Publishing Co.

Stevenson, Ian (1974a). *Twenty Cases Suggestive of Reincarnation.* Charlottesville: University Press of Virginia.

——— (1974b). *Xenoglossy.* Charlottesville: University Press of Virginia.

——— (1975). *Cases of the Reincarnation Type.* Vol. 1: *Ten Cases in India.* Charlottesville: University Press of Virginia.

——— (1977a). *Cases of the Reincarnation Type.* Vol. 2: *Ten Cases in Sri Lanka.* Charlottesville: University Press of Virginia.

——— (1977b). "The Explanatory Value of the Idea of Reincarnation." *Journal of Nervous and Mental Diseases,* 164: 305–326.

——— (1980). *Cases of the Reincarnation Type.* Vol. 3: *Twelve Cases in Lebanon and Turkey* Charlottesville: University Press of Virginia.

——— (1983a). *Cases of the Reincarnation Type.* Vol. 4: *Twelve Cases in Thailand and Burma.* Charlottesville: University Press of Virginia.

——— (1983b). "American Children Who Claim to Remember Previous Lives." *The Journal of Nervous and Mental Disease,* 171 (12): 742–748.

——— (1984). *Unlearned Languages: New Studies in Xenoglossy.* Charlottesville: University Press of Virginia.

——— (1987). *Children Who Remember Previous Lives: A Question of Reincarnation.* Charlottesville: University Press of Virgnia.

Thera, Nyanaponika (1962). *The Heart of Buddhist Meditation.* New York: Samuel Weiser.

Thomas, Lewis (1975). *Lives of the Cell* New York: Bantam.

Trager, Milton (1982). "Psychophysical Integration and Mentastics." *Journal of Holistic Health,* 7:15ff.

Wambach, Helen (1978). *Reliving Past Lives: The Evidence Under Hypnosis.* New York: Bantam.

—— (1979). *Life Before Life.* New York: Bantam.

Weber, Renée (1986). *Dialogues with Scientists and Sages.* New York: Routledge & Kegan Paul.

White, John, ed. *What is Enlightenment?* (1984). Los Angeles: Jeremy P. Tarcher, Inc.

—— (1990). *Kundalini, Evolution and Enlightenment.* New York: Paragon House.

Whitton, Joel, and Joe Fisher (1986). *Life Between Life.* Garden City, N.Y.: Doubleday.

Wilson, Ian (1982). *All in the Mind.* Garden City, N.Y.: Doubleday. (Previously published as *Mind Out of Time?*)

Wolf, Fred Alan (1981). *Taking the Quantum Leap: The New Physics for Non-Scientists.* New York: Harper.

—— (1984). *Star Wave.* New York: Macmillan.

Woolger, Roger (1988). *Other Lives, Other Selves: A Jungian Therapist Discovers Past Lives.* New York: Bantam.

Zukav, Gary (1979). *The Dancing Wu Li Masters.* New York: Morrow.

INDEX

Abraham, 221
Adler, 143
The Adventure of Self-Discovery, 53–
54
Adventures in Immortality, 60–61
After the Beyond, 112–113
Afterlife: An Investigation of the Evidence for Life after Death, 43
n.24
Agape and agapic love, 65, 143–
144, 210–214
Agnihotri, Mr. and Mrs., 34
Ajaya, Swami, 69n.5, 142n.7
Allah, 117
Amnesia of previous incarnations,
128–129, 130–131
Animal incarnations, 58–59
"An Apparent Intention of the Fate
of the Individual," 191n.3
"Are the Chakras Real?" 142
n.8
Atman, 110n.4
Atwater, P.H.M., 57n.40
Aurobindo, Sri, 59
Autistic children, 41

Ballentine, Rudolph, 142n.7
Banerjee, Hemendra, 2, 34
Bardo, 84, 85, 86, 92
    Chonyid Bardo, 137
    Earth plane, reasons for returning to, 89–90
    identity assumed in, 87
    life plan, 132
    planes of, 87n.19
    and religious expectations, 86n.18
    Sidpa Bardo, 137
    time spent in, 86–87
    tribunal, 87–89, 96
*Bardo Thdol. See The Tibetan Book of
    the Dead.*
Being-Consciousness-Bliss, 147
Being of Light, 133n.7
Belle, 57n.40
Bengali songs and dances, 37–38
Bernstein, Morey, 43n.24
Beyond the Brain, 51–53
Biological families, 178–179
Birth, 178
Bocchi, Elena, 78
Brody, Eugene, 33

Bryant, Ray, 43n.24
Buddha, 215
Buddhism, 8, 26, 89n.22, 201
  death, 57
  vipassana meditation, 199, 211–
    212, 214

Campbell, Joseph, 191
Camus, Albert, xiv
Cannon, Alexander, 45
Capra, Frijhof, 18
Case histories
  from past-life therapy; and
    karma, 63
  from past-life therapy, 70–79
  see also names of specific people, i.e.,
    Crees, Romy
Cases of the Reincarnation Type, 28,
  33
Cause and effect, 11–12
Chakra system
  brow chakra, 144–145
  crown chakra, 145
  defined, 141
  genital chakra, 143
  heart chakra, 143–144
  map of soul age, 141–145
  root chakra, 142–143
  solar plexus chakra, 143
  throat chakra, 144
Chance, 98–99, 101
  and suffering, 101–102
Change, growthful, 194–195
Channeling, 83
Chicago American, 43n.24
Chicago Daily News, 43n.24
Children and childhood, 40, 175–
  176, 179, 180, 181
  autism, 41
  pathological disturbance attrib-
    uted to adult awareness in
    childhood, 40–41
Children Who Remember Previous
  Lives, 28, 38n.15, 62n.1
Chiristianity, 19, 67
  agape and agapic love, 65, 212–
    213
  early; reincarnation in, 214–219
  Gnostic, 18, 150, 154, 222

historical impact, 163–164
  oral phase, 221–222
  reincarnationist, 149–174
  rejection of reincarnation, reasons
    for, 166–167
  unproductive approaches to rein-
    carnation, 153–157
Cliness, David, 122–124
COEX systems, 46
Collective perspective, 111–112,
  169–170
  analogies for, 170–174
Coming Back to Life, 57n.40
Compassion, 143–144
Compensation, 68
Concentration camps, 99–100
Connection to specific people,
  places, and conditions. See Web
  of life.
Consciousness, 18–19
  evolution across many lives, 59
  thresholds, 59
  transpersonal states of, 208n.7
Creativity, 144
Crees, Romy, 1–3, 8
Cryptomnesia, 32
Cycle of death and rebirth, 116
Cynchronicities, 189–190

Dale, 70–72
Dark Night of the Soul, 212n.11
Death, 57
  one's thoughts at the moment of,
    71n.6
  violence of, 38
Denver Post, 43n.24
Dhammapada, 201
The Dharma, 89n.22
Drummond, Isobel, 48, 95–96
Dunanoir, 54

Eastern religions, 170, 209
Elijah the prophet, 220
Emanation, theory of, 118
Enlightenment, 145
"Enlightenment and the Christian
    Tradition," 161n.5
Eternity, 115
Ethical relativism, 145n.9

Evans, Jane, 43n.24
Evidence for reincarnation, 26–61
  evoked memories, 42–56
  spontaneous memories, 28–42
Evolutionary potential, 145–148
Existentialism, xiv, 10, 11
Exoteric and esoteric levels of religion, 15–19, 63
  analogy of the ellipse, 16–17
  convergence of, 17
  public side, 15–16
  secret side, 16
Experience, field of. See Field effect.

The family and reincarnation, 175–184
  biological families, 178–179
  childhood, 175–176, 179, 180, 181
  infancy, 175–176
  parents, 182–183
  soul families, 177–178
Far Journeys, 58, 89n.22, 110–112, 137–138
Fetal self-awareness and identity, 73n.11
Field effect, 24, 201–214
  intervening in karmic cycles, 204–205
  two-sided field, 201–204
Fifth Ecumenical Council, 166
Fiore, Edith, 70–72
Fisher, Joe, 63, 76, 83–84
Flynn, Charles, 112–113
Forgiveness, 171n.9, 213
Former lives, 125
Forte de Oro, 54
Freud, Sigmund, 143, 197
Fromm, Erich, 144

Gallup poll, 60–61
Garonzi, Ben, 95
Gender, 55–56
Gnostic Christianity, 18, 63, 150, 154, 222
The Gnostic Gospels, 222–224
God, 86, 92n.25, 138, 162, 171, 173
  Judeo-Christian, 151–152
  monotheism, 158–159n.4

as our essence, 158
and the Oversoul, 116–119
will of, 10
Godhead consciousness, 145
Golden fortress, 54
Golden Rule, 171n.9, 216
Grof, Stanislav, 19, 51–53, 73n.11, 83, 206–208
Group regressions, 54–56
Guides, spirit, 82–83, 96n.28
  karmic scripts proposed by, 91

Hargreaves, Peter, 77
Hasidic Judaism, 17, 63, 150
Heading Toward Omega, 57n.40, 102–103, 113n.7
Heaven, 136–138
Hell, 136–138, 162
Hesed, 65, 143–144
Hinduism, 8, 26, 141, 158n.4, 199
  Lords of Karma, 82n.13
  Upanishads, 64, 68
Historical details, verification of, 43
Historical periods, male/female ratios, 55–56
Holonomic therapy, 46
Human beings
  bodies as a hierarchy of interdependent systems, 118–119
  innermost essence, 66
Hypnosis and hypnotherapy, 42–43, 91–92, 122–124, 206
  the Collective, 123
  regression to famous personalities, 56
  self-hypnosis, 48

I Ching, 188–189, 193
India
  animal incarnations, 58–59
  consciousness through meditation, 26–27
  folk belief, 39
  religions of, 171
Infancy, 175–176
Inspect (Intelligent Species). See Oversoul.
Intuition, 144–145, 197–198
  "insight" meditation, 211–212

Intuition (*continued*)
  paranormal insight, 144
Islam, 17–18
  Sufism, 18, 63, 150
Iverson, Jeffrey, 43*n*.24

Jain, Nirmal, 4–7
Janis, 57*n*.40
Jeremy, 79
Jesus, 24, 67, 154–155, 157*n*.3,
  160–164, 165–166, 167–168,
  215, 219, 223
  possible belief in reincarnation,
  220–222
Joe, 70–72
John the Baptist, 220
John's Gospel, 154, 223
Journal of the American Medical Association, 33
Journal of Nervous and Mental Disease, 33
Judaism, 17
  Hasidic, 63, 150
  hesed, 65, 143–144
Judgment, 161
Judgment, Board of, 87–89, 96
Jung, Carl G., 18, 189
Justice, retributive, 68

Karl, 53–54
Karma, 12, 182, 210–214
  case histories from past-life therapy, 70–79
  cycles of; intervention, 204–205
  esoteric teaching, 63, 64–70
  intelligence demonstrated by, 80–82
  life between life, 84–97
  machine metaphor for, inappropriateness of, 80–81
  as moral reciprocity, 65
  and rebirth, 62–104
  as retributive justice, 68
  and social passivity, 97–98
  tests of, 94–96
Karmic scripts, 91, 92, 93
  absence of, 96
King, Lester S., 33

Kin-hin (walking meditation), 199
Knowledge, 112–113

Lao-Tzu, 215
Learning, 64–65, 68–69, 112–113,
  131, 134, 140, 216
Life
  analogy of hills and valleys, 132–133
  expansion and integration, 131–132
  rhythms of, 128–148
  two phases of, 129–136
Life Before Life, 91–92
Life Between Life, 47, 63, 76, 83–84
Life, web of. *See* Web of life.
The Lives of the Cell, 119
Logan, Steve, 94–95
Lords of Karma, 82*n*.13
LSD-assisted psychotherapy, 46
Luke, 167*n*.6

MacGregor, Geddes, 155*n*.2, 166
Matter and materialism, 19–23
Meditation, 26–27, 170, 210–214
  vipassana, 199, 211–212, 214
  walking (kin-hin), 199
Mehra, Parmanand, 29–30
Memories
  evoked, 42–56
  hidden (cryptomnesia), 32
  spontaneous, 28–42
  surfacing, reasons for, 59–61
  therapeutic impact, 46–47
Merton, Thomas, 170
Metaconsciousness, 85
Metaphysics, 93–94
  naturalism, 20, 22
Mishra, Swarnlata, 33–38
  second incarnation, memories of,
  37
Monism, 158–159*n*.4
Monotheism, 158–159*n*.4
Monroe Institute of Applied Science, 83
Monroe, Robert, 58, 89*n*.22, 110–112, 115, 137–138, 140
Moral reciprocity, 66
  karma as, 65

More Lives Than One? The Evidence of the Remarkable Bloxham Tapes, 43n.24
Morphogenetic fields, 61n.43
Murphey, Bridey, 43n.24

Nadia: A Case of Extraordinary Drawing in an Autistic Child, 41n.20
Nag Hammadi texts, 154, 166, 222–224
Naturalism. *See* Metaphysics, naturalism.
Nautilus, large-chambered; analogy of the Oversoul as, 108–109
"Near-Death Experiences: Implications for Human Evolution and Planetary Transformation," 57n.40
Near-death experiences, *xiii–xiv*, 102–103, 104, 112
and reincarnation, 56–57
Netherton, Morris, 72
A New Science of Life: The Hypothesis of Formative Causation, 61n.43
New Testament, 154, 155–157
reincarnation in, 219–222
Nonphysical domain, 115

Ocean as an analogy of life on earth, 67
Oneness, 67
Other Lives, Other Selves: A Jungian Discovers Past Lives Therapy, 43n.25
Out-of-body research, 93
Oversoul, 105–127, 147, 164, 165
analogy of a large-chambered nautilus, 108–109
assistance, request for, 113
defined, 87n.20
and God, 116–119
individual identity and, 119–128
as our bridge to the cosmos, 114–115
possibilities, opening to the, 114–116
reincarnation within the perspective of, 110n.3
time and, 115–116

Pagel, Elaine, 222–224
Pal (Prof.), 37
Pandey, Biya Pathak, 34
Parents, 182–183
Parsons, Carl, 72–76
Pasricha, Satwant, 39n.17
Past Lives Therapy, 72
Pathak, Biya, 34
Paul, 67, 155
early epistles, 221
Pennington, Gary and Elizabeth, 76–79
Perl, Fritz, 59–60
Personality, 145
Phobias, 38
Physical life on Earth
analogy of the ocean, 67
living in the present, 198–200
as realm of effect, 93–94
reasons for, 64–65, 89–90
returning to, reasons for, 89–90
as training plan for future endeavors, 90
Physical universe, 11
Pistia Sophia (Faith Wisdom), 223
Plato, 118n.10
Power, 143
The Power Within, 45
Psychotherapy
LSD-assisted, 46
past-life, 120–121
Psychotherapy East and West, 69n.5

Quantum physics, 54
Quantum research, 121n.12

Raleigh, Walter, 54
Rama, Swami, 142n.7
Randomness, 10
Rebirth, 26
broader implications of, 167–174
Reincarnation, 114
adoption of theory of, 12–13
Cliness's analogy of playing cards, 124
critical investigation of, 13
and ever-enlarging populations, 57–58
gender during, 59

Reincarnation (*continued*)
  group regressions, 54–56
  negative attitude toward specific
    rebirth, reasons for, 29
  noteworthy individuals who be-
    lieve in, 3–4
  procedure for verifying former
    lives, 27–28
  sources of study, 14–15
  spontaneous recall of a former
    life, 38
  see also specific topics, i.e., Evidence
    for reincarnation; The family
    and reincarnation
Reincarnation in Christianity, 155n.2,
  166
Relativity theory, 115
Religion, 65, 167, 216
  comparatives, 169
  Eastern, 15, 118n.9, 170
  esoteric spiritual traditions and
    karma, 63
  exoteric and esoteric levels. *See*
    Exoteric and esoteric levels of
    religion
  heaven and hell, 136–138
  of India, 171
  Western, 10–11, 127, 149–150,
    165, 170–171
  see also specific religions, i.e.,
    Christianity
Reliving Past Lives, 40–41, 55
Ring, Kenneth, 57, 102–103,
  113n.7
Rinpoche, Kalu, 89n.22
Rogers, Carl, 144

Saccidananda (Being-Consciousness-
    Bliss), 147
Sambhava, Padma, 136
Samskara, 64n.3, 182
Satan, 1n.9
Schopenhauer, 191
Schuon, Frithjof, 16–17
Scientific method, 20
Scientism, 21
The Search for Bridey Murphey,
  43n.24
Selfe, Lorna, 41n.20

Self-hypnosis, 48
Self-programming, 64–65
Sharma, Parmod, 28–32
Sheldrake, Rupert, 61n.43
Shiffrin, Nancy, 72
Sin, 161
Smith, Huston, 16–17, 21
Social reform, 170–171
Son of Man, 219–220
Soul, 163
  Western view of, 127
  see also Oversoul; Soul age; Soul
    families.
Soul age, 24, 138–141, 145–146
  Chakra system map of, 141–145
Soul families, 177–178
Spiritual domain, as realm of cause,
  93–94
Spiritual path, 217
Spiritual traditions, Eastern, 209
Spontaneous memories of a former
    life, 28–42
Star Wave, 121n.12
Stevenson, Ian, 4, 28, 32, 33, 34–
    35, 36, 38, 43, 56, 60, 62n.1
  follow-up studies on children with
    spontaneous memories of for-
    mer lives, 40
The Stranger, xiv
St. John of the Cross, 1n.16,
  212n.11
St. Teresa of Avila, 212n.11
Suffering, 9, 10–11, 91, 97–98, 103
  of great masses, 99–100
  role of chance in, 101–102
Sufism, 18, 63, 150
Survival of the species, 143
Synchronism, 207

Tagore, Rabindranath, 37
Talents, 72
Tanya, 52–53
Taoism, 191
  t'zu, 65, 143–144
  wu wei, 65
Theology, 20–21
Therapy, 46, 59–60
  past-life; case histories, 70–79
Thomas, Lewis, 119

The Tibetan Book of the Dead, 57, 84,
    85–86, 136
Time
    in the bardo, 86–87
    interval between lives, 38, 86–87
    linear, 115
    our relationship to, 186
    and the Oversoul, 115–116
*Twenty Cases Suggestive of Reincarna-
    tion*, 28, 33
T'zu, 65, 143–144

Umnov, Sevastjan, 78
Unlearned Languages, 28
Upanishads, 64, 68

Varshnay, Prakash, 4–7
Vipaka, 65
Vipassana meditation, 199, 211–
    212, 214
Vissudhimaga, 212n.11

Wambach, Helen, 40–41, 60, 91–
    92
    group regressions, 54–56
Web of life, 24, 185–200
    canges in, 194–197
    as conscious and reactive, 187–
    188

as a field of energy, 202–203
    intuition, 197–198
    living in the present, 198–200
    working with the web, 188–194
Western countries, reasons for
    scarcity of strong cases of re-
    birth in, 40
Western religions, 149–150, 165,
    170–171
Whiteholme, Heather, 47–51, 95–
    96
White, John, 161n.5
Whitton, Joel, 47, 63, 76, 83–84,
    86n.18, 102
Wilber, Ken, 142n.8
Williams, Joe, 1–3, 8
Williams, Louise, 2–3
Wilson, Colin, 43n.24
Wolf, Fred, 18, 121n.12
Woolger, Roger, 43n.25
Wu Wei, 65

Yoga and Psychotherapy, 142n.7
You Have Been Here Before, 70–72

Zen, 198
Zukav, Gary, 18